SIGN TALK

A UNIVERSAL SIGNAL CODE WITHOUT APPARATUS

FOR USE IN ARMY, NAVY, CAMPING HUNTING AND DAILY LIFE

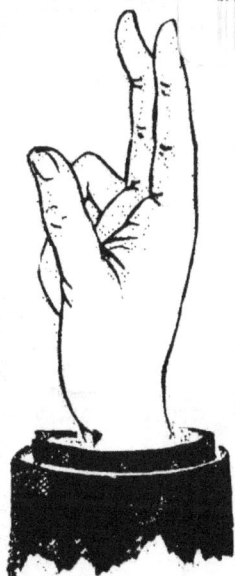

ERNEST THOMPSON SETON

British Library Cataloguing-in-Publication Data
A catalogue record for this book is available from the
British Library

Ernest Thompson Seton

Ernest Thompson Seton was born on 14th August 1860, in South Shields, County Durham, England. He grew up to be a pioneering author, wildlife artist, founder of the Woodcraft Indians, and one of the originators of the Boy Scouts of America (BSA).

The Seton family emigrated to Canada when Ernest was just six years old, and most of his childhood was consequently spent in Toronto. As a youth, he retreated to the woods to draw and study animals as a way of avoiding his abusive father – a practice which shaped the rest of his adult life. On his twenty-first birthday, Seton's father presented him with a bill for all the expenses connected with his childhood and youth, including the fee charged by the doctor who delivered him. He paid the bill, but never spoke to his father again.

Originally known as Ernest Evan Thompson, Ernest changed his name to Ernest Thompson Seton, believing that Seton had been an important name in his paternal line. He became successful as a writer, artist and naturalist, and moved to New York City to further his career. Seton later lived at 'Wyndygoul', an estate that he built in Cos Cob, a section of Greenwich, Connecticut. After experiencing vandalism by some local youths, Seton invited the young miscreants to his estate for a weekend, where he told them what he claimed were stories of the American Indians and of nature.

After this experience, he formed the Woodcraft Indians (an American youth programme) in 1902 and invited the local youth to join (at first just boys, but later girls as well). The stories that Seton told became a series of articles written for the *Ladies Home Journal*, and were eventually collected in *The Birch Bark Roll of the Woodcraft Indians* in 1906. Seton also met Scouting's founder, Lord Baden-Powell, in 1906. Baden-Powell had read Seton's book of stories, and was greatly intrigued by it. After the pair had met and shared ideas, Baden-Powell went on to found the Scouting movement worldwide, and Seton became vital in the foundation of the Boy Scouts of America (BSA) and was its first Chief Scout (from 1910 – 1915). Despite this large achievement, Seton quickly became embroiled in disputes with the BSA's other founders, Daniel Carter Beard and James E. West.

In addition to disputes about the content of Seton's contributions to the Boy Scout Handbook, conflicts also arose about the suffrage activities of his wife, Grace, and his British citizenship (it being *an American* organization). In his personal life, Seton was married twice. The first time was to Grace Gallatin in 1896, with whom he had one daughter, Ann (who later changed her name to Anya), and secondly to Julia M. Buttree, with whom he adopted an infant daughter, Beulah (who also changed her first name, to Dee). Alongside his work with the Woodcraft Indians and the BSA, Seton also found time to pursue his primary interest – that of nature writing.

Seton was an early pioneer of animal fiction writing, his most popular work being *Wild Animals I Have Known* (1898), which contains the story of his killing of the wolf Lobo. He later became involved in a literary debate known as the nature fakers controversy, after John Burroughs published an article in 1903 in the *Atlantic Monthly* attacking writers of sentimental animal stories. The controversy lasted for four years and included important

American environmental and political figures of the day, including President Theodore Roosevelt. Seton was also associated with the Santa Fe arts and literary community during the mid-1930s and early 1940s, which comprised a group of artists and authors including author and artist Alfred Morang, sculptor and potter Clem Hull, painter Georgia O'Keeffe, painter Randall Davey, painter Raymond Jonson, leader of the Transcendental Painters Group, and artist Eliseo Rodriguez.

In 1931, Seton became a United States citizen. He died on 23rd October, 1946 (aged eighty-six) in Seton Village in northern New Mexico. Seton was cremated in Albuquerque. In 1960, in honour of his 100th birthday and the 350th anniversary of Santa Fe, his daughter Dee and his grandson, Seton Cottier (son of Anya), in a fitting tribute to the man who loved his surrounding countryside so much, scattered his ashes over Seton Village from an airplane.

SIGN TALK

A Universal Signal Code, Without Apparatus, for Use in the Army, the Navy, Camping, Hunting, and Daily Life

By
Ernest Thompson Seton

*Author of "Wild Animals I Have Known," "Life Histories of Northern Animals," "The Book of Woodcraft," etc., etc.
Chief of the Woodcraft League of America*

THE GESTURE LANGUAGE OF THE CHEYENNE INDIANS

With additional Signs used by other tribes, also a few necessary Signs from the code of the Deaf in Europe and America, and others that are established among our Policemen, Firemen, Railroad Men, and School Children

IN ALL 1,725

Prepared with assistance from
General Hugh L. Scott, U. S. A.

The French and German equivalent words added by
Lillian Delger Powers, M. D.

700 ILLUSTRATIONS BY THE AUTHOR

PREFACE

IN OFFERING this book to the public after having had the manuscript actually on my desk for more than nine years, let me say frankly that no one realizes better than myself, now, the magnitude of the subject and the many faults of my attempt to handle it.

My attention was first directed to the Sign Language in 1882 when I went to live in Western Manitoba. There I found it used among the various Indian tribes as a common language, whenever they were unable to understand each other's speech. In later years I found it a daily necessity when traveling among the natives of New Mexico and Montana, and in 1897, while living among the Crow Indians at their agency near Fort Custer, I met White Swan, who had served under General George A. Custer as a Scout. He had been sent across country with a message to Major Reno, so escaped the fatal battle; but fell in with a party of Sioux, by whom he was severely wounded, clubbed on the head, and left for dead. He recovered and escaped, but ever after was deaf and practically dumb. However, sign-talk was familiar to his people and he was at little disadvantage in daytime. Always skilled in the gesture code, he now became very expert; I was glad indeed to be his pupil, and thus in 1897 began seriously to study the Sign Language.

In 1900 I included a chapter on Sign Language in my

projected Woodcraft Dictionary, and began by collecting
all the literature. There was much more than I expected, for almost all early travellers in our Western
Country have had something to say about this *lingua
franca* of the Plains.

As the material continued to accumulate, the chapter
grew into a Dictionary, and the work, of course, turned
out manifold greater than was expected. The Deaf,
our School children, and various European nations, as
well as the Indians, had large sign vocabularies need-
ing consideration. With all important print on the
subject I am fairly well conversant, besides which I have
had large opportunities in the field and have tried to
avail myself of them to the fullest extent, carrying my
manuscript from one Indian tribe to another, seeking
out always the best sign-talkers among them, collecting
and revising, aiming to add all the best signs in use to
those already on record.

The following are the chief printed works on Sign
Language:

1823. The Indian Language of Signs by Major
Stephen H. Long, published in his Expedition to the
Rocky Mts., 1823, Vol. I, pp. 378-394. Gives 104 signs.
The earliest extensive vocabulary on record.

**1880. Gesture Signs and Signals of the North
American Indians** by Lieut. Col. Garrick Mallery. An
elaborate and valuable 330 page quarto compilation
from many contributors; published by the Bureau
of American Ethnology of the Smithsonian Institution, 1880.

It was preliminary to the much more extended work published the year following, and combines in itself all the important vocabularies published up to that time, including: *Wm. Dunbar's List* pub. Trans. Am. Phil. Soc., January 16, 1801; about 60 signs; *Prince Maximilian von Wied-Neuwied's List*, Reise, Nord. Am., 1832-34, 1837; *Capt. R. F. Burton's List* pub. in "The City of the Saints," 1862; *Dr. D. G. MacGowan's List* pub. in *Historical Magazine*, Vol. X, 1866, pp. 86-97; also Manuscript Lists supplied by *Col. R. I. Dodge, Dr. William H. Corbusier*, U. S. A., and about forty other contributors.

1881. Sign Language Among the North American Indians compared with that among other peoples and Deaf Mutes, by Col. Garrick Mallery; 290 page quarto, 286 illustrations, an elaborate examination of the history, origin, and nature of the Sign Language, with extensive vocabularies. Published in 1st Annual Report, Bureau of American Ethnology, 1881.

1885. The Indian Sign Language by Capt. William Philo Clark, U. S. A., 244 pp. octavo, quite the best book on the subject, giving over 1,000 signs with photographic exactness; it is also one of the best early encyclopedic books on Indians in general; unfortunately, it is without illustrations and is out of print. Published by Hamersly & Co., of Philadelphia, 1885.

This is practically the only publication quoted in preparing this work. I have referred to it continually as a standard—as the highest available authority. (W. P. Clark was born July 27, 1845, at Deer River, Lewis Co., New York. Graduated from West Point June 15, 1868. Served on the Plains in 2d Cavalry during the Indian wars of 1876 to 1880. Died at Washington, D. C., September 23, 1884.)

HADLEY INDIAN SIGN PRINTS

About twenty-five years ago there lived in Anadarko, Indian Territory, an enthusiastic missionary worker named Lewis F. Hadley, known to the Indians as Ingonompashi.

He made a study of Sign Language in order to furnish the Indians with a pictographic writing, based on diagrams of the signs, and meant to be read by all Indians, without regard to their speech. Pointing to the Chinese writing as a model and parallel, he made a Sign Language font of 4,000 pictographic types for use in his projected works. He maintained that 110,793 Indians were at that time sign-talkers and he proposed to reach them by Sign-Language publications.

In pursuance of his plan, he issued the following:

1887. List of the Primary Gestures in Indian Sign Talk. "Only 19 copies were printed." It was intended as a prodrome to *"extended works and a magazine in Hands-tal[k]ing."*

It consists of 63 pages with 684 crude woodblocks of white lines on black ground, illustrating signs, alphabetically arranged, but without captions or text of any kind, except the explanation on the title page, abridged as above.

1890. A Lesson in Sign Talk, designed to show the use of the line showing the movement of the hands in the Indian Gesture Language, by In-go-nom-pa-shi, Fort Smith, Ark., 1890. Copyrighted by Lewis F. Hadley, 12 pp. A portrait of him by himself is on p. 11, inscribed "In-go-nom-pa-shi, drawn by himself at 60 years."

It devotes 3 pages to general discussion of Sign Talk, 1½ pages to reform of our spelling, the rest is given to general remarks with 12 poor illustrations in white line, also a Scripture text with 15 signs drawn, the Lord's Prayer with 55 drawn signs, and on p. 12, The Indian Little Star, a novel version of "Twinkle, Twinkle," rendered in 97 drawn signs.

1893. Indian Sign Talk. Being a Book of Proofs of the matter printed or equivalent cards designed for teaching sign-talking Indians as much English as can be explained through the medium of their "Universal" Gesture Language, by Ingonompashi, copyrighted May 15, 1893, "only 75 copies are saved."

This is Hadley's most extended work. It is a dictionary of the Sign Language, in 268 large octavo leaves printed on one side only of each sheet.

It consists of 9 pages of Preface and general matter, 192 pp. of dictionary alphabetically arranged, each page having three gestures figured and beside each the equivalent in English. A total of 577 signs (including a double). Pages 193 to 205 are given to small reproductions of the sign drawings to illustrate "measurements of type"— his font—about 800 illustrations, two pages of appendix with compound sign words, and 14 illustrations, 1 page of black type, 18 in number, 53 pages of reading matter in signs, the above cited version of "Twinkle, Twinkle, Little Star" and the story of "Wolf and the White Man" in signs; the rest being Scripture texts and exhortations and the 19th Psalm, ending with the Lord's Prayer.

The cards referred to I have. They consist of 571 separate cards with an illustrated sign on each and additional matter on the back. Besides which there are about 100 separate cards each with a scripture text, chapter, or sermonette on it, about 1,000 illustrations in all. The same being the matter of the dictionary proper reproduced on separate cards, the diagram on one side and the text on the other. The front matter and the type measurements do not, however, appear on the cards. Though poor as art, the drawings are of some value to the student.

This is the most ambitious work extant on the subject of Sign Language, but seems to be quite unknown to most ethnologists, and is not in any library, so far as I can learn, except the Library of Congress, the Smithsonian Institution, the New York Public Library, the Library of Prof. J. C. Elsom of Wisconsin State University, and my own collection.

Of the 75 copies issued, only these 5 have been accounted for, but cards comprising the dictionary part were issued to the extent of 100,000 in sets of 571 each, and the reading matter on cards to the number of over 27,000.

1910. The Sign Language, by Prof. J. Schuyler Long, State School for the Deaf, Council Bluffs, Iowa, published at Washington, D. C., 1910. A valuable dictionary of about 1,500 signs used by the deaf, with 500 admirable photographic illustrations. Of these signs a large number seem to be arbitrary, but many are evidently of good construction and quite acceptable to Indian sign-talkers.

To these should be added:

1832. La Mimica, by Andrea de Jorio. "La mimica degli antichi investigata nel Gestire Napoletano." Napoli, 1832, 8vo, 372 pp., 21 plates.

This interesting Italian work on Sign Language was written to show that the gestures figured on antique vases, etc., may be explained by their modern parallels, especially as observed in Naples. The 21 plates illustrate about one hundred of these gestures—about half of these are reproduced in Mallery's 1881 publication.

1854. **Dactylologie** by Louis de Mas-Latrie. "Dictionnaire de Paleographie." *Tome Quarante-septième,* pp. 179 to 366.

An extended study of Finger-talking as used by the deaf, the savages, etc. About 30 American Indian signs are described and compared with those of the deaf. No illustrations.

1878. **The Gesture Language,** by E. B. Tyler, in his studies in "Early History of Mankind," third edition, 1878, pp. 14-81.

An interesting but not very important dissertation on the Gesture Language in use among the deaf, the Cistercian Monks, and the American Indians. No illustrations.

1883. **Sign Language, Remarks on,** by Wilfred Powells in his "Wanderings in a Wild Country." An account of a three years' residence in New Britain (to the north of New Guinea), 1883, pp. 254-261, with 14 good figures, showing the digital origin of numbers.

1896. **Arunta Sign Language,** E. C. Stirling. Rep. Horn Scientific Exped. to Central Australia; IV, pp. 111-125.

A considerable discourse on the Sign Language as used by the very primitive races. Many figures.

My thanks are due to General Hugh Lenox Scott,

U. S. A., one of the best living sign-talkers, for a general review of the text, with new signs and explanations as indicated.

To John Homer Seger of Colony, Oklahoma, for much assistance. He was for 45 years in official control of the Indians at Darlington and Colony, Oklahoma. They were of the Southern Cheyenne, Kiowa, and Arapaho tribes chiefly. All his communications with them were in the Sign Language, so that he became one of our best experts. We have corresponded much, and during a prolonged visit to his home in August, 1915, we together went over every sign in this Manual. His signs were of the Cheyenne dialect.

To the Reverend Walter C. Roe (since dead) of Colony, Oklahoma, for many notes and comments. He was so expert that he preached every Sunday in the Sign Language.

To Sheeaka, or Cyiaka (The Mudhen), a Yanktonnais Sioux living at Standing Rock. He worked over my entire manuscript with me in 1912, endorsing most of the signs given by Clark, as well as adding those that are accredited to him. He was considered the best sign-talker on the reservation. His familiarity with the Sign Language was largely due to the fact that a member of his family was a deaf-mute, so that he has kept up the method while others of his generation are forgetting it. Frank Zahn, an intelligent and educated half-breed, acted as interpreter and helped with many suggestions.

In the autumn of 1916 I took my manuscript to Montana and received valuable help from the following Blackfoot Indians:

Bearhead, an old-time, full-blooded Piegan Indian,

with a pronounced contempt for modern ways and modern signs; George Starr or Bull Calf, a half-blood, who acted as interpreter for Bearhead; Medicine Owl, Eagle Child, Three Bears, Two-Guns Whitecalf; all full-blooded Piegans and excellent sign-talkers.

Heavy Breast, a half-blood, acted as interpreter, with assistance from James C. Grant.

I am also indebted to Chasing Bear (Ma-to Hu-wa-pi), a Santee, and to Chief Tom Frosted, a Yanktonnais; both of Standing Rock. About a dozen good signs were given me by C. B. Ruggles, of Taos, New Mexico; and helpful information was received from Thomas La Forge, official interpreter for the Crow Nation, and Clitzo Deadman, an educated Navaho at Ganado, Arizona.

In the spring of 1917 I spent some time among the Cheyennes at Concho, Oklahoma, checking up my lists. My chief source of information was Robert Burns, an intelligent and educated Cheyenne, who spoke excellent English and was also a good sign-talker. At the same time I got much valuable assistance from Cheyenne Fanny (Mrs. Hamilton), Deafy Fletcher, and numerous old Cheyennes and Arapahoes about the Post. Father Isadore, of the St. Patrick's Mission, Anadarko, Oklahoma, and the Reverend Sherman Coolidge (Arapahoe), of Sheridan, Wyoming, also contributed.

In the case of special or unusual signs, I give the name of the best of my authorities; but when, according to my own observation, the sign is in general use and indorsed by practically all, no authority is cited.

I have to thank my friends James Mooney and F. W. Hodge of the Smithsonian Institution, and Professor J. Schuyler Long, of Council Bluffs, Iowa, for much help-

ful criticism; Professor Elmer D. Read, of the Pennsylvania School for the Deaf, for a review of the Introduction; also, Doctor Charles A. Eastman (Ohiyesa), Col-
onel W. F. Cody (Buffalo Bill), Hamlin Garland, Miss
Frances Densmore, and Mrs. Mary Austin for contributions or criticism.

For the French and German equivalent words I am
chiefly indebted to Doctor Lillian Delger Powers, of
Mt. Kisco, New York. Some assistance was given by
Miss Dorothy Dwenger, of Greenwich, Connecticut, and
Harry G. Seides, Professor of German, Jersey City High
School, New Jersey.

The drawings throughout are by myself.

ERNEST THOMPSON SETON.

INTRODUCTION

MANY thoughtful men have been trying for a century, at least, to give mankind a world-speech which would overstep all linguistic barriers, and one cannot help wondering why they have overlooked the Sign Language, the one mode common to all mankind, already established and as old as Babel. Yes, more ancient than the hills.

As far back as the records go, we find the Sign Language in use. General Hugh L. Scott has pointed out nineteen examples in Homer. Greek vases, Japanese bronzes, ancient Hindu statuary, as well as songs and legends older than history, give testimony in like tenor. While Egyptologists remind us that the oldest records show, not only that the Sign Language was then used, but that the one original code was much like that in use to-day. The fact that it is yet found all over the world wherever man is man, is proof of its being built on human nature in the beginnings. We might even argue that it is more ancient than speech.

Ideas certainly came before the words that express them. The idea of "hunger" must be a thousand times as old as any existing "word" for "hunger." When it became necessary to communicate to another the idea of hunger, it certainly was easier and more direct to communicate it by gesture than by word. The word had, perforce, to be more or less arbitrary, but the gesture was logical, and could at once indicate the pain, its place, and even hint at the cause.

The possible variations of a mere squeak in a concealed pipe are obviously less in number and far less graphic and logical than the various movements of two active, free-moving, compound, visible parts of the body that utilize all the dimensions of space, all the suggestions of speed, motion, physical form and action, juxtaposition, yes, even a measure of sound, and that could in a multitude of cases reproduce the very idea itself.

Animals have far more gestures to express thoughts and emotions than they have sounds, and children instinctively use gestures for various ideas long before they acquire the sound for them. In all races as a rule the very young children's gestures are the same, but the different words imposed by the different mothers have little or nothing in common, and no obvious basis in logic. All of which goes to prove the greater antiquity of eye-talk over ear-talk. To which conclusion we are forced also by the superiority of sight over hearing as a sense. "Seeing is believing," is convincement: hearing is more open to challenge.

Nor can the sign-talk have changed radically, for it is founded on the basic elements of human make-up, and on mathematics, and is so perfectly ideographic that no amount of bad presentation can completely divert attention from the essential thought to the vehicle; while punning is an impossibility.

It had all the inherent possibilities of speech, was indeed capable of even greater subtleties, as we have noted, and had a far greater distance range, three or four times that of spoken words.

In view of the greater antiquity and many advantages
that hand gestures have over spoken language, one is
prompted to ask: Why did it not develop and continue
man's chief mode of inter-communication?   The answer
is, doubtless, partly because it was useless in the dark or
when the person was out of sight or partly hidden by
intervening things.   Diagrammatically expressed it was
thus:

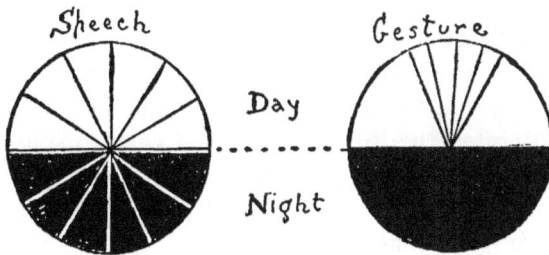

Speech therefore covers all directions night and day.
Gesture covers one-third of the circle in hours of light.
Therefore speech serves six times as many occasions as
gesture.

But the chief reason for the triumph of the appeal to
the ear is doubtless because the hands were in constant
use for other things; the tongue was not; was indeed practically free to specialize for this end.

ITS UNIVERSALITY

Being so fundamental, ancient, and persistent, Sign
Language is, *perforce*, universal.   In some measure it is
used by every race on earth to-day.   Eskimo and Zulu,
Japanese and Frenchman, Turk and Aztec, Greek and
Patagonian.   And whenever two men of hopelessly di-

verse speech have met, they have found a medium of
thought exchange in the old Sign Language—the pantomimic suggestion of ideas.

Latin races are proverbially hand-talkers, so that the
Sign Language is more widely used among them than
with Anglo-Saxons.

But the American Plains Indian is undoubtedly the
best sign-talker the world knows to-day.   There are, or
were, some thirty different tribes with a peculiar speech
of their own, and each of these communicated with the
others by use of the simple and convenient sign-talk of the
plains.   It is, or was, the language of Western trade and
diplomacy as far back as the records go. Every traveller
who visited the Buffalo Plains had need to study and
practise this Western Volapuk, and all attest its simplicity,
its picturesqueness, its grace, and its practical utility.

Many of the best observers among these have left us
long lists of signs in use, Alexander Henry in his gossipy
journal among the Mandans of the Missouri in 1806 tells
us of the surprise and interest he felt in watching two
Indian chiefs of different tribes who conversed freely for
hours on all subjects of common interest, conveying their
ideas accurately by nothing but simple gestures.

The European races are much less gifted as sign-
talkers.   But we all have a measure of it that is a surprise
to most persons when first confronted with the facts.
Our school children especially make daily use of the
ancient signals.

AMONG SCHOOL CHILDREN

In taking observations among school-boys and girls, I
had this uniform experience: All denied any knowledge

of the Sign Language, *at first*, but were themselves surprised on discovering how much of it they had in established use.

One very shy little girl—so shy that she dared not speak—furnished a good illustration:

"Do you use the Sign Language in your school?" I asked.

She shook her head.

"Do you learn any language but English?"

She nodded.

"What is the use of learning any other than English?"

She raised her right shoulder in the faintest possible shrug and at the same time turned her right palm slightly up.

"Now," was my reply, "don't you see you have answered all my three questions in signs which you said you did not use?"

Following the subject, I said: "What does this mean?" and held up my right hand with the first and second fingers crossed.

"Pax," she whispered; and then, after further trials, I learned that at least thirty signs were in daily use in that local school.

This was in England. In America the sign "Pax," or "King's cross," is called "King's X," "Fines" or "Fins" or "Fends," "Bars up" or "Truce," meaning always, "I claim immunity."

This is a very ancient sign and seems to refer to the right of sanctuary. The name "King's cross," used occasionally in England, means probably the sanctuary in the King's palace.

In general I found about 150 gesture signals in

established use among American school children, namely:

Me (Tap one's own chest).

You (Pointing to you).

Yes (Nod).

No (Shake head).

Good (Nod and clap hands).

Bad (Shake head and grimace).

Go (Pushing flat hand forward, palm forward).

Come (Drawing in flat hand, palm toward one).

Hurry (The same repeated vigorously several times).

Come for a moment (Beckon with forefinger, hand unmoved).

Stop (Flat hand held up, palm forward).

Gently (Flat hand held low, palm down, gently waved).

Good-bye (Flat hand held high, palm down and forward, fingers quickly waved up and down).

Up (Point up).

High (Flat hand, palm down, held up at arm's length).

Deep (Left flat hand palm down at level of mouth, right palm up, as low as possible).

Heaven (Point up very high and look up).

Down (Point down).

Forward (Swing index forward and down in a curve).

Backward (Jerk thumb over shoulder).

Across (Hold left hand out flat, palm down, run right index across it).

Over or Above (Hold out flat left, palm down, and above it hold ditto right).

Under (Reverse of foregoing).

Hush (Index finger on lips).

Listen   (Curved hand behind ear).

Look   (Flat hand over eyes).

Look there   (Point and look in same direction).

Touch   (Reach out and touch with index).

Taste   (Lay finger on tongue).

Smell   (Hold palm to nose).

Friendship   (Hand shake).

Warning   (Index finger held up).

Threatening   (Fist held up).

Weeping   (With index finger at each eye, trace course of tears).

Shame on you   (Point one index at the person and draw the other along it several times in same direction).

You make me ashamed   (Cover eyes and face with hands).

Mockery   (Stick tongue out at person).

Disdain   (Snap fingers toward person).

Scorn   (Throw an imaginary pinch of sand at person).

Insolent defiance   (Thumb to nose, hand spread).

Arrogant   (Indicate swelled head).

Pompous   (Indicate big chest).

Incredulity   (Expose white of eye with finger, as though proving "No green there").

I am no fool   (Tap one side of the nose).

Joke   (Rub side of nose with index).

Connivance   (Winking one eye).

Puzzled   (Scratch the head).

Crazy   (Tap forehead with index then describe a circle with it).

Despair   (Pulling the hair).

Sleepy   (Put a fist in each eye).

Bellyache   (Hands clasped across the belly).

Sick   (A grimace and a limp dropping of the hands).

Applause   (Clap hands).

Victory   (Swing an imaginary flag over head).

Upon my honor   (Draw a cross over heart or cross the hands over breast).

I am seeking   (Looking about and pointing finger in same directions).

I am thinking   (Lay index on brow, lower head and look out under brows).

I have my doubts   (Slowly swing head from side to side).

I will not listen   (Hold flat hands on ears).

I will not look   (Cover eyes with hands).

I forget   (Slowly shake head, and brush away something in air, near the forehead).

I claim exemption, or "Fins" or "Bar up" (Middle finger crossed on index).

I beg of you   (Flat hand palm to palm, pointing to the person).

I pray   (Clasped hands held up).

I am afraid, or surrender   (Hold up both flat hands, palm forward).

I wind him around my finger   (Make the action with right thumb and index around left index).

I have him under my thumb   (Press firmly down with top of right thumb).

You surprise me   (Flat hand on open mouth).

I send you a kiss   (Kiss the finger tips of right hand and throw it forward).

Search me   (Hold the coat flaps open, one in each hand).

Swim   (Strike out with flat hands).

Dive (Flat hands together, moved in a curve, forward and down).

Will you come swimming? (Two fingers in V shape held up level).

Will you? or Is it so? (Look, nod and raise brows).

Fool or Ass (A thumb in each ear, flat hands up).

Cut-throat (Draw index across throat).

Indifference (A shoulder shrug).

Ignorance (A shrug and a head shake).

Pay (Hold out closed hand, palm up, rubbing thumb and index tips together).

Jew (Flat hands waved near shoulders, palms up).

Bribe (Hold hollow hand, palm up, behind one).

It is in my pocket (Slap pocket with flat hand).

Give me my bill (Beckon, then write on air).

Match (Make the sign of striking a match on the thigh).

Set it afire (Sign match, and then thrust it forward).

Pistol (Making barrel with left index, stock and hammer with right hooked on; snapping right index from thumb).

That tastes good (Smack the lips).

The food was good (Pat the stomach).

Bad taste (Grimace and spitting out).

Bad smell (Hold the nose).

Bend (With right hand bend left index).

Break (With fists touching, make as though to bend a stick, then swing the fists apart).

Hot (Wet middle finger in mouth, reach it forward and jerk it back).

Cold (Fists near shoulder and shaken).

Paint (Use flat right as a brush to paint flat left).

Shave   (Use finger or thumb on face as a razor).

Wash   (Revolve hands on each other as in washing).

Knife   (With right fist as though holding knife, whittle left index).

Revolver   (Hold out right fist with index extended and thumb up).

Gun or shooting   (Hold hands as in aiming a gun).

Drive horses   (Work the two fists, side by side).

Give me   (Hold out flat hand, palm up).

Write   (Make the action with index).

Strike   (Strike down with fist).

Fighting   (Make the fists menace each other).

Drinking   (Lift right hand to mouth as though it held a glass).

Smoking   (Make as though holding a pipe and drawing).

Rub it out   (Wet tips of right fingers, and seem to rub).

Thank you   (Bow and, at the same time, swing flat right, palm up, a little way down and to one side).

Church   (Hands clasped, fingers in, but index fingers up and touching).

Get up   (Raise flat right, palm up, from low up high).

Sit down   (Drop flat right, palm down, from high, down low).

Here   (Pointing down, hand swung in small circle).*

In all, 110; besides the compass points, the features of the face, the parts of the body, the numerals up to 20 or 30, and a great many half-established signs, such as

---

*Professor Elmer D. Read writes me that all of these are in use among the deaf also, except the signs for "shame" and "church"; for these they make the Indian signs "*red*" and "*house prayer*," respectively.

book, telephone, ring the bell, etc., which, if allowed, would bring the number up to nearly 200.

As another line of observation, I have asked New York boys, "How many signs does the Broadway policeman use in regulating the traffic?" Any bright child remembers presently that the officer seldom speaks, could scarcely be heard if he did. Indeed, he relies chiefly on Sign Language and hourly uses the established signs for "Stop," "Come on," "Come here," "Go right," "Go left," "Go back," "Hurry up," "Go easy," "I warn you," "I'll punish you," "Pass," "Keep behind me," "Scorn," and, perhaps, one or two others.

While not infrequently the small boy responds with the sign of "insolent defiance" that is used the world 'round, and was probably invented by Cain and Abel.

Similarly, the car conductor uses the signs for "Do you want this car?" "Do you want transfer?" "How many?" "Go on," as well as most of the above.

Evidently, then, the Sign Language is used of necessity in much of our life where speech is impossible.

CODES, ETC.

It is inevitable that a world-wide language be split into variant forms. Besides the fragmentary Sign Code among our children, the more copious list of signs among Latins, and the code of the Cistercian or Trappist Monks, there are the Deaf Code and the Sign Language of the American Indians. Only the two last are widely established and at all complete as languages to-day.

DEAF CODE

The Sign Language used by the deaf was originated in France by Abbé de l'Epée about 1759, with a view to

facilitating the intercommunication of the deaf.   His
signs were largely arbitrary or founded on the spelling
of French words, usually in abbreviated form, so that it
was merely a short-hand of French done into finger-
spelling.

While this was the case at its beginning, the deaf
themselves had instinctively done so much in the way
of introducing pantomime and expressive gesture, that
they have half redeemed the Code from its unfortunate
original plan, and, in so doing, have made themselves in-
telligible to an immensely larger audience.

THE INDIAN CODE

So far as I can learn, no student hitherto has compared the various methods without being convinced that
the American Indian Sign Language is the best extant.
It is theoretically perfect and practically complete.   In
order to make this evident, I must offer a definition and
some comparative details.

*A true Sign Language is an established code of logical
gestures to convey ideas; and is designed as an appeal to
the eye, without the assistance of sounds, grimaces, apparatus, personal contact, written or spoken language, or
reference to words or letters; preferably made by using only
the hands and adjoining parts of the body.*

Measured by these standards, there is only one true
Gesture Language in the field to-day; that is the sign-
talk of the American Indians.   It is established over
the whole area of the Great Plains; and, though varied
locally, is essentially the same from Saskatchewan to
Rio Grande.

In general, it is claimed that there are two well-marked

dialects of this: the northern, which is a *whole hand* and a
two-hand dialect; the central and southern, which is a
finger and *one-hand* dialect.

The former is better for far signalling; the latter
for conversation. There are, however, many exceptions to these rules; and, in any case, they are so
close akin that Indians from opposite extremes of
the Plains have no difficulty in conversing with each
other.

The Cheyennes originally lived in a central region
where they had intercourse with a dozen tribes whose
spoken language differed from their own; so they became very expert sign-talkers, perhaps the best. They
have amplified to the number of several thousand signs,
and simplified until theirs has become largely a one-hand
code; therefore, as far as possible, I make the Cheyenne
sign-talk my standard. All signs herein given I have
found in use among the southern Cheyennes and are
understood to be Cheyenne except when another source
is specifically mentioned.

Clark gives first place among gesture talkers to the
Cheyennes and their associates the Arapahoes, whose
sign-talk was the same, though their speech was very
different, so that the signs for which he is authority may
also be considered Cheyenne.

The signs given me as Indian by Sheeaka and his
friend, Tom Frosted, should be cautiously received if
one would study the ancient code. Sheeaka had in his
family a deaf-mute, who probably imported some signs
from the Deaf Code, as indicated.

In cases where there were different signs for the same
idea, I have selected the simplest and clearest, the least

like other signs; or, other things equal, the one most ex-
tensively used, preferring a one-hand to a two-hand sign.

Usually that sign is best from the locality where the
idea is most familiar.   Thus the Sioux sign for "tree
squirrel" is poor; the Modoc sign is very good.   The
Navaho signs for "domestic sheep" are numerous and
clearly differentiated; those of the north are not, and
refer back to the "bighorn."   Southern signs for "snow"
are descriptive and cumbrous, while those of the northern tribes are simple and perfect.

A COMPARISON OF THE TWO CODES

A comparison of the Deaf and Indian Codes seems to
emphasize the superiority of the Indian.   The Deaf
was intended to convey, word by word, a vocal language;
it assumes that you know the other man's speech, and can
spell.   Whereas, the Indian was invented to over-ride
linguistic barriers and, knowing nothing of spelling,
deals only with ideas.

The next great advantage of Indian style is its picturesqueness.   The two systems can be illustrated and
fairly compared by the signs for the months.

First the Deaf:

January—Sign for *Month*, then *J, N*, and *R*, that is
4 signs.

June—Sign for *Month*, then *J* and *N*, that is 3 signs.

July—Sign for *Month*, then *J* and *L*, again 3 signs.

Whereas the Indian calls January the *Snow Moon*,
thus *moon* or "Horns in the sky" and *snow*, that is two
signs.   June is *Rose Moon* i.e., *horns* or *Crescent in the
sky* and *rose* (the right hand plucking an imaginary
petal from each finger tip of the left).   July is the

Thunder Moon, i.e., *horns in the sky*, then the right index darted downward in a quick zigzag to imitate *lightning*. All need but two signs each.

The first involving a certain amount of spelling is limited to those who can read, and who use that word. The second, touching nothing but the idea, is widely acceptable, much shorter, and visible much farther off. It was apparently developed for the safe distance beyond arrow range.

Again the Indian method is strong in its dignity. The deaf often spoil their sign-talk by grimacing, the Indian never does so. One may occasionally help the idea by facial expression, but it should be used with great reserve, as there is nothing more unlovely or likely to harm the study of the Sign Language than the excessive grimacing that one sometimes sees in an uneducated deaf-mute. The Indian sign-talker's face is calm and little changed, his head is moved in graceful sweeps, and never jerked unless to express some jerky action. His communication is indeed a study in beautiful, dignified gesture. There is not an Indian sign in this book that depends on facial expression for its usefulness, and there are but few that involve the face in any way.

Last year (1910) my friend Hamlin Garland met a party of moving picture men returning from a business tour among the Indians. He asked, "Did you get two old chiefs talking together in the Sign Language?" They said "No, hadn't heard of it."

"Then," he replied, "you have missed one of the most graceful and rewarding chances for your special art that the western country affords."

They were so much impressed with his description

that they went back. Having brought together two
chiefs of diverse speech they got results on their films
which amply justified their time and trouble.

Finally a large number of the signs used by the deaf
are conventional and arbitrarily fixed, dating back about
100 years, whereas each Indian sign is the slow evolu-
tionary product of ages, with its roots deep in human
nature. It is never arbitrary, but so logical and so
reasonable that it is easily and quickly learned.

Every interested person, therefore, must regret pro-
foundly that the teachers of the deaf should have gone
out of their way to fabricate an unnatural, localized code,
when there was awaiting them ready-made, and already
established, a system founded on universal human nature, old as the hills, full of the charms of grace and
poetry, and so logical that any one of any race can learn
it in a tithe of the time required for the acquisition of the
merest smattering of a spoken language, and the adoption
of which would at once have greatly lessened the handi-
cap of the deaf.   One can only suppose that the founders
of the code were unaware of the other's existence.

Undoubtedly actual service has done much to reform
and redeem the Deaf Code and make it more nearly
a true Sign Language, but one cannot help wishing that
their teachers would take the inevitable step at once and
adopt the natural system.

Thus we have logic with us as well as the opinion of
ethnologic students in giving preference to the Indian
System. While in the extent of usage honors are about
even, I am credibly assured that about 100,000 people
are daily using the Deaf Code and an equal number
using the Indian.

It is my belief that an available popular Manual will soon establish the latter as the universal code and result in its further and full development.

ATTITUDE TOWARD THE SIGN LANGUAGE

There are two distinct attitudes toward Indian Sign Language:

First, that of the student who sees in it a beautiful product of evolution, a perfect demonstration of the subtle laws of speech growth, the outcome of human mind yearning for converse with human mind, rebellious at its shut-in loneliness, battering with its hands the prison walls, till it could reach out and signal to the next locked-in, before it had yet found the way of modulated sounds. This, then, was the means which responded to the demand for communion and mental fellowship before there was a spoken speech. It began, as all codes must, with the broadest, simplest root ideas, and expressed their inter-relationships at most by context, sequence, proximity, or emphasis, but not by inflection.

Every student of the Sign Language is impressed by this thought and very naturally considers every true sign of the old Sign Language a thing sacred, precious as a pre-Homeric manuscript. He believes that to modify it or tamper with it would be to rob it of all value as a living expression of growth, and much like trying to read-just the crystalline forms on a frost-covered pane by shaping them with a hot iron. The student recognizes it as his first and highest duty to make faithful, unadulterated, untooled records of the oldest types of signs. This is the academic attitude. I am fully in sympathy with it.

Second, the practical attitude which realizes that Sign Language, never dead, is coming to its renaissance and can serve many useful ends among us here to-day. But to complete its possibilities it must be brought up to date by the addition of elements that stand for the latest modern ideas; and therefore does not hesitate to seize on and adopt these elements wherever they may be found. Thus, it may be held, is a contamination of the thought by interminglement of spurious recent creations. But it is merely submitting the code to the ordinary rules of all language. We should remember, further, that the ancient signs, as well as the modern, were *invented by men who had need of them.* The only difference is that the one was invented recently, the other maybe thousands of years ago; and that without such changes the Sign Language could not serve its beneficent purpose to-day among the deaf, the distant, the roar-environed, the moving picture folk, and those of unknown speech about us. Hand-talk fully developed will find much good work to do; and it matters little where the elements of the code were gathered so long as they meet with general acceptation; which implies that they be *needed, serviceable,* and of *sound construction.* The forty odd Deaf Signs included here have been admitted on this basis.

PROPER NAMES

There is at least one place where all pure Sign Language must fail; that is in dealing with proper names, especially new proper names. If I wish to signal "New York State" to an expert sign-talker, I can use the nickname "Empire State" and signal *"Country great crowned";* or, for "Kentucky" I can signal *"Country blue grass"*; or Boston, *"The Hub City"*; or Chicago *"Windy City"*; but when I come to South America or Oberammergau or Poughkeepsie, I am obliged to fall back on the white man's method and spell the name. For this reason then we begin our sign-talk by teaching the one-handed sign alphabet of the deaf. The two-handed will answer, but obviously a one-handed sign is better than a two-handed, other things equal. We aim at simplicity; and there are many occasions when one has but one hand free.

TO WHAT PURPOSE?

My own interest in the study had been growing for thirty years, and to satisfy myself that it was not a mere fad of slight and passing import, I set down carefully the reasons for studying and using the Sign Language, not forgetting its limitations. I set these also in hostile array and will give them first:

It is useless in the dark.

It cannot serve over the telephone.

It can scarcely be written, except by cumbrous pictographs.

It cannot give new proper names; they must be spelled.

But the reasons for the study were more numerous and stronger.

1st. *It develops observation and accurate thinking.* All races that excel in sign-talking are noted for their keenness of observation. Which is cause and which effect one cannot certainly determine, but it is sure that this method of communication is excellent practice to develop observation, and it makes for a wonderfully graphic descriptive power.

Herein, perhaps, is its most enduring, the least obvious, claim to a high place. There is a sweet reasonableness, a mathematical accuracy, in the fabric of the Sign Language that has an insistent and reactionary effect on the mental processes and pictures of those who use it. Therefore, it is valuable for the kind of mind it makes.

2d. *It is easily learned.* Unlike most languages, it is very easily acquired, for most of the signs are natural in concept, and so logical that they explain themselves where their history is known. Six hundred signs (that is ideas) make a fairly good sign-talker.

3d. *It is Indian talk.* By means of this you can talk to any Plains Indian no matter what his speech; and there are many tribes each with its own tongue or dialect. In some measure it is understood and used by savages and keen observers all over the globe.

4th. *A cognate code is the talk of the deaf;* and is used the world round by them in preference to the manual alphabet when possible; so that a wide use of the much better Indian Sign Language will certainly result in their accepting it and thus tend to lessen the barrier between the deaf and their more fortunate brethren.

5th. *It is silent talk.* It can be used on occasions when it is necessary to give information, but improper or impossible to speak aloud. Thus, lecturers use it in directing their lanternist; friends use it for necessary information during musical performances; it is used at the bedside of the sick, the actors in a moving picture can utilize it, and so be comprehended the world round; the pantomime stage, forbidden to use speech, can easily make clear the plot by sign-talk.

In a recent letter, Prof. J. S. Long has furnished me with a touching instance (one that has since recurred) that indicates another and final service that the silent method can render: An eminent divine was on his deathbed. His life had been devoted to ministering to the deaf, he knew the Sign Language perfectly; for several hours before the end his power of ordinary speech had deserted him, but his mind was clear, and to the last he conversed freely with those about him, in this, the universal talk, the one which for its exercise depended on muscular powers, that in his case were the last of all to fail.

6th. *It allows talk in an uproar.* It can be used when great noise makes it impossible to use the voice; therefore it can be of daily service in modern life, city or country, and each year it discovers new uses. Friends talk across a rackety thoroughfare or from a moving train; firemen and policemen, or sailors in a storm find it of growing service. The baseball umpire uses it when the roar of the multitude makes him voiceless; the catcher talks to the pitcher; the aeroplanist talks to his friends on earth; the stockholder on the curb buys and sells in it; the football captain or the army officer issues clear sign orders when the uproar of fight would drown even the trumpet call. The politician facing a shrieking mob may find it useful for conveying a few crude truths to his crude, unruly audience, thus opening the way for a more usual form of harangue, or failing in the attempt, he can at least inform his friends of his next move and his audience what he thinks of them. In St. Paul's epoch-making address on the stairs of Jerusalem we have a good illustration of the first part of this.

7th. *It is practical far-talk.* It is a valuable method of talking at a distance, far beyond earshot. Compared with the other modes of far-signalling it has the great advantages of speed, for it gives a sentence while semaphore, Morse, or Myer code give a letter, and of inconspicuousness at short range, or in a crowd; also it is independent of apparatus.

8th. *It is a true universal language.* It is already established. Instinctively the whole world has adopted it in a measure; and daily proofs of this are seen. Rasmussen among the Eskimo would have been helpless, he tells us, for he knew not their tongue, and they not a word of his, but they were expert sign-talkers and the lingual barrier was swept away. So also Henry among the Mandans, and Butler among the Basutos, while a thousand other cases could be aligned.

It is so complete that Dr. W. C. Roe and many others regularly *preach* and *lecture* in the language of Signs, to congregations in which several spoken tongues are used and would be necessary to the preacher were he limited to sounds.

It is so fundamental indeed that it is the easiest means of communicating with animals; the best trainers of dogs and horses use Sign Language as the principal medium of command.

But, for lack of standards and codification, its use is much smaller than it might be; and yet larger than commonly supposed. At least 100 of the 725 signs herein given are in daily employ among hearing white folk in America. After a little extension of the study, as is inevitable with a standard code, one will be able to travel all over Europe, the world indeed, on Sign Language alone.

No matter what the other man's language may be, French, German, Russian, Greek, all are the same in the Sign Language because it expresses *ideas, not words*. This, then, is its chief obvious strength—*It is a universal language.*

It was with this in view that the French and German equivalents were added after each sign; and since it is impossible to render in one word a sign that stands for a broad idea and is capable of conveying many meanings, according to the context and sense, the foreign equivalents are understood to deal only with the simplest root idea, that which usually is expressed by the first of the English words given.

It is my earnest hope that we may have an International Society of the Sign Language whose functions would be to keep it pure, to add new signs as they are needed, and to aim at its complete development.

Also, that in furtherance of this a thorough, full, and careful record of the old Indian Sign Language will be made before it is too late; that is, before all the old-time Indians of the Plains are dead.

My own effort is meant not as a record of the past, but a starting point for the future.

SYNTAX OF THE SIGN LANGUAGE*

The Sign Language is a system of root *ideas* expressed by *gestures*, preferably made only by the hands, without

---

*"After going carefully over your syntax I approve it in the main but I think it quite likely that many of the rules are not so inflexible as this makes them seem; besides which, there must be always a certain amount of modification by transliteration from the spoken language of those using the signs. This would manifest itself in a growing comformity of the Sign Language syntax to that of the more dominant spoken language."
—*F. W. Hodge (Ethnologist, Smithsonian Institution).*

sounds or reference to letters, or words, spoken or written, and not delimited by anything corresponding to words. There can be but little doubt that Sign Language preceded all audible speech.

Being fundamentally a true spontaneous language, wholly removed from any spoken language, it must necessarily have its own syntax and idiom.

Its syntax is simple and primitive, much like that of spoken language in its earliest or monosyllabic stage, as defined by Hovelacque. Yet clearly many signs are amplified by an associated but subsidiary root, so that we may consider it entering the second or agglutinative stage. Thus *deer*, signed by holding up the hands to indicate *branching horns*, is a simple or isolated root; but *white-tailed deer* which gives first *deer*, then adds the qualifying sign *banner tail* by waving the right index up high, is in close correspondence with agglutinative language. Still more so are the signs *finished* or *done* added to a verb to show the past tense, or the different twists to the sign *give* that turns it respectively into *give me* or *give you*, or the variations of *talk* which make it mean *I talk to you, you talk to me*, or *they talk to each other*.

The sentence construction is elemental. Dependent sentences are not used nor are negative or involved questions.

The relation of one idea to another is indicated chiefly by proximity and sequence, rarely by connectives and (with a few exceptions) never by inflection. So that the same sign may be the equivalent of a noun, a verb, or a phrase, etc., according as it is used.

NOUNS AND PRONOUNS

The **Nominative** and **Objective cases** are not distinguished except by context and sequence, that is, the Nominative precedes, the Objective usually follows, the verb.

A partial exception is the first personal pronoun—the starting point of most inflection—for *I*, *mine*, and *me* are sometimes given as cognate but distinctive signs.

The **Possessive case** is usually shown by the addition of the possessive sign, equivalent to "his," "hers," "its," etc. "That man's" horse would be signed: *Man, that, his horse*, or *Man, that there, possession, horse.*

The **Gender** of nouns is indicated when necessary by adding the signs *male* or *man* and *female* or *woman.* Thus "A She bear" would be rendered *Bear Woman.*

The **Number** of nouns is indicated by the signs 1, 2, 3, 4, etc., *many* or *few.*

In the Personal Pronouns the plural is made by adding *all* to the singular. Thus *Me all* is the equivalent of "We," *You all* of "Ye." *He all* is the equivalent of "they."

The **Person** by pointing to *myself*, to *you*, or to the *third person.* The first person is understood unless otherwise indicated.

VERBS

The **Verb** is usually placed between the subject and the object, but need of emphasis may change this so the verb comes last.

The **Tense** of verbs is marked by the auxiliary prefixes *now, future* and *past, finished* or *done.* Thus "I have eaten" would be *I done eat*, "I shall eat" will be *I time ahead, eat.*

The present is understood, unless otherwise stated; but the sign is plastic and may be any part of the verb, according to context. Thus *Arrange, Arranged,* or *Arranging* are the same.

The **Number** of the verb is shown by the context.

The **Voice** is assumed to be active, indeed the passive is not used.

The **Imperative** is shown by following the verb with the sign *must,* that is, strike down with right fist, giving the significance of command, or else by emphasis.

The **Subjunctive** is shown by the signs *if, so that, perhaps.*

ADJECTIVE AND ADVERB

The **Adjective** usually follows the substantive. Thus "A bad man" would be rendered *Man bad.* But numerals are exceptions to this rule.

The **Adverb** of time precedes the verb.

Qualities are compared by the use of the signs *little, more, much, most, ahead,* and *behind.* They are further modified by adding such signs as *strong, brave, very much,* or *very strong.*

The **Numeral sign** is often prefaced to small numbers to prevent confusion. Thus when prefaced by the numeral sign the sign *Wolf* may become *two* and *Man* become *one.*

Mere particles and expletives, as "a" "the," etc., have no equivalent signs.

PREPOSITIONS

Prepositions were little used by the Indian sign-talkers, though they did have *above, about, across, around, at, below, beside, beyond, by, for, from, in, near, on, out, to,*

under, upon, with, etc. *Of* or *pertaining to* has been
added by the deaf.

CONJUNCTIONS

And or *also* (add on) *but* or *if* (*pick out* or *cut off*), *so
that,with* are the equivalents of conjunctions.   Sometimes
the close continuity of two signs serves the purpose of
"and," conversely a pause may indicate a full stop.

INTERROGATION

The sign of interrogation always precedes the question,
but is sometimes added after it as well, for emphasis or
certainty.

. PERIOD OR FULL STOP

For period, the sign *finished* is generally used.   The
Blackfeet make the sign *broken off* and often clap the flat
right down on the flat left, palm to palm, for both beginning and end of a sentence.

ABSTRACT IDEAS

Abstract ideas are not copiously rendered in signs.
But it often happens that a gesture with the index alone
is specific, while the same gesture with the flat hand becomes abstract.   For example, compare *yonder* and *far,*
up and *up there.*

OPPOSITION

The principle of opposition as pointed out by Mallery
plays an important part in the pairing of signs.   Thus
above being fixed, *below* is the reverse; the sign *come*
is reversed in *go,* and *out* reversed in *in,* etc.

EMPHASIS

Emphasis is sometimes given by using both hands for a sign that can be made by one, sometimes by repeating the sign, sometimes by energetic rendering, and sometimes by adding the sign *very much* or *heap*.

PARALLEL OR DUPLICATE SIGNS

Many signs are made by parallel action of both hands. Most of these are permissibly rendered by using only one hand as, *woman, abandon, gratitude*, etc.

ENUNCIATION OR DELIVERY

In actual and expert practice most signs are abbreviated. But the beginner, as in all new arts, should go slowly and be careful to make each sign clear-cut and complete in itself.

The hands are always held or moved so as to illustrate-as far as possible, the action in mind or its manner, or its direction, or the point where it takes place, or the shape of an object, or their relative positions if two objects are being considered.

ELEGANCE

Grace and dignity are of large importance in all good sign-talk. Ugly or vulgar gestures should be abandoned. Even angular gestures should be avoided, except to express some angular idea.

Many times my Indian teachers have said to me as I imitated their signs, "Yes, that is correct enough in a way, but it is awkward"; or "it is not graceful. We do it this way." Then they sketched the same structure, but in sweeping lines. In this work many movements are indicated in straight lines, for the sake of simplicity. As a matter of fact, I never saw a Cheyenne make a straight-line movement, all had a graceful curve.

Many signs are followed by a changeable *liaison;* that is, by an introduced sweep to join it on to the sign that follows and avoid a jerk or unpleasant movement. This elegant manner is what I call an Indian accent, few whites achieve it.

In a dignified way, the expression of face and the pose were used in elucidation of the gesture, but very sparingly.

THE CONCEPT AND ITS VALUE

The student of vocal language finds vital help in remembering the derivation of words; so also the sign-talker.

Most signs were pantomimic originally, but through much use have become shortened, till now they are conventional. Yet it is well worth while in each case to note the original concept as fully as possible; first as a great help to the memory, and second as a guard against slovenly gesture and a guarantee of point, power, and structural accuracy. Some of the concepts given are evidently right, but some are mere guesses, probably wrong in many cases. It is quite permissible in any one to challenge any of them.

Nevertheless, the fact that most signs are capable of logical explanation does not mean that they are self-explanatory. Indeed nearly all have become conventional, and each must be learned separately before it can be rightly used.

Signs which make the heart the seat of the mind are,

I think, older than those which give the place of honor
to the brain.

Although not at all Indian, it is exceedingly helpful to
know the single-hand alphabet as given in the cut on
page II; partly because it must sometimes be used for
giving proper names and also because it saves time in
describing *hand positions*. For example, we say "position A or B" instead of describing each hand all over
again for each new sign.

Fingers and *numbers* are nearly synonymous the world
round when making signs, manual or written, hence the
universality of the decimal system. The Indian Code,
the Popular Code, and the Deaf Code are nearly alike in
this, but in most points of difference the Indian is best.

To prevent mistakes in certain cases preface the number with the sign of *numbers* or *arithmetic*.

For Ordinals, make the figure sign, 1, 2, or whatever it
is, then without changing the position of hand or arm,
give the hand a twisting from the wrist, to add point or
emphasis, meaning "number-so-and-so." This is not
Indian but adopted from the Deaf, nevertheless quite
logical.

ILLUSTRATIONS OF SIGN LANGUAGE

Clark gives the following (pp. 17-18) as a good illustration of the syntax of the Sign Language:

In English. "I arrived here to-day to make a treaty
—my one hundred lodges are camped beyond the Black

Hills, near the Yellowstone River. You are a great chief—pity me, I am poor, my five children are sick and have nothing to eat. The snow is deep and the weather intensely cold. Perhaps God sees me. I am going. In one month I shall reach my camp."

In Signs, this literally translated would read, I—arrive here—to-day—to make—treaty. My—hundred —lodge—camp—beyond—Hills—Black—n e a r—r i v e r —called—Elk—you—chief—g r e a t—pity me—I—poor —My—five—child—sick—food—all gone (or wiped out) —Snow—deep—cold—brave (or strong). Perhaps— Chief Great (or Great Mystery)—above—see—me—I —go. Moon—die—I—arrive there—my—camp.

"An Indian in closing or terminating a talk or speech wishing to say, 'I have finished my speech or conversation,' or, 'I have nothing more to say,' simply makes the sign for *'Done'* or *'Finished.'* "

THE LORD'S PRAYER

FATHER ISADORE'S VERSION

Our Father up high, medicine thy name. Thy sit-aboard down here on earth as up high. Give us all bread. Forgive our bad as we forgive bad. Lead us bad not. Ended.

Professor Elmer D. Read has supplied me with the foregoing two examples done into the Sign Language of the deaf, as below:

I—came—here—to-day—make—agreement (t h i n k parallel)—name (written). My—1 C (100) tents— beyond—B-l-a-c-k H-i-l-l-s, near Y-e-l-l-o-w-s-t-o-n-e

water flow. You—most—chief, feel—tender—me. I—
ragged sleeve (poor). My—five—children (sign size)
—sick—nothing—eat. Snow—deep. Weather (air,
wind)—very cold. Perhaps—God—look down on (see)
me. I—go. In—one—month—I—shall—arrive—tents
—home (eat, sleep).

The Lord's Prayer in Deaf Signs:

Our—Father—sky—into.
Honored—thy—name—truly.
Thy—kingdom—come;
Thy—law—do—on—earth—as—in—sky.
Give—us—our—bread—daily.
Forgive—us—our—lawbreaking—as—we — forgive —
those—injure—us.
Lead—us—not—in—temptation,
But—save (break our tied hands)—us—from—law-
breaking.
Because—thine—kingdom, power, and—glory—for-
ever.
Amen.

PICTURE-WRITING

As already noted, a weakness of Sign Language is the difficulty of writing it without translating it into words, and thereby changing its nature and its world-wide application. Yet it can be written; and some mention of its recorded form may fitly round out this introduction.

The characters used, because they represent ideas, not words or letters, are called ideographs or picture-writing. It is widely believed that Sign Language is the oldest of all languages, that indeed it existed among animals before man appeared on earth. It is universally accepted that the ideograph is the oldest of all writing. The Chinese writing, for instance, is merely picture-writing done with as few lines as possible.

Thus, it is said that their curious character for *Hearing* was once a complete picture of a person listening behind a screen, but in time it was reduced by hasty hands to a few scratches; and *War*, now a few spider marks, was originally a sketch of *Two women in one house.*

We may also record our Sign Language in picture-writing, as was the custom of many Indian tribes; and we shall find it worth while for several reasons: it is picturesque and useful for decoration; and it is likely that a pictographic inscription dug up 10,000 years from now would be read, whether our language was understood or not.*

---

*Since the above was written, I have come across L. F. Hadley's pictographic writing of the Sign Language, fully set forth in the bibliographical matter. E. T. S.

When the French Government set up the Obelisk of Luxor, in Paris, and wished to inscribe it for all time, they made record, not in French or Latin, but in pictographs.

It is, moreover, a good thing to take the young through the stages of race development; just as the young bird must run for a send-off, before it flies, so pictography, being its earliest form, is the natural first step to writing.

In this dictionary I give the written form after many of the signs that have an established pictograph. These are chiefly from Mallery, 10th Annual Report Bureau of American Ethnology. A few are popularly accepted among ourselves.

NOTE

The letters, initials, etc., after the paragraphs indicate the chief authority for the sign.

Where no authority is given, it means that the sign was observed by myself among the Cheyenne Indians. Those ascribed to other Indians also were observed by myself. Besides these the following are cited:

C. Standing for Captain William Philo Clark, U. S. A.

Scott, for General Hugh L. Scott, U. S. A.

Seger, for John M. Seger, of Colony, Oklahoma.

R. B., for Robert Burns, the Cheyenne interpreter at Concho, Oklahoma.

Long, for Major Stephen H. Long, U. S. A.

Pop. for Popular; that is, established among ourselves.

D. for Deaf Sign, as given in J. Schuyler Long's Dictionary.

GENERAL INSTRUCTIONS

The drawing shows the hands as seen by the second person.

The digits are named: thumb, first or index finger, second or middle finger, third or ring-finger, and fourth or little finger.

The following marks, etc., are used in the illustrations:

Unless otherwise stated the *solid outline* indicates the position of the hands at the beginning of a sign, the *dotted outlines* indicate the position of the hands at the finish.

............Dotted lines indicate the course of hand employed in the sign.

⟩ Indicates the commencement point of the movement.

→Indicates the direction of movement.

✕ Indicates the point in the gesture line at which the hand position is (x) changed.

⊙Or full stop represents the termination of the movement.

"A hand" means like A, and "B hand" means like B, etc., in the one-handed Deaf Alphabet (Cut 1) on next page. The positions meant by "4 hand," "5 hand," "flat hand," "flat fist," or "compressed hand," are figured on the same page.

Begin by learning the Single-hand Manual alphabet as noted above.

Next learn the *Numbers* and the signs for *Question* and its combinations; also *Yes* and *No, Good* and *Bad, Come* and *Go, Big* and *Small, Truth* and *Lie, Strong* and *Weak, Understand, Perhaps, Talk* and *Sign-talk*, after this refer to the Dictionary for the signs that serve your purpose and use them according to the rules of syntax as herein set forth.

Never lose a chance of talking the Sign Language with an old Plains Indian, preferably of the Cheyenne or Arapahoe tribes. Their wonderful facility and grace are as hard to convey on paper as the pronunciation of French, and are as essential for the best style in Sign Talk. One may, indeed, know every sign in this book and not be a good sign-talker, so fundamental is this correct accent, or manner.

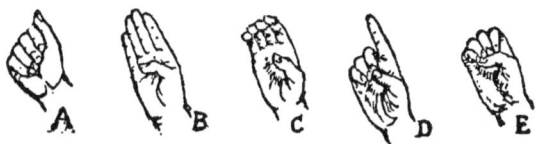

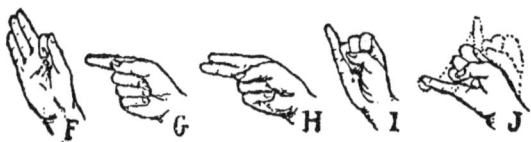

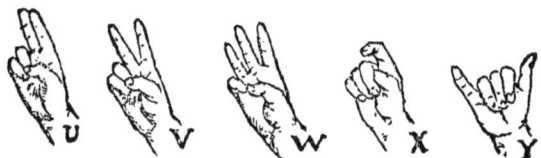

and

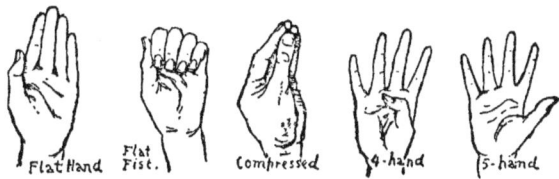

Flat Hand   Flat Fist.   Compressed   4-hand   5-hand

li

SIGN TALK

*A Universal Signal Code, Without Apparatus, for Use in
the Army, the Navy, Camping, Hunting, Daily
Life and Among the Plains Indians*

SIGN TALK
OF THE AMERICAN INDIANS

BY

ERNEST THOMPSON SETON

"A hand," "G hand," "flat hand" etc., mean like "A," "G," "flat," etc., on page li.

A

Abandon, Give It up (Thrown away, chucked). Hold both S hands, backs up, near left breast, briskly swing both down to left side, opening them with a snap and giving a slight rebound to the hands after the movement, as though emphatically throwing away something. Sometimes only one hand is used. Compare *Bad, Hate,* and *Charge.* See *Divorce.*

Fr. *abandonner;* Ger. *aufgeben.*

Able. See *Can.*

Aboard (Sitting down on). Left hand out flat, palm up, right S hand on it, thumb up. Compare *Sit down.*

Fr. *à bord;* Ger. *an Bord.*

About or **Around.** Hold the flat left hand pointing forward, up and to the right, encircle it several times with the right G finger. If possible, make it concrete by indicating the very thing that was encircled.

Fr. *autour;* Ger. *um . . . herum.*

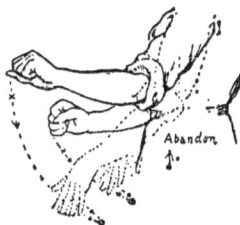

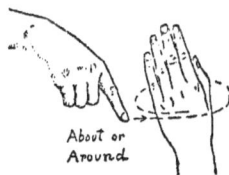

3

About, in the sense of *Near by* or *Almost.* See *Close.*

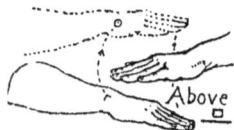

Above or **Over** (One thing above another).   Bring the flat left hand, back up, in front of and a little to the left of body; left forearm horizontal, fingers pointing to right and front; bring the flat right hand, back up over the left in a semi-circle upward large or small, as best suggests the actual distance.   Has been used for *More than.*   Compare *Beyond.*

      Fr. *au-dessus;* Ger. *über.*

(Below is the reverse of this.)

Absent. See *Empty.*

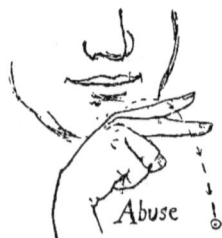

Abuse to **Scold** or **Defame** (Throwing lies against one). Hold the right V hand near the mouth, pointing to left. Jerk it forward toward person once or twice.   For **Abusing me** make the sign lower opposite the left breast and inward toward one's self.

      Fr. *calomnier, injurier;* Ger. *schmähen, beschimpfen.*

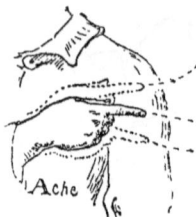

Accident. See *Free,* also *Luck.*

Ache or **Pain.** Thrust G finger many times in different directions over and parallel to the part.   Compare *Wound* and *Sick.*

      Fr. *la douleur;* Ger. *der Schmerz.*

Across, Cross, or **Over** (Crossing a ridge).   Hold the flat left hand out, palm down, and pointing forward and toward the right, pass the flat right hand edgewise across the back of the left.   If but one person is meant, the right G is sometimes used. This sign as illustrated is often used for *Council*. See *Council* and *Laws*.

Fr. *d'un côté à l'autre, traverser;* Ger. *hinüber.*

Act, as in a theatre play. Hold A hands in front perpendicularly, move up and down alternately as though the thumbs were two puppets. (Deaf sign, not used or understood by Indians.) Compare *Play* and *Follow*.

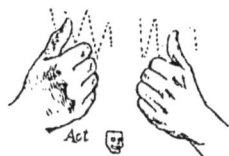

Act, as in a play. Sign *Face, Two, Dance* (that is dancing with a mask) (not established).

Fr. *jouer;* Ger. *spielen.*

Act or **Deed.** See *Work*.

Add to (Piling up). Flat left hand pointing to the right and front, palm up, forearm horizontal; the palm of flat right hand is placed on top of left hand a number of times, the left hand being raised a couple of inches each time, to meet it; the movement ends with left hand as high as top of the head. Often it is done as in the illustration but with palm of left down.

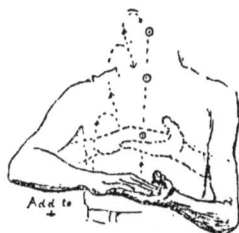

Adjectives, see *Comparative*.

Adulation. Kissing the back of the hand. (Pop.) Not Indian, but they understand it now. (R. B.)

Fr. *la flatterie;* Ger. *die Schmeichelei.*

Advance. Both flat hands back up, pointing forward, tandem, right in advance, six inches ahead (the fingers extended) moved forward together in gentle jerks. Compare *Move camp.*

Fr. *avancer;* Ger. *vorschreiten.*

Advance Guard (The one ahead, looking). Flat left hand back up, pointing forward, breast high; place G right just before it, then turn right G into V to mean *Looking*. Also used for *Scout*. Compare *Ahead*.

Fr. *l'avant-garde;* Ger. *die Vorhut.*

Advise or **Advice**. Sign *Talk, Make, Way*. (C) Sign *Help* and *Talk* would be near it.

Fr. *conseiller;* Ger. *raten.*

Afraid (Shaking heart). Sign *Heart* then shake it up and down two or three times, to indicate the throbbing action of the heart under influence of fear. Or more strongly, sign *Heart* and then finish by raising the hand until its back strikes the chin, to mean the heart rises in the throat.

Fr. *effrayé;* Ger. *ängstlich.*

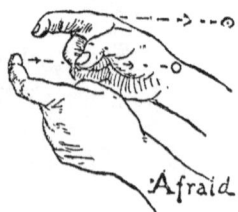

Afraid or **Cowardly** (Seger says this means Buffalo backing out of fight; that is, " drawing in his horns.") Hold out both G hands level, backs out, G fingers hooked like horns, draw them straight back together for six inches. Mostly but one hand is used. Compare *Bring*.

Fr. *lâche, poltron;* Ger. *feige.*

Afraid of no one. Point right G in several directions, then add *Afraid, Not*.

Fr. *peur de personne;* Ger. *vor niemand Angst haben.*

After, Behind, or **Late** (Time or space). G fingers pointing forward at an angle in front of body; left in advance. Draw the right over and behind the left. Draw it back a little way for a *little bit after;* but far back and low down for *a long way behind.* Some finish by clenching the right hand.

If it meant that *one* is behind *the rest,* use the flat left hand, palm down, in advance, with right G behind.

Fr. *après;* Ger. *hinter, nach.*

Afternoon. Make a circle of right thumb and index and sweep it over the afternoon half of the sky from the zenith down. Compare *Sunset.*

Fr. *l'après-midi;* Ger. *der Nachmittag.*

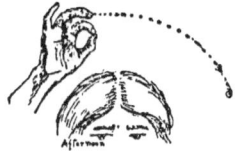

Again. See *Repeat* or *More.*

Against, i.e., **Go Against.** Thrust the tips of the flat right, back out, square against the palm of the flat left held pointing level forward, back to left. See also *Oppose.* Compare *Quandary.*

Fr. *contre;* Ger. *wider.*

Agent, Indian. Sign *Whiteman* and *Chief, Give all.* The Southern Cheyennes sign *Chief* and *pull teeth,* because their first agent had false upper teeth.

Agitate. See *Excite.*

Agree. Sign *You, I, think, same.* Sometimes use *Equal.* See also *Treaty.*

Fr. *s'accorder;* Ger. *übereinstimmen.*

Agreement. See *Treaty.*

Ago, Time back, Past, or **Back.** Sign *Time* and point back over the right shoulder with right finger G. Sometimes the thumb or the whole hand is used instead of the index.   See *Back*.

Fr. *passé, il y a quelque temps;* Ger. *vorher, früher.*

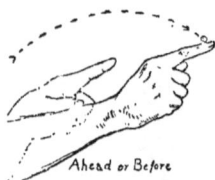

Ahead or **Before** (In time).   Hold out the left G pointing forward and up; swing the right G over the left to a place in front of it, both pointing the same way.   Some finish by closing and lowering the right fist.   Compare *After*.

Fr. *avant;* Ger. *vor.*

Ahead or **Before others** (In space or rank).   Hold out flat left, back up, near breast, pointing forward and slightly upward; then hold right G just before it.   Compare *Advance Guard*, which it exactly resembles, except that this omits *Looking*.

Fr. *en avant;* Ger. *vor.*

Air.   See *Wind*.

Alight or **Descend.**   Indicate from what, then drop right V fingers downward onto flat left palm.   See *Dismount*.

Fr. *descendre;* Ger. *absteigen, hinuntersteigen.*

Alike, to **Look like** or **Resemble** (Of persons).   Make the signs *Face* and *Equal*.

Fr. *semblable;* Ger. *ähnlich sein.*

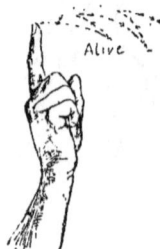

Alive, Live, Life, or **All right** (Walking about, upright). Hold index of right hand upright, move it about shoulder high, forward in long slow zigzags sidewise, always turning it so as to move palm forward.   Also used for *Be* or *Exist*.   See *Life, Deer,* and *Nothing*.   The Blackfeet use the sign *Grow* for this idea.   See *Wandering*.

Fr. *vivant;* Ger. *lebendig.*

All. With right hand flat and back up, describe a large horizontal circle, shoulder high.

Fr. *tout;* Ger. *alles.*

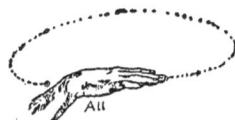

All gone or **Empty** (Hands swept clean). Both 5 hands in front of body, backs out, right nearer; loosely brush fingers of right on left palm, moving right outward, then reverse and repeat. Sometimes begin with sign *All.* See *Wipe out.*

Fr. *vide;* Ger. *leer.*

Alliance or **Friendship** (Linked together). Form two circles with thumbs and index fingers, and link them together, other fingers closed. Some use only index fingers hooked together.

Fr. *l'alliance;* Ger. *das Bündnis.*

All right. See *Good* or sometimes *Alive.*

All the time. Hold up the left G, pointing upward, forward, and to the right; strike on it with right G near the tip, then every inch or so up to the arm. See *Many times, Cheyenne* and *Buy.*

Fr. *toujours;* Ger. *immerzu.*

Alone or **Only** (Living and moving singly). Move the right G hand, pointed upward, slowly forward and to left in a line slightly waving to right and left. Compare *Alive, Life, Man, One* and *Up there.*

Fr. *seul;* Ger. *allein.*

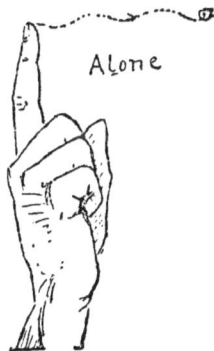

Already. See *Now.*

Always, Ever, or **Forever** (Going on in cycles). With elbow at side, hold the right G hand pointing forward; move hand forward, describing circles with the index, the result a spiral, ending with the index raised. (Frosted, borrowed from the Deaf Code.)

Always. Sign *Long time*, *Wiped out*, and *Not*. Sometimes sign *Stop*, *Not*. (Blackfoot signs.) See *All the time*.
  Fr. *toujours;* Ger. *immer.*

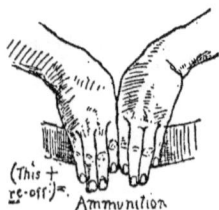

Ambitious (Pushing to rise). Indicate a person, then sign *Push* and *Rising man*, or omit last.
  Fr. *ambitieux;* Ger. *ehrgeizig.*

American. See *Nationalities.*

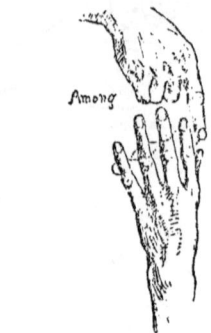

Ammunition (Cartridges in belt). Lay the flat hands, palm in, on belt, then add *Shoot* by shooting the right G forward. (Not Cheyenne, but understood.)
  Fr. *les munitions;* Ger. *die Munition.*

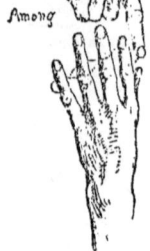

Among. Hold the left 5 hand in front of neck, pointing upward, move right G index (pointing down) in and through. Sometimes use *With*.
  Fr. *parmi;* Ger. *unter.*

Ancestor. Repeat the sign for *Father* several times, with the flat left hand held back out on the breast, and each time pushed farther away, the *Father* sign made beyond it. (Crow sign.) The Cheyennes sign *Father* and *Old*.
  Fr. *l'ancêtre;* Ger. *der Vorvater.*

And or **Also** (Meet and go together). The spread flat right hand, breast high, back forward, drawn six inches to the right and closed to flat hand. (Deaf sign.) Compare *Horse*. The Cheyennes use *Equal* or *Increase*, according to the sense; or sometimes *With* or *Add*.

Fr. *et, aussi;* Ger. *und, auch.*

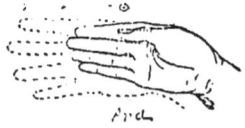

Angry (Mind twisted). Twist the A hand against or near the forehead.

Seger maintains that this means a " mad buffalo breaking off his own horns." Possibly he is right; for the older signs make the heart, not the head, the place of the mind, and this must be a very old sign. Some of the Blackfeet make this sign over the heart. Some grind on the heart with the flat right fist, palm in, after pointing to the person; meaning, " he grinds my heart." See *Sorrow*.

Fr. *en colère;* Ger. *böse, zornig.*

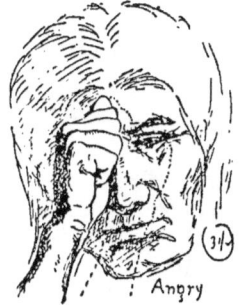

Animal or **Quadruped** (Jumper). The compressed right hand, back up, advanced in short jumps, as in *Frog* and *Weasel*. Sometimes the sign *Ground* is made first by sweeping the flat right across, palm up. " Leaping " is generic for the quadruped as " Flying " is generic for *Bird*. Compare *Jump*. Used by Blackfeet. The Cheyennes considered it incomplete.

Fr. *l'animal;* Ger. *das Tier.*

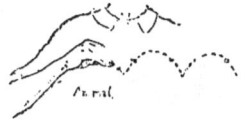

Annihilate. See *Exterminate* or *Wipe out*.

Annoyance. See *Trouble*.

Annul. See *Rub it out*.

Another or **Other** (one other). Hold out flat right, back up, swing it slowly up, out, *far to right* and down low, turning it palm up. Compare *Fall* and *Lie down*.
Fr. *un autre;* Ger. *ein anderer*.

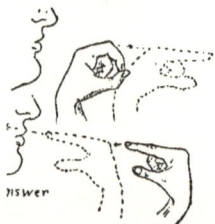

Another person. As above, but use right G. (Blackfoot.) In this, as usual, the index up alone means *Man*. This gesture is so natural that many whites use it; as, for example, in saying impatiently: " That was another man altogether."

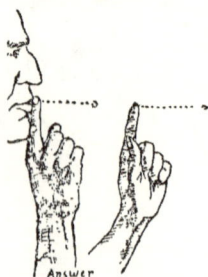

Answer (Talk come back). Push right G from the mouth in the sign *Talk*, then draw back reversed; that is, pointing to one's own face or ear. (Blackfoot.) The Cheyennes use *Talk, Arrived here*.

Answer, Reply, Respond (The word that follows the other). Right G index upright on lips, left six inches ahead and parallel; move them together toward the person. (Frosted, borrowed from the Deaf Code.)
Fr. *la réponse;* Ger. *die Antwort*.

Antelope (Pronged horns of the animal). Bring the L hands palm toward and alongside of the head, near the base of the ears.
Fr. *l'antelope;* Ger. *die Antilope*.

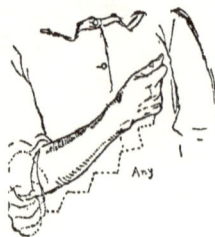

Anxious. See *Want*.

Any (Scattering). Place the right A hand near left side, elbow high; draw it down and out to right side in a shaky curve. (Deaf sign.) Use *Here* and *There*. (Cheyennes.)
Fr. *quelconque, quelque;* Ger. *irgend ein*.

Apache. See *Indian.*

Appear, To come into view. See *Come into view.*

Appears, Seems, or **Looks like** (See and Same). Hold up flat right hand, thumb toward self, shoulder high; throw it forward and turn palm toward self, fixing the eyes on it and sign *Same.* Sometimes use the sign for *Look* before *Same.* (Frosted; probably adopted from Deaf Code.)

Fr. *paraître;* Ger. *aussehen, erscheinen.*

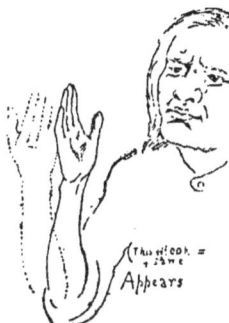

Applause. See *Approval.*

Approach or **Moving toward.** Hold partly bent left hand well in front, breast high, to left side, palm to you and right similarly to right, but quite near to you; move the latter *slowly* forward toward former, but not to touch it by several inches. Some use right G. See *Arrive there* and *Quandary.*

Fr. *approcher;* Ger. *näher kommen.*

Approval, Applause, or **Praise.** Make the motion of clapping the hands, but without noise. A white man's sign, but now generally understood.

Fr. *l'approbation;* Ger. *der Beifall.*

Arise or **Get up.** Hold out right G, back down; raise the arm with a swing and snap and bend the wrist till the finger points straight up. For a large number, use both 5 hands.

Fr. *se lever;* Ger. *aufstehen.*

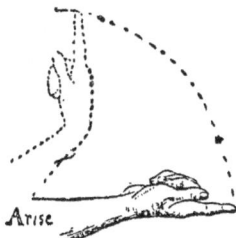

Arithmetic. See *Numeral.*

Around. See *About*.

Arrange (Parfleches placed in teepee). With flat right, slightly curved, back out, strike half a dozen times in a circle, turning to watch the hand; then add *Good*. Sometimes omit *Good*. Or, sign *Work* and *Fix*. See *Ready*.

> Fr. *arranger;* Ger. *ordnen, einrichten*.

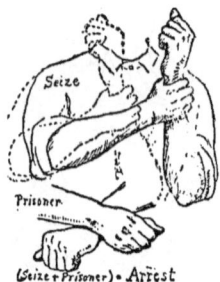

Arrest or **Imprison** (To seize hold of and tie at wrists). Sign *Seize* and then add *Prisoner;* that is, cross the wrists, hands closed. Sometimes the upright left forearm with S hand, back to left, is held near the left shoulder, grasp left wrist with right hand and pull it a little distance to right.

> Fr. *arrêter;* Ger. *verhaften*.

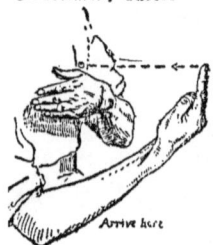

Arrive here or **Get here.** Hold the flat left hand, back out, near the breast, fingers pointing to right; carry right G, back to front, well out in front of body; bring the right hand briskly against back of left. Often the flat right is used instead of right G.

> Fr. *arriver ici;* Ger. *hier ankommen*.

Arrive there or **Reach.** Hold the flat left hand, back to front, well out in front of body, about height of neck, pointing to right; bring right G hand, palm outward, in front of and close to neck, carry the right hand out sharply to strike the palm of the left.

> Fr. *y arriver;* Ger. *hinkommen*.

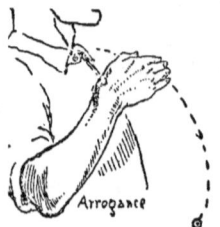

Arrogance. A haughty lifting of the eyebrows and side-long, disdainful look down as upon an inferior. (Scott.)

Sign *Head, Big.* In the popular code, indicate big chest. See *Conceit* and *Pride.*

Fr. *l'arrogance;* Ger. *die Anmaszung.*

Arrow. Make, with a long swing, the motion of drawing an arrow from the left hand.

Fr. *la flèche;* Ger. *der Pfeil.*

As or **Than.** Both hands, G fingers parallel, level, forward near right side; carry them over to left in similar position. (A sign borrowed from the Deaf, Frosted.) This is the same as *Who;* only the context can show which is meant. Sign *Same* or *Beside.*

Fr. *comme, que;* Ger. *wie, als.*

Ascend. Indicate the object (hill, tree, etc.), then press right G against it, raising the same in jerks. Compare *Famous.*

Fr. *monter;* Ger. *hinaufsteigen.*

Ashamed or **Bashful** (Drawing blanket over face). Flat hands pointing up, palms in, close to face and moved in till the *wrists crossed*, right nearest the face; bow the head a little. Compare *Blind* and *Dark.* The bowing of the head was not generally done, yet is the only feature to distinguish it from *Dark.*

Fr. *honteux;* Ger. *verschämt, verlegen.*

Ashamed (I am ashamed). Cover the face and eyes with both hands. (Pop.)

Fr. *avoir honte;* Ger. *sich schämen.*

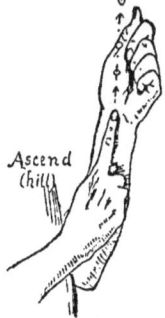

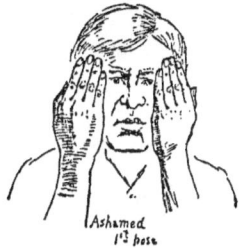

Ashamed (You should be). See *Shame*.

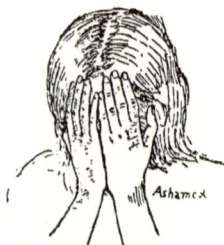

Ashes. Sign *Fire* and *Powder*.
Fr. *la cendre;* Ger. *die Asche.*

Ask. See *Beg.*

Assiniboine. See *Indian.*

Astonishment or **Wonder.** Lay the flat palm of left hand over the open mouth and draw the body backward. Sometimes, also, raise right hand flat, palm forward.
Fr. *l'étonnement;* Ger. *die Verwunderung.*

Astray. See *Lost.*

Astride. See *Horseman.*

At. Hold left flat hand, back up, pointing partly up; strike the back with right flat hand.
Fr. *à;* Ger. *an, auf.*

Attempt. See *Try.*

Attention (A command). See *Call.*

Aunt. Sign *Father* (or *Mother*) and *Sister*. Or, sign *Woman* with right, then tuck compressed right, point down, under left arm pit. (R. B.)
Fr. *la tante;* Ger. *die Tante.*

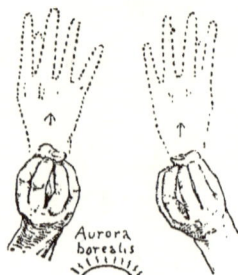

Aurora or **Northern Lights.** Both hands, backs down,

half closed, thumb and finger tips together, raised very
high and spread with a sweep to indicate flashes. It
should be done facing north. It is helped if the hands
when at the highest are swung apart in an arch.

Fr. *l'aurore boréale;* Ger. *das Nordlicht.*

Automobile. See *Motor car.*

Autumn (Leaf-falling time). Make the sign for *Tree*
with both hands, then for *Leaf* with the right near the
left finger tips, then drop the leaf with tremulous, wavy
motion down and to right.

Fr. *l'automne;* Ger. *der Herbst.*

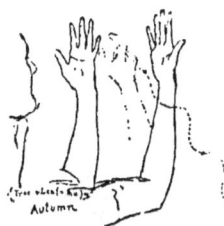
Autumn

Avoid or **Miss.** Hold up G hands, move them toward
each other as in *Meet*, but carry left well outside, past
and beyond without meeting. Compare *Meet, Trade,*
and *Mistake.*

Fr. *éviter;* Ger. *vermeiden.*

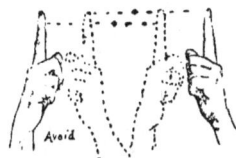
Avoid

Awl. Bore right G finger into left palm. Or, over the
left G as in sewing.

Fr. *l'alêne;* Ger. *die Ahle.*

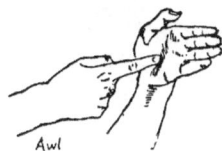
Awl

Axe or **Hatchet.** Hold out the flat right hand, back to
right, wrist bent downward. Make as though chopping with it; that is, strike down once or twice. Some
also grasp it near the elbow with left index and thumb,
but the Cheyennes omit this. For *Hatchet,* indicate
Size. See *Tomahawk.*

Fr. *la hache;* Ger. *das Beil.*

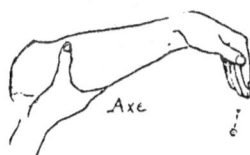
Axe

B

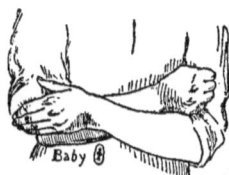

Baby. Swing the flat right hand (sometimes S hand) in the hollow of the left arm as though it were a baby. Add signs for sex and size when needed. Compare *Tomahawk.*

Fr. *le bébé;* Ger. *das Kindchen, der Säugling.*

Bachelor. Sign *Man, Marriage, No.* (C)

Fr. *le célibataire;* Ger. *der Junggeselle.*

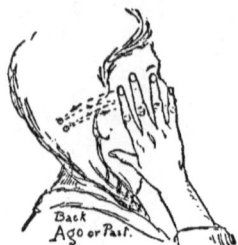

Back or **Again.** See *Repeat.*

Back, Backward, Ago, or **Past** (In time or space). Throw right 5 hand thumb first back over right shoulder once or twice. See *Ago.*

Fr. *en arrière;* Ger. *hinten, zurück.*

Backbite. Lay the right V hand on the mouth, as in *Lie,* then lay it on the back of the right shoulder. (Blackfoot.)

Backbite. Sign *Scold, Talk,* and *Hide.*

Fr. *médire de;* Ger. *verleumden.*

Bacon (Meat and thin). Hold out the flat left hand, thumb edge up; with thumb and finger tips of right back down, rub little finger of left. Hadley gives this with the right hand over. It makes a better sign, but I never saw it used that way. Compare *Meat* and *Thin* and *Oil.*

Fr. *le lard;* Ger. *der Speck.*

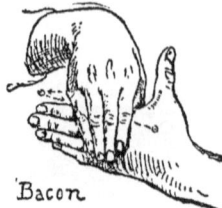

Bad or **Evil** (Suddenly thrown away). Hold clenched fist, back up, near breast; throw it forward, down, and aside, opening the hand. Sometimes for emphasis both hands are used. Compare *Abandon, Charge,* and *Hate.*

Fr. *mauvais;* Ger. *schlecht.*

Badger (Walks under ground). Sign *Hole, Enter,* and *Walk.* The Blackfeet sign is *Striped-face* with size and pawing indicated.

Fr. *le blaireau;* Ger. *der Dachs.*

Bad Taste. See *Taste Bad.*

Bag. Left C hand, back out; drop compressed right into this; then sometimes indicate thickness with flat hands pointing straight up.

Fr. *le sac;* Ger. *der Sack.*

Bald. Lay the flat right hand on the forehead, draw it up and back to the top of the head. Touch the hair and sign *Wiped-out.* (Blackfoot.)

Fr. *chauve;* Ger. *kahlköpfig.*

Band or **Patrol** (Banded together). Hold the compressed left hand pointing up; encircle it with the right forefinger and thumb. (Chasing Bear.) Not a true Indian sign and not used, but would understand it. (Seger.) Sometimes use *Bunch* or *Few.* See *Tribe* or *Troop.*

Fr. *la bande, la patrouille;* Ger. *die Schar, die Truppe.*

Bankrupt. See *Done.*

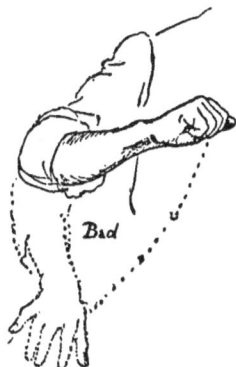

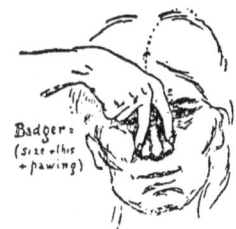

Bar or **Saloon** (House of drink). Sign *Crazy, Drink, House.*

> Fr. *le cabaret, la buvette;* Ger. *die Bierstube, die Kneipe.*

Bark (Like a dog). Sign *Talk,* but use index and middle finger against thumb.

> Fr. *aboyer;* Ger. *bellen.*

Barracks. Sign *White, Soldier, House.*

> Fr. *la caserne;* Ger. *die Kaserne.*

Barren. Sign *Born* and *All gone.*

> Fr. *stérile;* Ger. *unfruchtbar.*

Bar up. See *Fins.*

Baseball signs. These, of course, are not Indian; they differ locally, but the three following are used by most umpires:

> *A strike.* The sign "Yes."
> *Out.* The Same as the "No" sign (as tho striking something to one side with the back of hand).
> *Safe.* Hand raised as in "Easy."

Bashful. See *Ashamed.*

Basin or **Hollow** (A spread out circle). Hold the L hands low in front, backs up, forming an incomplete horizontal circle, not touching, the index fingers nearer each other than thumbs; swing the hands apart by wrist action so the index fingers point nearly forward.

> Fr. *le bassin;* Ger. *die Vertiefung, die Grube.*

Basket. Sign *Kettle*, then interlock fingers as in *House of logs*, to show structure. The Cheyennes understand this, though usually they sign *Kettle* and *Sew*.

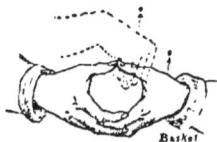

Basket. Lock the fingers of the hollowed hands, backs down, join the thumbs as for a handle, then with the right hand grasp left thumb and raise the hand a few inches. (Sioux.) Compare *Corral*.
  Fr. *le panier;* Ger. *der Korb*.

Bat. Sign *Night* and zigzag flight; i. e., flat hands side by side, breast high, flapped first to right side next to left. (C)
  Fr. *la chauve-souris;* Ger. *die Fledermaus*.

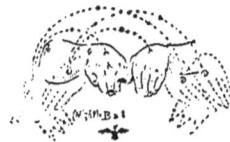

Battle, Combat. Sign *Fight*, after which make *Shoot* with each hand toward the other. (C) Compare *Fight* and *Kill*.
  Fr. *la bataille, le combat;* Ger. *die Schlacht*.

Battle-cry or **War-cry.** Open the mouth as in saying "O" and pat it with flattened fingers of right hand. (C) The Cheyennes use *Yell*.
  Fr. *le cri de bataille;* Ger. *der Schlachtruf*.

Bay. Sign *Water*, then bring right L hand well out in front of body, forming a horizontal half-circle. (C)
  Fr. *la baie;* Ger. *die Bucht*.

Bayonet. Sign *Gun*, then lay left G index alongside right G, the latter one-third ahead. If there is doubt, indicate drawing it on the barrel tip.
  Fr. *la baïonnette;* Ger. *das Bajonett*.

Be, to be or exist (Living). Sign *Alive* and then finish with *Now* or *Past* to indicate tense, and *Many* to indicate plural. Sometimes use *Dwell* or *Recover* for this idea. Compare *Alone*.

Fr. *être;* Ger. *existieren, sein.*

Beads. Hold out the flat right, slightly hollow; drop it a little with a sidewise quivering to suggest the shimmering of a handful of beads. (C)

Beads. Simulate holding beads between the left index and thumb, while threading them with a needle in the right. For *Beadwork* add a design or sign for *Work*.

Fr. *les perles;* Ger. *die Perlen.*

Beans (One picked out of a handful). Right hand flat, palm up, index and thumb joined with the tip of index projecting. (Chasing Bear. Understood by Cheyennes.)

Fr. *les haricots;* Ger. *die Bohnen.*

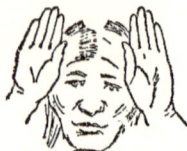

Bear. Hold out the Y hands, backs up, and strike both down; push both forward in a series of jerks, or swing down, forward and up.

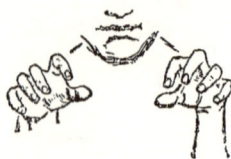

Bear. Hold up flat fists near ears, palms forward, to indicate round ears. (Blackfoot.) Some indicate the paws by holding up both curved 5 hands.

Fr. *l'ours;* Ger. *der Bär.*

Bear, Grizzly. As above, but indicate the gray color.

Fr. *l'ours gris;* Ger. *der graue Bär.*

Beard. Hang the compressed right hand, point down, under chin. The hand or hands are differently placed for different cuts of whiskers.

Fr. *la barbe;* Ger. *der Bart.*

Beat, or **Overcome.** Use *Kill.*

Beautiful, Handsome, or **Pretty.** Hold up flat right hand, and look on the palm as in a mirror, then make the sign *Good.*

Beautiful. Draw the flat hand down near the face, back forward, and sign *Good.*

Fr. *beau;* Ger. *schön.*

Beaver (Tail of beaver striking mud or water). Hold left flat hand in front of body, left arm horizontal; strike up against the left palm once or twice with back of right flat hand.

Fr. *le castor;* Ger. *der Biber.*

Because. Sign *Consider,* then *Behold.* Understood by Cheyennes and Blackfeet, though not well established.

Fr. *parce que;* Ger. *weil.*

Become or **Turn into.** Sign *Grow* and *Same* or *Arrive there.*

Fr. *devenir;* Ger. *werden.*

Bed (Spreading blanket for sleep). Hold flat hands palms up, points forward, one behind the other, left ahead, push it forward, at same time draw back right, then add *Sleep.*

Fr. *le lit;* Ger. *das Bett.*

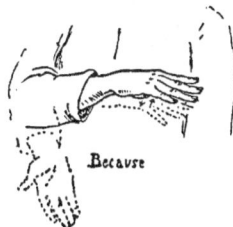

Bee. Sign *Fly*, *Arrow*, and *One*. (C) In Cheyenne, sign *Small*, *Bird*, *Make*, *Taste*.
Fr. *l'abeille;* Ger. *die Biene*.

Before. See *Ahead*.

Before, that is, **Future.** Sign for *Time*, but hold left hand near breast and swing right forward, up and over. Or sign *After*, *Many Sleeps*.
Fr. *avant;* Ger. *ehe*.

Beg (To ask alms). Hold out the flat right hand, palm up, as a beggar does. Swing it forward and upward, then draw it toward self, slightly curving the fingers.
Fr. *mendier;* Ger. *betteln*.

Beg, I beg of you, Ask, I pray you. Lay the flat hands together, palms touching, fingers pointing up (or clasp them) and hold them toward the person. A white sign now understood by the Indians. Compare *Pray*.
Fr. *supplier;* Ger. *bitten*.

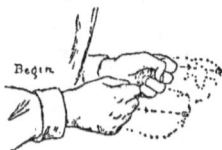

Begin, Commence, Must, Push, Try, Go ahead (Start in a race). With elbow at sides and arms level, push fists forward two or three inches, right a little behind. Or use *Go*. See *Strong*.
Fr. *commencer;* Ger. *anfangen, beginnen*.

Behavior. See *Way*.

Behind. See *After*.

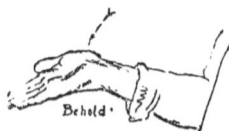

Behold. Hold out flat right, palm up, pointing forward and moved slowly down to below level. Sometimes use both hands. Compare *Show*.
Fr. *regardez!;* Ger. *siehe da!*

Believe. Sign *Think, Straight.*
Fr. *croire;* Ger. *glauben.*

Belonging to. See *Possession.*

Below, Beneath, or **Under.** Is the reverse of *Above;* which see.
Fr. *dessous, sous;* Ger. *unter.*

Belt. With both hands, make as though putting on a belt.
Fr. *la ceinture;* Ger. *der Gürtel.*

Beneath. See *Below.*

Bend or **Bent.** Take left index in right finger and thumb and bend the middle joint of it at right angles. Or sign *Break* very slowly.
Fr. *plier;* Ger. *biegen.*

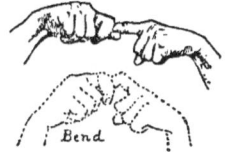

Berry. With right middle finger and thumb hold tip of right index, letting it project a little; add *Bushes.* Or, sign *Tree, Pick,* and *Eat.* This is a descriptive phrase rather than an established sign, but it is a good illustration of impromptu constructions which are continually made and are at once understood because in harmony with the main principles of Sign Talk. Compare *Fruit, Cherry,* and *Bullet.*
Fr. *la baie;* Ger. *die Beere.*

Beside or **By** (By the side of). Like *With,* but right G about three inches off left palm. Sometimes use *Close.*
Fr. *à côté de, près de;* Ger. *neben.*

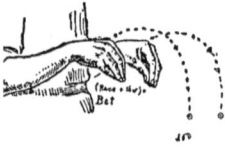

Bet or **Wager** (Placing on each of two piles). Indicate the event, as *Race,* then sign *Place;* that is, hold out partly compressed hands backs up; swing both forward up and down nearly *together* at finish.

Fr. *le pari;* Ger. *die Wette.*

Between. Hold up the flat hands, palm to palm, six inches apart; then thrust the right G on line close past left palm.

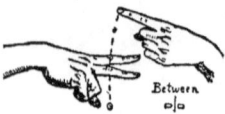

Between. Hold left V hand, fingers level, pointing to right (or straight up) and drop right G down between.

Fr. *entre;* Ger. *zwischen.*

Beware, Caution, or **Look out.** See *Warning.*

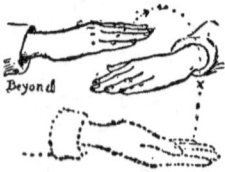

Beyond or **Other side.** Hold the flat left hand, back up, in front of body about ten inches, fingers pointing to right; bring flat right hand, back up, between left and body at same height, fingers pointing to left; swing the right hand upward, outward, and then downward on curve, beyond left hand, turning right hand back down in movement. Compare *Fall* and *Other.*

Fr. *au-delà de;* Ger. *jenseits.*

Bible. Sign *Book* and *Medicine.*

Fr. *la Bible;* Ger. *die Bibel.*

Big. Hold the curved 5 hands with palms toward each other, well out in front of the body, hands a little lower than shoulders and a few inches apart, pointing forward; separate hands, carrying right to right, left to left, keeping them opposite each other. Also used for *Long.* Compare *Great* and *Long.*

Fr. *grand, gros;* Ger. *grosz.*

Bighorn. See *Sheep*.

Bird. With flat hands at the shoulders, palms down, imitate the motion of wings. Using different speeds for different birds. Compare *Fly*, which progresses.
   Fr. *l'oiseau;* Ger. *der Vogel*.

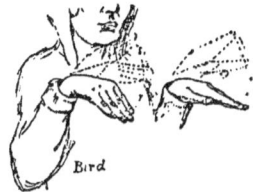

Birth. See *Born*.

Bison. See *Buffalo*.

Bit (Of a bridle). Place the L hand palm down on the mouth.
   Fr. *le frein;* Ger. *das Gebisz*.

Bite. Bring the right C hand, back outward and upward, a little in front of the body; snap sharply together the tips of the first and second fingers and the tip of thumb against the back of the left flat hand, repeating the motion. Some omit left hand. The Blackfeet make this from the mouth.
   Fr. *mordre;* Ger. *beiszen*.

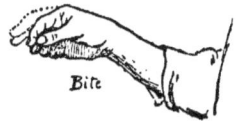

Bitter or **Sour.** Touch tongue with tip of right G and add *Bad*. Compare *Salt, Sugar, Taste, Taste bad*.
   Fr. *amer;* Ger. *bitter*.

Black. See *Color*.

Blackfoot. See *Indian*.

Blackguarding or **Reviling** (Lies from both). Hold up right V, pointing nearly level forward, opposite right shoulder; left ditto at left shoulder; swing them alternately at each other.
   Fr. *outrager, insulter;* Ger. *jemanden beschimpfen*.

Blanket or **Robe** (Wrapping about shoulder). Bring the A hands palms toward each other, opposite and above each shoulder *near the neck;* move the right hand to left and left to right till the wrists are crossed, right hand nearest body. Compare *Fond.*

Fr. *la couverture;* Ger. *die Decke.*

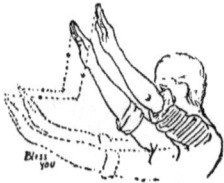

Bless you (Drawing from above and spreading out). Hold the flat hands high up in front, palms forward, apart, at arm's length. Lower them a little and slightly push toward the person meant. (C)

Fr. *que Dieu vous bénisse;* Ger. *Gott segne dich!*

Blessing the food. Hold both 5 hands over the food, then add *Talk* upward.

Blind. Bring both flat hands, backs outward, in front of and close to eyes, right hand nearest and both hands parallel to face; move right hand slightly to left, left to right; then place the tips of the fingers against closed eyes. (C)

Fr. *aveugle;* Ger. *blind.*

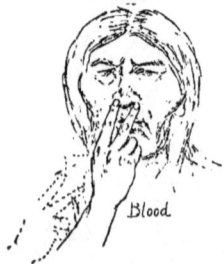

Blood (A wounded buffalo bleeds at the nostrils). Raise the right V hand so the tips of the fingers are pressed one against each nostril; move the hand to the right and downward, giving it a tremulous motion. Add *Red.* Some omit *Red.*

Fr. *le sang;* Ger. *das Blut.*

Bloom or **Blossom.** See *Flower.*

Bluff. See *Hill.*

Boat. Bring the hands together hollowed, fingers straight, little fingers joining, the thumbs somewhat apart, to represent the body of a boat, held before the breast. Push it forward to indicate movement. Add the motion of paddling for *Canoe*, or *Rowing* for bigger boat. Usually the *Boat* sign is omitted; *Paddling* or *Rowing* being enough by itself. Compare *Bowl*.

Fr. *le bateau;* Ger. *der Kahn.*

Boil. See *Cook.*

Fr. *bouillir;* Ger. *kochen.*

Bone. Hold up the left hand, palm down, wrist a little bent; with right G tap the wrist bone on outer side of left; then add *Hard*.

Fr. *l'os;* Ger. *der Knochen.*

Bonnet, that is, *Warbonnet*. Sweep 5 hands along near each side of head from front to back. Sometimes also sweep right 5 hand down behind for the *Tail*.

Fr. *le bonnet de guerre;* Ger. *die Federkappe.*

Book. Open and close the flat hands like cover of a book, then indicate the lines of writing. Sometimes show the thickness to distinguish it from *Letter*. Compare *Open* and *Shut*.

Fr. *le livre;* Ger. *das Buch.*

Born, Birth, or **Parturition** (Issuing from loins). Flat right in front of and near the body, pointing downward and to front, moved downward and outward on a curve. Compare *Dive*.

Fr. *né;* Ger. *geboren.*

Borrow. See *Lend.*

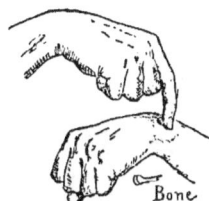

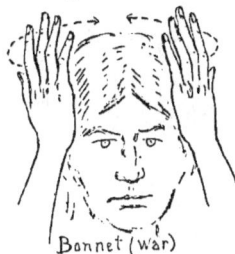

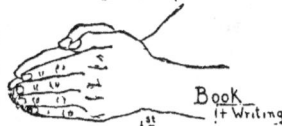

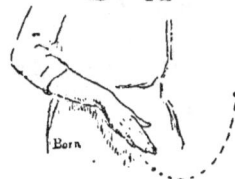

Boss. Use *Chief*.

Both. Sign *Or*, that is, hold up the left V, pointing forward, and tap each tip of V, and in turn, with right G; then over left V add *All* with right. Sometimes point to each and add *Two*. Sometimes use *All*. Blackfeet use *Two* and *Same*.

Fr. *tous les deux;* Ger. *beide.*

Bow (Weapon). The left A hand held still, a little advanced, the right A hand touches it and makes the motion of drawing the cord of the bow.

Fr. *l'arc;* Ger. *der Schiessbogen.*

Bowl (A vessel). With curved hands side by side, fingers bent, palms up, indicate shape. (C) Compare *Boat*. For a larger vessel, use *Basin*.

Fr. *le bol;* Ger. *die Schale, die Schüssel.*

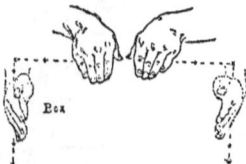

Box. Hold out both flat hands side by side, backs up; then swing apart and down at right angles, turning the hands at the angle so the backs are out.

Fr. *la boîte;* Ger. *der Kasten.*

Boy. Sign *Man, Young.*

Fr. *le garçon;* Ger. *der Knabe.*

Brag. See *Bravado*.

Brain. Touch forehead with N hand.

Fr. *le cerveau;* Ger. *das Gehirn.*

Brand or **Name.** All fingers of right closed but thumb and index, these form a "C," which lay on the palm of flat left, pointing forward, thumb up. Sometimes lay it on left shoulder outside. Compare *Name*.

> Fr. *la marque, marquer avec un fer rouge;* Ger. *das Zeichen, das Brandmal, einbrennen.*

Brand

Bravado or **Brag.** Sign *Fire, Talk, True*, and *No*. (C)
> Fr. *la bravade;* Ger. *die Prahlerei.*

Brave (Strong heart). Sign *Heart* and *Strong*.
> Fr. *brave;* Ger. *mutig, tapfer.*

Brave, as an intensive. See *Very much*.

Bread (Making a cake). Gently clap the slightly hollow right hand over slightly hollow left hand, then reverse so left is on right and clap them together again; repeat.
> Fr. *le pain;* Ger. *das Brot.*

Break. Make the motion of seizing a stick, hold it horizontally with both hands and breaking it in the middle. The thumbs finish wide apart.
> Fr. *casser, briser;* Ger. *zerbrechen.*

Break

Breakfast. Sign *Sunrise* and *Eat*.
> Fr. *le déjeuner;* Ger. *das Frühstück.*

Breeze. See *Wind*.

Bribe. Hold the hand behind the back, hollowed, open and palm up. (Pop.)
> Fr. *corrompre;* Ger. *bestechen.*

Bridge (Lifting over water). Sign *Water;* hold out the

Bridge = (Water + flat + Across)

flat hands horizontally in front of body, pointing forward, palms up; and *Across.*
   Fr. *le pont;* Ger. *die Brücke.*

Bridle.   Like *Bit;* but raise the hand till near the eyes.
   Fr. *la bride;* Ger. *der Zaum.*

Bring, Take, or **Fetch.**   Move the right G hand briskly
well in front or to right or left of body; draw the hand
with a sweep in toward the body, at the same time
curving index finger.   Compare *Come* in which the index is held vertically, and *Steal.*
   Fr. *apporter, prendre;* Ger. *bringen, nehmen, holen.*

Broad or **Wide.**   Same as *Big,* but keep the hands flat
and palms up.

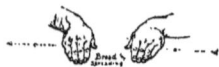

Broad and Spreading is the same as above but with
palms down.   Compare *Prairie.*
   Fr. *large;* Ger. *breit.*

Broke or **Dead broke.**   See *Done* (No.2.)

Broken down.   See *Decrepit.*

Brook.   See *Creek.*

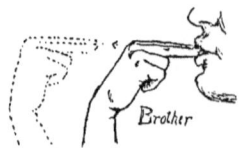

Brother (Suck together).   Lay nearly horizontal N of
right hand on lips; draw it away and down, then add
Male.
   Fr. *le frère;* Ger. *der Bruder.*

Brother-in-Law.   Left forearm across breast; with
lower edge of flat right, strike down past left elbow.
Probably means relative on the side.   (R. B.)
   Fr. *le beau-frère;* Ger. *der Schwager.*

Bucket. Sign *Bowl*, then indicate the handle.
Fr. *le seau;* Ger. *der Eimer.*

Buffalo (Curved horns). Hold the curved G fingers palms toward and close to sides of head; raise the hands slightly and carry them a little to the front. To distinguish domestic cattle, add *Spotted.* The Navahos reverse this; that is, with them the curved horns as above means *Cattle*, to which they add *Beard*, to mean *Buffalo.*
Fr. *le bison;* Ger. *der Büffel.*

Bullet. Sign *Fire off;* then grasp the forefinger of the hand with the second finger and thumb, so that the tip of it will so extend beyond them and represent the ball.
Fr. *la balle;* Ger. *die Kugel.*

Bunch (Of fruit). Hold out the compressed right hand opposite throat, fingers pointing down. Compare *Beard.*

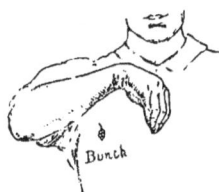

Bunch (A small herd grazing). Hold out curved right 5 hand, back up and forward. See *Herd.* Sometimes use *Enclosure.*
Fr. *le troupeau;* Ger. *die Anzahl, die kleine Herde.*

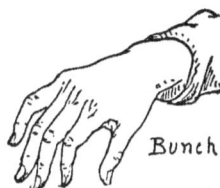

Burn. Sign *Fire* and *Wipe out.*
Fr. *brûler;* Ger. *brennen.*

Bushes or **Brush.** Like *Grass*, but breast high; and draw right hand to you and left far ahead.
Fr. *la broussaille;* Ger. *das Gebüsch.*

Busy. Sign *Push* and *Work.*
Fr. *occupé;* Ger. *beschäftigt.*

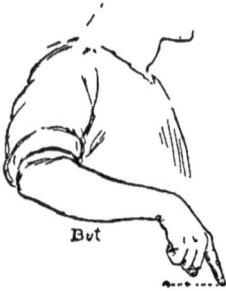

But, Except, Save, or **Unless** (Of all one pulled back). Sign *All*, with right swung to left; then sign *One*, with left at left side, and pull it to right side between forefinger and thumb of right.

But. Sign *All Go, One, Sits.*

But (One drawn back). Point right G down, forward and to right; hold it a second, then jerk it back four or five inches. (Hadley.)

Fr. *mais;* Ger. *aber.*

Butte. See *Hill.*

Buy. Sign *Money* and *Trade*, making it clear who gives the money.

Buy or **Sell** i.e., **Market.** Tap three times on side of left G index with side of right G index. Compare, *All the time, Peas,* and *While.* See *Sell.*

Fr. *acheter;* Ger. *kaufen.*

By. See *Beside.*

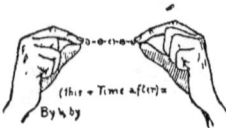

By and By (After a little time). Hold the pinched index and thumb of each hand as in *Time*, but half an inch apart. Or sign *Time afterward.* Compare *Sometime.*

Fr. *plus tard;* (C) Ger. *später.*

C

Cache. See *Hide.*

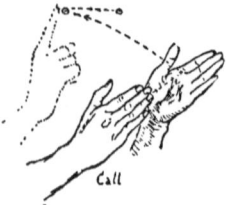

Call, Attention! Say! Strike the palm of the open left hand with the tips of right fingers, then swing right G a little toward the person.

Fr. *dites donc;* Ger. *hören Sie!*

Called or **Named.** Lay the back of the crooked right G *on lips*, pointing to front and left, its tip pressed against the thumb, which is nearly straight; then move the hand upward and forward in a curve, straightening out the index finally with a snap, pointing toward the person or thing. Compare *Talk* in which the action is repeated. See also *Name.*

Fr. *appelé;* Ger. *genannt.*

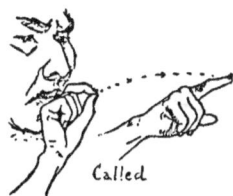

Camera. Sign *Picture* and *See.* Compare *Photograph.*

Camp (Set up the lodge). Sign *Teepee*, holding the hands face high; drop the hands together for a foot with energy.

Fr. *le camp;* Ger. *das Lager.*

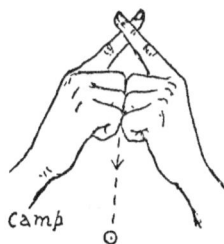

Camp-fire. Hold left hand flat, palm down, fingers a little spread; then lay right hand fingers similarly held across at right angles, to indicate the wood laid ready, and add the sign for *Fire.* (Sheeaka.) Not a true Indian sign, but sufficiently descriptive for the Cheyennes to understand it.

Fr. *le feu de camp;* Ger. *das Lagerfeuer.*

Camp-fire Girls. Sign *Camp-fire*, then raise the right index in a spiral for *Smoke.*

Camp-fire man are you? Give the signs *Question, you, camp-fire*, and *man* or briefly make the *Camp-fire* sign and look inquiringly.

Fr. *Êtes vous membre du Camp-fire Club;* Ger. *Sind Sie ein Mitglied des Lagerfeuer Klubs?*

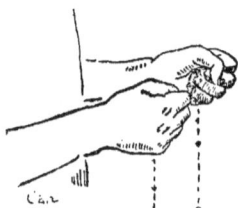

Can, Able, or **Power.** Hold both S hands in front, elbows at sides, thumbs up; drop the hands for six inches with a jerk. (Sheeaka and the Blackfeet.) Sometimes use only one hand. The Cheyennes sign *Own, Strong, Medicine.*

> Fr. *pouvoir;* Ger. *können.*

Candid (True, clear as day and good). Sign *True, Day,* and *Good.* (C)

> Fr. *sincère;* Ger. *aufrichtig.*

Candle. Hold up left G finger and with right hand sign *Fire* on its tip, then indicate length on left arm.

> Fr. *la bougie;* Ger. *die Kerze.*

Candy-stick. Sign *Sugar;* then on left G index held upright, show stripes. (C)

> Fr. *le bonbon;* Ger. *das Zuckerwerk.*

Cannon. Sign *Gun* and *Big.*

> Fr. *le canon;* Ger. *die Kanone.*

Cannot, or **Unable, Fail, Failure** (The arrow that failed to stick). Hold the flat left hand out in front, thumb edge up; strike the palm of it with the forefinger of the right G hand, which then at once rebounds and is thrown forward and down to rest on its back.

> Fr. *ne pas pouvoir, incapable;* Ger. *nicht können, unfähig.*

Canoe. Sign *Boat* and *Paddle.*

Canoe of birch bark. Push forward compressed right, back down, to represent the curved prow, then add *Paddle*.

Fr. *la pirogue, le canot;* Ger. *das Kanu, der Rinden-kahn.*

Canyon (Between hills). Hold up the fists, palms toward each other, about six inches apart, face high; then indicate *Go between;* that is, hold the left unchanged but thrust forward the flat right hand, palm to left. (Blackfoot.) Compare *Between.*

Fr. *le canyon, le grand ravin;* Ger. *die Schlucht.*

Cards. Hold imaginary cards in left and deal with right hand.

Fr. *les cartes;* Ger. *die Karten.*

Caribou. Sign *Deer, High,* and lay the flat right hand on forehead so the fingers slightly spread point forward, showing the *brow shovel.* (Blackfoot.) Sometimes omit *High.*

Fr. *le renne, le caribou;* Ger. *das Karibu.*

Carriage, or **Covered Wagon.** Sign *Wagon,* then raise the hands, palms down, flat, but bent at an angle, up above the head, and move forward about two feet to represent the carriage top.

Carriage or **Buggy.** Sign *Wagon, Small,* and sometimes add *Black.*

Fr. *la voiture;* Ger. *der Wagen.*

Carry or **Pack.** Both closed hands held opposite the temple as if holding the tump line, the shoulders slightly forward as though bearing a pack.

Fr. *porter;* Ger. *tragen.*

Carry in the hand. With one hand make as though carrying a basket by the handle.

Cars. See *Railroad train.*

Cartridge . (this + shoot)

Cartridge. Hold right G hand, back up, in front of body, index horizontal and pointing to front, thumb pressed against side of index, with the thumb tip just back of second joint; add *Shoot.* See *Ammunition.*
> Fr. *la cartouche;* Ger. *die Patrone,* (*artill*) *die Kartusche.*

Cat

Cat (Flattened or turned-up nose). Lay A hand on nose, rotating a little out and up. (C) Sign *Nose, Short, Dog.*
> Fr. *le chat;* Ger. *die Katze.*

Catch. Same as *Get* but action quicker. See *Get.*
> Fr. *attraper;* Ger. *fangen.*

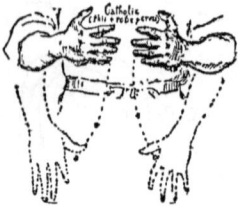
Catholic (this + robe+cross)

Catholic. Indicate gown by sweeping the 5 hands down over the sides and outward; then add *Black.* Sometimes make the sign of the Cross.
> Fr. *catholique;* Ger. *katholisch.*

Cattle. Sign *Buffalo* and *Spotted.* (Blackfoot.) Compare *Buffalo.* Or, sign *Buffalo* and *Whiteman.*
> Fr. *les bestiaux;* Ger. *das Vieh.*

Caution. See *Warning.*

Cavalry. *Soldier* and *Ride.*
> Fr. *la cavalerie;* Ger. *die Kavallerie.*

Centre. With thumbs and index fingers of L hands make a horizontal circle; then, keeping the left unchanged, indicate centre with right G finger. Sometimes draw a horizontal circle with right G, then drop same down into its centre.

Fr. *le centre;* Ger. *die Mitte.*

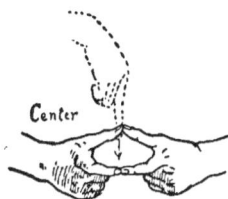

Certain. Sign *I, Know, Good.* Or use *True.*
Fr. *certain;* Ger. *sicher.*

Challenge, Defy, or **Dare.** Spring the middle finger with a vigorous snap toward the person, the other fingers closed; hand held face high, back up. A European sign given by Butler. Compare *There* and *Defiance.*

Fr. *défier;* Ger. *herausfordern.*

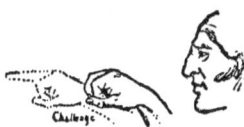

Chance. See *Luck.*

Character (Shape of heart). Lay right C hand on heart, draw it out, that is, forward, a little and with both A hands outline a human figure. (D) Sign *Heart, Good, Bad.* (Blackfoot.)

Fr. *le caractère;* Ger. *der Charakter.*

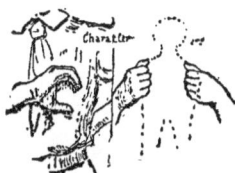

Charge (Military, against others). Swing both fists from right shoulder forward and a little down in an up curve, away, rising a little, at the same time springing them open.

Fr. *la charge (contre les autres);* Ger. *die Attacke, der Angriff (gegen andere).*

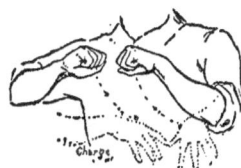

Charge (Military, against us). Similar but reversed, springing the hands open toward one's face.

Fr. *la charge (contre nous);* Ger. *die Attacke (gegen uns).*

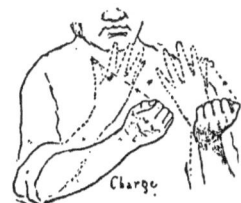

Chase. See *Follow.*

Cherries (Choke). Sign, *Tree*, *Pick*, and *Pound*. (Blackfoot.) See *Berry.*
Fr. *les cerises;* Ger. *die Kirschen.*

Cheyenne. See *Indian.*

Chicken. Sign *Bird*, then *Red* and with 5 hand on crown show *Comb.* (C) Or sign *Bird* and *Whiteman.*
Fr. *le poulet;* Ger. *das Huhn.*

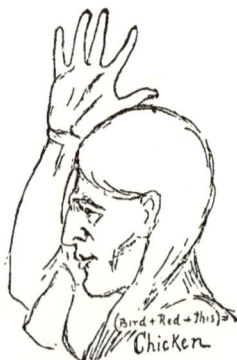

Chief (People with one man rising above them). Hold up left 5 hand, palm to right, pass index of right G hand at several inches above left. (Scott.) The Cheyennes omit left hand; they shoot the right G up over and much down in a long sweep, finishing lower than it began.
Fr. *le commandant;* Ger. *der Häuptling.*

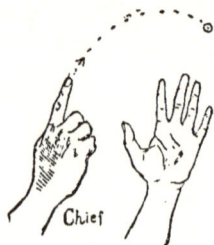

Child or **Offspring.** Compressed right hand, points up, swung well out in front and dropped a foot to the height of the child. Compare *Young.*
Fr. *l'enfant;* Ger. *das Kind.*

Children (Springing up). Hold out both hands, palms up, very low, fingers pointing up and scarcely spread; alternately swing them up and down for six inches. Compare *Grass*, in which they are held low and are spread widely; also *Bushes.*
Fr. *les enfants;* Ger. *die Kinder.*

Choose, Make choice, or **Select.** Hold right G shoulder high, back up, a foot in front of the breast, swing it in a

circle with a succession of little bounds or up curves, as though pointing at many different objects in succession, the head turned to follow always; then finish by throwing the G finger forward in a curve; or, in some cases, finish by picking up the imaginary object selected, using index and thumb for this. Compare *Find, Hunting,* and *Look.*

Fr. *choisir;* Ger. *wählen.*

Chop. Use the flat right hand, little finger down, as an axe, chopping first from right, then from left, once on each side. Sometimes do this on back of left hand, which stands for the log. Compare *Free,* which is two or three cuts on right side only.

Fr. *couper, trancher;* Ger. *hauen, hacken.*

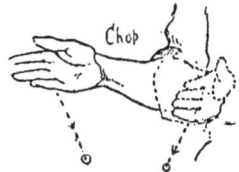

Christmas (The day of the shining tree). Sign *Tree,* then hold hand with fingers spread and crooked, palm down, level of face. Lower it six inches in short, quick zigzags to suggest glittering or shimmering. (W. C. Roe.) In *Snow* the hand is lowered in long zigzags for about two feet. See *Shimmer.* Or sign *Middle, Winter, Tree,* and *Hanging;* for the last, hold the curved 5 hands, backs up, at level of the eyes; jerk them a little apart. (R. B.)

Fr. *le Noël;* Ger. *Weihnachten.*

Church (Steeple house). Cross clasp the fingers so the tips are within, then raise both index fingers to form the steeple. (Pop.)

Church. Sign *Medicine, Talk, House.*

Fr. *l'église;* Ger. *die Kirche.*

(Tobacco—this) + Cigarette

Cigarette. Sign *Tobacco;* then lay G fingers side by side pointing opposite ways; roll one about the other. Sometimes omit *Tobacco;* sometimes give *Cigar* (2nd sign) and *Little.*

Fr. *la cigarette;* Ger. *die Zigarette.*

Cigar (2). Sign *Cigarette, Black,* and *Smoking.* Sometimes hold right G at corner of mouth, pointing forward. *Cigar* and *Cigarette* are recent signs and changing rapidly.

Fr. *le cigare;* Ger. *die Zigarre.*

City (Big town). Make sign for *Town,* then add sign for *Big.* Or omit *Big* but swing the hands far apart.

Fr. *la ville;* Ger. *die Stadt.*

Cities. Many are indicated by their initial letter enhanced with twisting motion. (D) For some we may use their nickname but this is merely a suggestion.

Boston (The Hub). Sign for *City* and *Centre.*

Chicago (Windy City). Sign for *City* and *Wind.* The Cheyennes call it *Big Lake City.*

Kansas City (Buffalo Head City). Sign *Buffalo Head* and point up high to the wall. (Cheyenne.)

London. Sign *City, Chief,* and *Red Coats.*

New York (Knickerbocker City). Sign for *City* and trousers cut off below the knee; i. e., draw flat of hand down over thigh then below knee and stop, turning edge of hand in. Or sign *Big Island City.* (Blackfoot.)

Ottawa. Sign *City*, *Chief*, and *Capotes*.

Philadelphia (Quaker City). Sign *City*, then make sign for broad hat with rim curled up by drawing both index fingers across mid-brow, level in front, then twisting them up at the place of the rim. Or "no name, just *Big City*, nothing distinctive." (Blackfoot.)

Pittsburg (Smoky City). Sign for *City* and *Smoky*.

Rome (Eternal City). Sign *City* and *Forever*.

Washington. Sign *Father*, *Chief*, *Sits*. (Cheyenne.)

Clean-handed or **Innocent** (Great Spirit see no blood on these hands). Lift hands over shoulder, palms up higher than head and add *Blood, No.* (C) Or, sign *Work, Bad, No.*
    Fr. *innocent*; Ger. *unschuldig*.

Clear (Clear Sky). Sign *Clouds*, then swing the hands wide apart, finishing with palms up at arm's length, up high. Or, sign *Clouds, Wiped out.* (Blackfoot.)

Clever. See *Cunning*.

Close, Near, Nearly, Soon, Early, About, or **Almost** (Draw near). Bring the flat curved right hand, back to right, well out in front of body, about height of shoulder; draw the hand in toward the body and slightly downward. Compare *Far*. See also *Soon*.
    Fr. *près, presque;* Ger. *nahe, beinahe.*

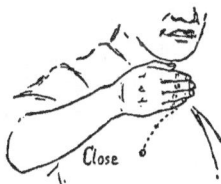

Clothes. See *Coat*.

Clouds (Rolling). Rotate the flat hands over each other from in front of the face, to over the head.

Clouds (Rain). Look upward, swing the flat hands at arm's length, palms down over the head; then add *Rain*.
Fr. *les nuages;* Ger. *die Wolken.*

Coal. Sign *Hard, Fire,* and *Good.*
Fr. *le charbon;* Ger. *die Kohle.*

Coat or **Clothes.** Hold the L hands near the breast, palms in; swing them down to the waist.
Fr. *l'habit;* Ger. *der Rock.*

Coffee (Grinding coffee in mill). A few inches over the flat left hand, back down, move the right A as though turning the crank of a coffee mill. Or, sign *Black Drink.* Compare *Tobacco.*
Fr. *le café;* Ger. *der Kaffee.*

Coin. Close hollow right over hollowed left and shake as tho jingling coin. (Sheeaka; not Indian, but now understood.) See *Dollar.*
Fr. *la pièce d'argent;* Ger. *die Münze.*

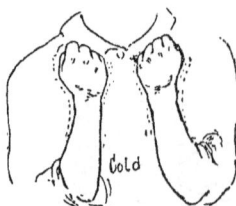

Cold (Shivering). Bring the fists in front of and close to body, height of shoulder, elbows at sides, shoulders drawn in, and shiver. See *Winter.* Compare *Blanket.*
Fr. *froid;* Ger. *kalt.*

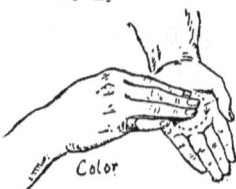

Color. With the finger tips of right hand (thumb crooked under) rub circularly on the palm of left hand as though rubbing color. Often add *Same* or *Equal,* to make more clear.
Fr. *la couleur;* Ger. *die Farbe.*

Color—*Continued*

Black. Sign *Color* and touch the hair or eyebrow.
Fr. *noir;* Ger. *schwarz.*

Blue. Sign *Sun* with left hand and then draw the
right G finger around it to mean color of sky around
the sun. (Sheeaka). Or, sign *Color* and *Sky.*
Fr. *bleu;* Ger. *blau.*

Brown. Sign *Color* and *Deer.*
Fr. *brun;* Ger. *braun.*

Gray. Sign *Color, Little,* and *White.*
Fr. *gris;* Ger. *grau.*

Green. Sign *Color* and *Grass.*
Fr. *vert;* Ger. *grün.*

Red (Cheek color). Sign *Color* and lightly brush
the right finger tips over the cheek, points to right.
Fr. *rouge;* Ger. *rot.*

White. Sign *Color* and rub thumb nail of left A
hand with tip of right G finger; i. e., nail color,
white in Indians.
Fr. *blanc;* Ger. *weiss.*

Yellow. Sign *Color* and point to any yellow ob-
ject, such as a straw or dead grass. Or sign *Color,
Grass,* and *Dead.*
Fr. *jaune;* Ger. *gelb.*
For other colors, touch or indicate some object of the
tint meant.

Comb. With all fingers of right 5 hand hooked, comb the right side of the head and down as far as the breast two or three times. Compare *Woman*.

Fr. *le peigne;* Ger. *der Kamm.*

Combat. See *Battle.*

Come. Carry right G hand, back out, fingers up, in a graceful sweep from arm's length to within a foot of one's face. Many use the flat hand swung down and to you, palm under and toward you. Railroad men use the whole arm, swinging it across the body at an angle of 45 degrees, so as to be seen in a dim light.

Fr. *venez;* Ger. *kommen Sie.*

Come back. Hold flat left, back forward, near breast; swing right ditto pointed up from arm's length in against back of left. See *Arrive here.*

Fr. *revenez;* Ger. *kommen Sie zurück.*

Come between or **Intervene.** Hold out left hand flat, back out, at arm's length and pass flat right, thumb up, between left and body.

Fr. *s'interposer, intervenir;* Ger. *dazwischen kommen.*

Come gently. See *Easy.*

Come for a moment. Right hand held forward and up, fingers closed except index, with which beckon by crooking and straightening, the hand not moved. (Pop.) White sign, now fully adopted by the Cheyennes.

Fr. *venez une seconde;* Ger. *kommen Sie einen. Augenblick her.*

Come into view or **Appear.** Hold out flat left hand, back forward, thrust right G index up, farther off, under and behind, until it appears above.

Fr. *paraître;* Ger. *erscheinen.*

Comfort (See how smooth or fat). Draw flat right hand, palm in, down breast, then off and up in curve forward, palm up. (Sheeaka.) Compare *Confess.* Sometimes use *Glad.* (Blackfoot.)

Fr. *le bien-être;* Ger. *die Behaglichkeit.*

Comfortable. Alternately rub left palm over back of right hand, then right over left back, always palm up; then swing both forward. (Sheeaka. Probably from Deaf.)

Fr. *confortable;* Ger. *gemütlich.*

Coming. Hold out the flat right, palm to you and pointing nearly up; draw it to you in little jerks.

Fr. *venant;* Ger. *kommend.*

Coming man. See *Rising man.*

Commence. See *Begin.*

Compass points. *North—Wind cold there.*
Fr. *le nord;* Ger. *der Norden.*
East—Sunrise there.
Fr. *l'est;* Ger. *der Osten.*
South—Wind warm there.
Fr. *le sud;* Ger. *der Süden.*
West—Sunset there.
Fr. *l'ouest;* Ger. *der Westen.*

Complete. See *Done*.

Comparative, etc., of *Adjectives*.

For **Positive**, give first the adjective then swing the
flat right hand out a little, level, palm up. (Sheeaka.)
For **Comparative**, give first the adjective then raise
the right G hand to the height of the chin, pointing
up. (Sheeaka.)   See *More*, and sometimes use
Ahead or *Above* after the adjective.

Fr. *le comparatif;* Ger. *der Komparativ.*

For **Superlative**, give first the adjective then add
Strong and *Ahead* or *Very much.*

Fr. *le superlatif;* Ger. *der Superlativ.*

Conceal. See *Hide*.

Conceit (Swelled Head).   Hold hands open and curved,
one on each side of the head, two or three inches away.
A whiteman's sign, but quite well known now to the
younger generation of Indians.

If in unbelievable degree, stretch the right hand at full
length sidewise, and work the first finger as though
scratching the ear which is supposed to be just above the
hand.   (Pop.)

Conceit. Sign *He, Think, Strong.*

Fr. *la vanité, la présomption;* Ger. *die Einbildung, der
Dünkel.*

Conduct. Same as *Way*.

Confess (Show the heart). Lay points of both compressed hands on centre of breast, then spring them
away, out and aside, turning them flat and palms up.
Sometimes but one hand is used.   I am inclined to

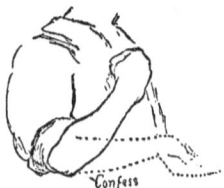

think that this should be simply *Heart* and *Behold*, although none of my Indians made it that way. Sometimes sign *You, Tell, True*.

Fr. *confesser;* Ger. *gestehen.*

Congress. Sign *Whiteman, Chief, Council* (No. 2).

Fr. *le Congrès;* Ger. *der Kongresz.*

Connivance (Wink, that is, close one eye). This ancient sign assumes that the person who should see, closes the eye next his accomplice. (Pop. Also Cheyenne.)

Fr. *la connivence;* Ger. *die Konnivenz, das* (*strafbare*) *Einverständnis.*

Consider, Ponder, or **Weigh** (Wisdom looking on the ground). Sign *Wolf* (i. e., *wisdom*, analogous with our word "foxy"), then turn downward the points of the two fingers representing the wolf ears, back of hand near the eyes and moving the hand from right to left as in surveying the ground. (Scott.)

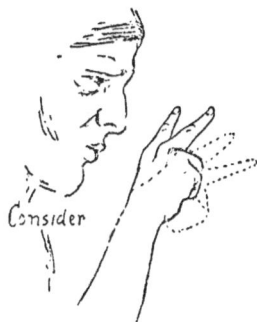

Consider. Hold the right "4" hand near the heart, pointing to left, rotate a little back and forth. (Blackfoot). The Cheyennes use V hand, which makes it the same as *If.* See *Because.*

Fr. *considérer;* Ger. *erwägen.*

Constable. See *Policeman.*

Contempt. See *Scorn.*

Contented. To make contented, Satisfied. Use *Glad* or *Sit, Good.* (Blackfoot.)

Fr. *content;* Ger. *zufrieden.*

Continue. Sign *Go* and *Long Time.* (Blackfoot.)

Fr. *continuer;* Ger. *fortsetzen.*

Conversation. See *Discussion*, *Speech*, and *Talk*.

Cook (In the abstract). See *Make* and *Food*.
Fr. *faire cuire, cuisiner;* Ger. *kochen.*

Cook (By boiling). With both L hands make a horizontal circle, then holding left unchanged, put something into it with right and add *Fire.* Compare *Centre* and *Hole.*
Fr. *cuire, bouillir;* Ger. *kochen.*

Cook (By frying). Place flat right on flat left hand, palm to palm, then flip the right like a pancake, turning it palm up as it drops on the left.

Cook (By broiling). As in the above *Frying*, but leave out the left hand entirely.
Fr. *griller;* Ger. *braten, rösten.*

Cook (noun). Sign *Man, Makes, Food.*
Fr. *le cuisinier;* Ger. *der Koch.*

Coon. See *Raccoon.*

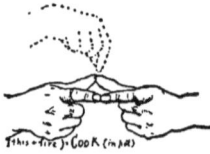

Corn (Shelling the corn). Hold out the left A hand, thumb straight and resting on index finger; place the ball of the thumb of right A hand on back of left thumb near its base; twist the right hand by wrist action to the right and downward until the right thumb slips off with a snap against the right index. Repeat once or twice.
Fr. *le maïs;* Ger. *der türkische Weizen, der Mais.*

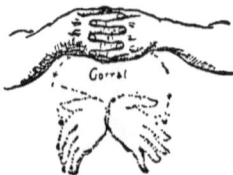

Corral or **Fenced Field** or **Pasture** (Area embraced or held). Interlock the fingers, hold arms curved in

front, horizontal; then add *Enclosure*, i. e., swing the
hands apart and draw back each in a half circle till their
heels meet near you.

Fr. *le corral;* Ger. *die Einzäunung.*

Council (Sitting in a circle and talking). Bring the
A hands, back outward, well out in front of body, a little
lower than the shoulders, little fingers touching; swing
them apart and toward the body so they meet close
to it, forming a horizontal circle; palms forward; then
add *Discussion.*

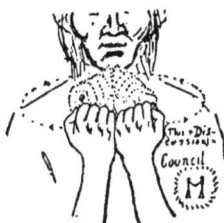

Council(2). Exactly like *Across*, but repeated two or
three times. This is a recent sign among the Cheyennes,
but is becoming popular. See *Across* and *Law.*

Fr. *le conseil;* Ger. *die Ratsversammlung.*

Counsel or **Advice.** See *Advice.*

Counting. See *Numbers.*

Count coup or **Make a hit** or a **Strike** (Striking a dead
body with the coup stick). Strike the top joint of the
right G index on the middle of the left G index, as the
right is swung from below up. *Grand Coup* sign *Coup*
and *Great.*

Fr. *le coup;* Ger. *der Treffschusz.*

Country. See *Land.*

Coup. See *Count coup.*

Courting (Driving or rounding up in secret). Thrust
the right L hand back nearly up under flat left, held

palm down, twisting the right by wrist action. Compare *Sweetheart* and *Glitter*.

Fr. *faire la cour;* Ger. *das Courmachen, das Hofmachen.*

Coward. See *Fear.*

Coyote. Sign *Wolf* and *Small.*

Fr. *le coyote, le loup des prairies;* Ger. *der Präriewolf.*

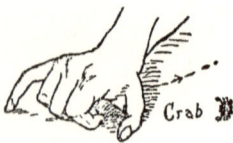

Crab. Place base of wrist of right hand, palm down, on some flat surface, thumb and little finger extended and curved (others closed) to represent claws. Then move the hand sidewise backward, waving the claws. (Scott.) Compare *Spider.*

Fr. *le crabe;* Ger. *die Krabbe.*

Crave. See *Want.*

Crayfish. Hold out the V hand level; draw it back, opening and shutting the V. Compare *Dog.*

Fr. *l'écrevisse;* Ger. *der Krebs.*

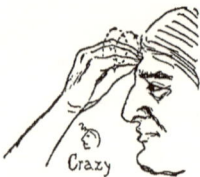

Crazy, Foolish, Mad, Demented (Brain in a whirl). Raise compressed right hand, all fingers together, tap the forehead with it and make one or two quick circles with finger tips in the air. (Sheeaka.) Tap the forehead, shake the head and point to the person. (Pop.)

Crazy. Swing the 5 hand in horizontal circles near the forehead, going with the sun. Going the reverse way always raises a laugh among Cheyennes; it both intensifies and makes the idea ridiculous.

Fr. *fou;* Ger. *verrückt.*

Cree. See *Indian.*

Creek, Brook, or **Rill.** Sign *Water,* then draw right G hand, back up, held low, from opposite left side, past body to right side; finger level, pointing to left and waved sidewise. Compare *River, Snake, Crooked,* and *Wire.*

> Fr. *le ruisseau;* Ger. *der Bach.*

Crime or **Sin.** Sign *Strong, Bad, Work.*
> Fr. *le crime;* Ger. *das Verbrechen.*

Crooked or **Wrong.** Point the right G forward and slightly down; push it slowly forward in a succession of large, horizontal zigzags, each arched a little.

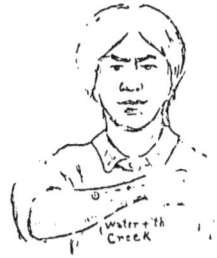

Cross or **Sulky.** Rest the forehead low on the left hand. Or sign *Heart, Bad.*
> Fr. *maussade;* Ger. *mürrisch.*

Cross (of Christ). Hold right G upright, left G at right angles across last joint of right.
> Fr. *le crucifix;* Ger. *das Kruzifix.*

Cross. See *Across.*

Cross the heart. With right index make a little cross over the heart. This means " I give you my word of honor." (Pop.)
> Fr. *parole d'honneur!;* Ger. *auf mein Ehrenwort!*

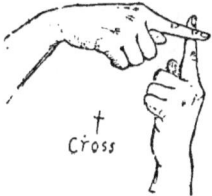

Crow. Sign *Bird* and *Black.*
> Fr. *la corneille;* Ger. *die Krähe.*

Crowded. See *Few.*

Crow Indian. See *Indian.*

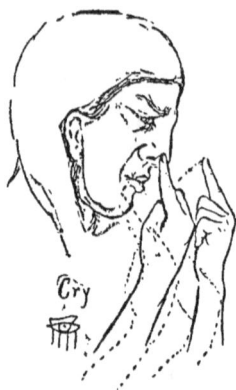

Crush. See *Exterminate*.

Cry out. See *Yell*.

Cry, To weep. With G forefingers near the eyes trace the courses of tears. If excessive, sign *Rain* from the eyes. (Blackfoot.) Compare *Pity*.
Fr. *pleurer;* Ger. *weinen.*

Cunning, Smart, or **Clever.** Make the sign for *Wolf* and add the sign *Equal*. Compare *Consider*.
Fr. *rusé;* Ger. *schlau.*

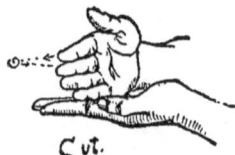

Cut. Saw the lower edge of the flat right across the palm or edge of the flat left.
Fr. *couper;* Ger. *schneiden.*

Cutting up. See *Meat*.

Cyclone or **Whirlwind.** With flat right hand, back to the right and level with the right shoulder, make a spiral upward. A very small one for a little dust whirlwind, and a large violent one for a dangerous cyclone.
Fr. *le cyclone;* Ger. *der Wirbelsturm.*

D

Dam. Sign for *Stream* or *River* and *Hold*. (Blackfoot.)
Fr. *la digue, l'écluse;* Ger. *der Damm.*

Dance (People jumping together). Bring the flat (or "5") hands in front of body about height of breast, with fingers pointing nearly up, palms toward each other

about six inches apart. Move the hands briskly upward and downward a few inches several times,
simultaneously, mostly by elbow action. Compare
People.

Dance (Drumming). Hold up one flat hand face high,
back to side, thumb raised and up: jerk up and down. (C)
    Fr. *danser; la danse;* Ger. *tanzen, der Tanz.*

Dance

Danger (The *Scout* or *Wolf* going ahead and coming
back to report danger). Right V hand, back upward,
moved directly and slowly forward in front of the right
shoulder and then suddenly and quickly drawn back at
the same time the body is thrown back a little. (Sheeaka.)

Danger

Danger. Sign *Look, Little, Afraid* (No. 2).
    Fr. *le danger;* Ger. *die Gefahr.*

Dangerous (Of a man). Sign *Strong* and *Bad.*
    Fr. *dangereux;* Ger. *gefährlich.*

Dare you. See *Challenge.*

Dark, Unknown, Obscure. Bring the flat hands, back
outward, in front of face, right hand nearest face, left a
little ahead, hands crossed, tips of fingers about opposite centre of forehead; bring the hands very slightly
toward face. Compare *Ashamed* and *Blind.*
    Fr. *obscur;* Ger. *dunkel.*

Dark

Daughter. Sign *Born* and *Female.*
    Fr. *la fille;* Ger. *die Tochter.*

Day. See *Time*.

Daybreak. Sign *Little, Sunrise*.

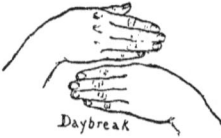

Daybreak (A peep through darkness). Hold right flat hand above left flat hand and in same plane; right little finger on left index then raise the right hand a few inches higher. (C)

Fr. *l'aube;* Ger. *der Tagesanbruch*.

Dead, Death. Make the sign for *Die* and *Sleep*. (C) The Cheyennes use *Die*.

Fr. *mort;* Ger. *tot*.

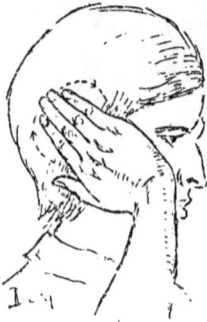

Deaf (Hearing ground out). Press the palm of extended right hand slightly against right ear, and move the hand in small circle parallel to and close to the ear. Sometimes add *Not*.

Fr. *sourd;* Ger. *taub*.

Debt. See *Owe*.

Deceive. Sign *Give* and *Lie*.

Fr. *tromper;* Ger. *betrügen*.

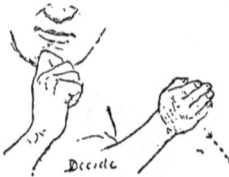

Decide, Determine, Make up one's mind (Think, then act or settle it). Lower the head and raise right fist to chin; then raise the head and cut down with the little finger edge of the flat right hand. (Sheeaka.)

Decide. This is a sentence rather than a sign. With 4 hand over heart, sign *Consider;* point slowly in two or three directions for *Ways;* sign *That* by vigorously swinging the right G index out, pointing down; then add *So* by raising it slightly up and then down. (Blackfoot.)

Fr. *décider;* Ger. *sich entscheiden.*

Decrease, Reduce, or **Make smaller.** Hold flat right hand, palm down, high above, a little to the side of flat left hand, palm up; move them together in succession of little jerks. Sometimes for emphasis finish by compressing all right fingers to a point in the left palm. Compare *Increase* and *Heap.*

Fr. *diminuer;* Ger. *verringern.*

Decrepit, Old, or **Broken down** (Bent with disease or age). Hold up G hand, back to right, higher than shoulder; lower the hand several inches, at same time bend the index. (C)

Decrepit. Hold up the right G, shoulder high, with index bent in a hook; rotate as in *Old.*

Fr. *décrépit;* Ger. *altersschwach, gebrechlich.*

Deed. See *Act.*

Deep. Hold the left flat hand horizontal, chin high, back up, fingers pointing to right; then drop right arm to full length down with flat right hand palm up, under left, fingers pointing forward.

Fr. *profond;* Ger. *tief.*

Deer. Both hands fully spread, palms in and held up to the side of the head to represent the horns of a deer. (Sheeaka.) This is generic for *Deer.* Compare *Elk.*

Fr. *le cerf;* Ger. *der Hirsch.*

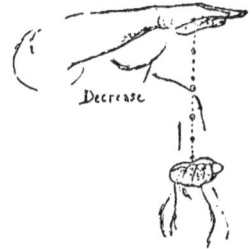

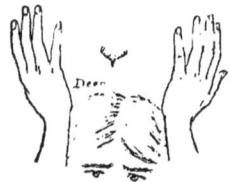

Deer, Mule or **Rocky Mountain Blacktail.** Sign *Deer* then set compressed hand at each ear pointing up and forward to indicate the large ears, as in a mule. (Scott.) Compare *Bear.*

> Fr. *le cerf mulet;* Ger. *der langohrige Hirsch.*

Deer, Whitetailed or **Virginian.** Raise the right G hand, pointing up and shoulder high; switch it from nearly horizontal right to nearly horizontal left and back, several times, pausing at the low point each time. Sign *Deer* if need for clearness.

> Fr. *le cerf de la Virginie;* Ger. *der Hirsch aus Virginien.*

Defame. See *Abuse.*

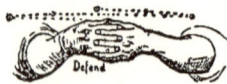

Defend, Protect, Defense, Forbid, or **Protection.** Sign the same as the first part of *Corral,* but swing the joined hands to left and right. So also to separate the hands means to *Loose* or *Remove* protection. See *Hold* or *Protect.*

> Fr. *défendre;* Ger. *verteidigen.*

Defiance, Defy, Dare, Challenge, or **I defy you.** Point the T hand toward the person. This is an extremely insulting challenge implying also the extreme of hatred and contempt. See *Challenge.*

> Fr. *le défi, défier;* Ger. *die Herausforderung, trotzen.*

Defiance, Insolent. See *Mockery.*

Delight. See *Excite.*

Depart. See *Go.*

Describe, Explain, or **Tell about** (Tell all about it). Sign *Talk* and *All*—that is, swing the curved flat right hand, palm down, and to left, in a horizontal circle in front of the right cheek.
Fr. *décrire;* Ger. *beschreiben.*

Desire. See *Want.*

Destroy. See *Exterminate.*

Determine. See *Decide.*

Devil. Sign *Medicine, Horns,* and *Tail.* A purely modern sign.
Fr. *le diable;* Ger. *der Teufel.*

Dew. Sign *Night, Grass,* and the *Shimmer;* i. e., pass curved right 5 hand, palm down, with a tremulous motion just above the grass and add *Water.* (C)
Fr. *la rosée;* Ger. *der Tau.*

Die (To go under; i. e., underground). Hold left hand flat, fingers horizontal, palm to you, breast high, pointing to right. Hold right G hand pointing to left above and within; pass it down, under and up beyond, still pointing to left.
This is capable of modification. Thus passing the right hand under and drawing it back means to be near death but to *Recover.* To make the sign *Little* after this means to *Faint.*
Fr. *mourir;* Ger. *sterben.*

Die out. See *Melt.*

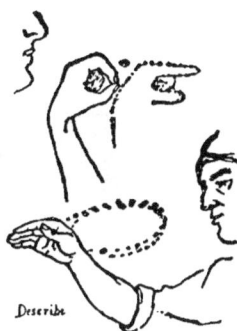

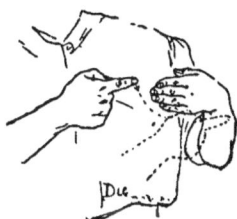

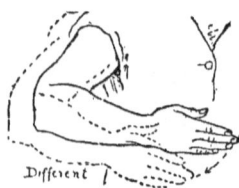

Different or **Wrong** (Push aside). Hold up the flat right, pointing forward and a little up, back to right. Swing the whole arm a foot to right, forward and upward, without bending the wrist, then back to first pose and repeat; a much-used and very plastic sign. Compare *Bad* and *No*.

Fr. *différent;* Ger. *anders.*

Difficulty. See *Trouble.*

Dig. Use flat right hand as a spade.
Fr. *creuser;* Ger. *graben.*

Dime. Sign *White, Little, Money.*

Dinner. Sign *Noon* or *Night*, as may be, and *Eat.*
Fr. *le dîner;* Ger *das Mittagessen, die Haupmahlzeit.*

Direction. Point the G finger forward and down, swing it forward in a curve till it is about horizontal and pointing in the line intended.
Fr. *la direction;* Ger. *die Richtung.*

Dirt or **Soil.** See *Earth.*

Dirty. Rub the tips of the 1st and 2nd fingers with the tip of the thumb, exactly as in *Powder*, and add *Bad.*
Fr. *sal;* Ger. *schmutzig.*

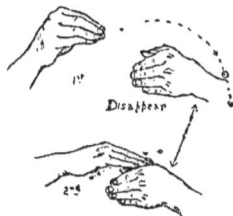

Disappear. Hold out the flat left, palm in, then shoot compressed right, points first, over and down; then rub upper edge of left with palm tips of right to mean *wiped out.*

Disappear. Look around and sign *See, Not.* Sometimes use *Hide.*

Fr. *disparaître;* Ger. *verschwinden.*

Disbelief. Sign *That, True, I think, No.*

Fr. *l'incrédulité;* Ger. *der Unglaube.*

Disciple. See *Learner.*

Discouraged. See *Sorrow.*

Discovery. *Found out.*

Discussion, Conversation, or Debate (In a general sense). Hold out both flat hands, palms, up, level, six inches apart, breast high; swing both to left, then back to right several times, to signify the handing of words back and forth.

Discussion or Conversation (Between two). Make the sign for *Talk* alternately right at left and left at right.

Fr. *la conversation;* Ger. *das Gespräch.*

Disgust or Dislike. Push both flat hands forward palms out, fingers up, and turn away head. Or *Heart, Tired.* (C) Sometimes use *Scorn.*

Fr. *le dégoût;* Ger. *der Ekel.*

Dismount. Sign *Horseman,* then separate and lower right V hand, points up. If the points of the A hand were down, it would mean "looking on the ground." See *Mount.*

Fr. *descendre de cheval;* Ger. *absteigen.*

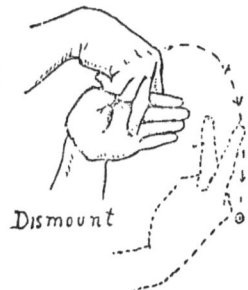

Disobey. Sign *Hear, Not.* Compare *Obey.*
Fr. *désobéir;* Ger. *nicht gehorchen.*

Distant. See *Far.*

Distress. See *Sorrow.*
Fr. *la misère;* Ger. *die Not.*

Dissolve. See *Melt.*

Dive (To plunge into water). Place flat hands palm to
palm and make the action of diving.
Fr. *plonger;* Ger. *tauchen.*

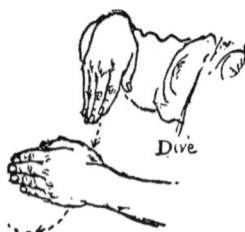
Dive

Dive or **Swoop** (Like a bird in air). Hold out flat left
hand, back outward, bring flat right hand, back out,
some inches in rear of and higher than left hand, pointing downward and forward; then shoot the right hand
downward and outward, back of hand grazing under
the left hand and up beyond. Compare *Born.*
Fr. *s'élancer;* Ger. *niederschiessen au.*

Divorce. Sign *Marry,* then swing the fingers apart
horizontally. This is a legal divorce. When *Abandon*
is used it means leaving one's mate without legal
divorce.

Do. See *Work.*

Doctor. Sign *Chief* and *Medicine.* (C) The Cheyennes omit *Chief.*
Fr. *le médecin, le docteur;* Ger. *der Arzt.*

Doer or **The one who does** or **Man who** (of all, that one).
Sign *Man,* then swing right G on the level a foot, and

back six inches; then raise and strike with same G down on middle of the line. (Sheeaka. Apparently no other Indian knew it.) The Cheyennes sign *Man* and *Work*, or *Man* and *Knows*.

Fr. *l'auteur, celui qui fait;* Ger. *der Täter.*

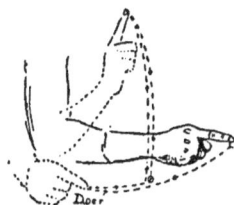

Dog (Drawing lodge poles). With V hand back up in front of body draw the double trail down and backward. Compare *Wolf.* Seger maintains that the idea here is the dog's ears point backward as he runs. See *Bark.*

Fr. *le chien;* Ger. *der Hund.*

Dollar. Sign *Money* and *One.* This would vary with the country, the sign stands for the unit of currency.

Fr. *le dollar;* Ger. *der Dollar.*

Done, Ended, Finished, Complete, Period, or **Full Stop** (Chopped off). Hold left hand flat, fingers touching, point forward, thumb up and with edge of right similarly held, chop down close past the tips of the fingers.

Also used as an auxiliary past tense, as *I done eat.*

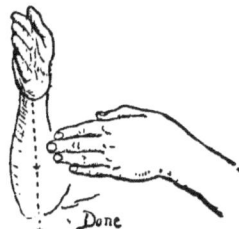

Done (2) **Finish, Quit, Break off.** Hold up both fists at level of chin, palms down, middle knuckles of left touching ditto of right; jerk them a foot apart as though breaking a cord; swing them apart, down, along and up. This is also used as a *Period* at the end of sentence and I have seen it used for *Bankrupt.* It is a northern sign recently established among the Cheyennes. Compare *Fat* and *Break.*

Fr. *fini;* Ger. *fertig.*

Don't Care (I am defiant). Tap chest with tips of right flat hand, then swing the hand briskly and high to right, keeping palm facing the left. (Sheeaka.) Merely shrug the shoulders. (Blackfoot.) The Cheyennes sign *Go ahead.*

> Fr. *cela m'est égal;* Ger. *ich mache mir nichts daraus.*

Do not or **Don't.** Hold up flat right hand, palm out, and forward at an angle; sharply shake the hand by wrist action back and forward (not sidewise), also sometimes the head. Compare *Easy* and *Rub it out.* Sometimes use *Stop.*

> Fr. *ne faites pas;* Ger. *tun Sie das nicht.*

Don't want. See under *Want.*

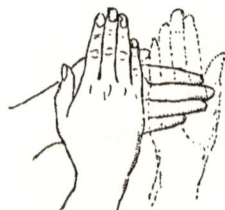

Door. Sign *Teepee* or *House,* then hold flat left hand, thumb up, and lay flat right across the palm with little finger of the right as the hinge; swing it till it lies flat on left palm. (C) The Cheyennes sign *House,* then pull and swing an imaginary door.

> Fr. *la porte;* Ger. *die Tür.*

Doubt, I am doubtful. Very slowly shake the head. (Pop.) Cheyennes and other Indians add—right hand held out palm forward and down, open and shaken; really a slow, slight *Question* sign. See *If.*

> Fr. *le doute, j'en doute;* Ger. *der Zweifel, ich bezweifle.*

Down, Downward, or **Below.** Point straight down with right G, lowering the same. (Blackfoot.) Some use flat hand for this. Compare *Here.*

> Fr. *en bas;* Ger. *unten.*

Down-hearted. See *Sorrow*.

Dream (See while sleeping). Sign *Sleep* and *See;* keeping the eyes closed.
Fr. *le rêve;* Ger. *der Traum.*

Dress. Pass the palm of the L hand over the part of the body to be covered. Compare *Hat, Moccasin, Robe*, etc.
Fr. *la robe;* Ger. *das Kleid.*

Drink or **Drinking** (From a cup). The O hand to the mouth as in drinking. Compare *Want.*

Drink

Drinking in the abstract would be: Draw the hollow hand level to the mouth from slightly above and down past chin, fingers pointing nearly forward. This combines *Water* and *Swallow*. See *Water*. Compare *Speech*.
Fr. *buvant;* Ger. *trinkend.*

Drinking liquor (Half a finger). Hold up right G hand back to you, then lay left G across back to indicate liquor, then add *Drink*. (Sheeaka.)
Fr. *buvant une boisson alcoolique;* Ger. *Schnaps trinkend.*

Drinking

Drive (Sense of driving a herd, or running off a herd). With L hands horizontal, opposite each other and same height, about an inch between tips of thumbs; move the hands simultaneously in the direction of the drive.
Fr. *mener;* Ger. *treiben.*

Drive

Drive a team

Driving (A team). Hold both hands, backs out, as though holding reins, thumbs straight, with index of each around its point. See-saw the hands on the same level.
Fr. *conduisant;* Ger. *lenkend, fahrend.*

Drouth. Sign, *Long time, Rain, No.*
Fr. *la sécheresse;* Ger. *die Dürre.*

Drown. Sign *Water* and *Die.*
Fr. *noyer;* Ger. *ertrinken.*

Drum. With G fingers draw a large circle, beginning together well forward, each making half-circle, ending near body; then strike on it several times with right A.
Fr. *le tambour;* Ger. *die Trommel.*

Drunk or **Drunkard.** Sign *Crazy, Drink,* and *Much.*
Fr. *ivre;* Ger. *betrunken.*

Dry (Of a stream or spring). Sign *Stream, Water, All gone.*
Fr. *sec;* Ger. *trocken.*

Dry. See *Thirsty.*

(Bird + Water + This) DUCK

Duck. Sign for *Bird* and make the broad bill with flat hand held under the nose, back up, pointing forward; push it forward a few inches, or else with thumb below and first and second fingers above.
Fr. *le canard;* Ger. *die Ente.*

Dull (Of a tool). Sign *Cut* and *Not* or *Bad.* Compare *Saw.*
Fr. *émoussé;* Ger. *stumpf.*

Dull. See *Dunce*.

Dumb. Press the finger tips of the flat hand on the mouth; add *Talk* and *No*.
  Fr. *muet;* Ger. *stumm*.

Dunce or **Dull** (Blockhead). Strike forehead with right fist knuckles. (D) A Cheyenne signed it *Behind, Book, Know, Not*.
  Fr. *le benêt, l'imbécile;* Ger. *der Dummkopf*.

During. See *While*.

Dust. Rub tips of right fingers with tip of right thumb, as in *Powder;* then with flat right hand horizontal, palm down, pat several times toward the earth. (Scott.) See *Earth* and *Land*.
  If the dust is in the air, pat down with one flat hand, then wave both 5 hands, points up, near the eyes; sometimes blink and draw back to make it more expressive.
  Fr. *la poussière;* Ger. *der Staub*.

Duty (That, me, sends). Sign for *That, Me,* and *Go* (emphatically).
  Fr. *le devoir;* Ger. *die Pflicht*.

Dwell or **Inhabit** (Alive and moving about in). Right flat hand, face high, pointing up, twisted slowly from left to right two or three times. Compare *Appear, Alive,* and *Doubt*.

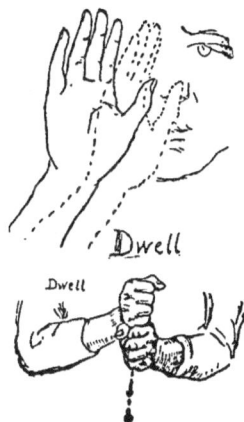

Dwell

Dwell

Dwell (2) (Sitting, emphatic). One fist above the other in front as though grasping a stake, then with both hands push it down and slightly forward. (Blackfoot.) Compare *Sit*.

Fr. *demeurer;* Ger. *bewohnen, wohnen.*

Dwindle. See *Decrease.*

E

Eagle. The sign for *Bird* is slowly made, then with the G hand in front of the face, back to right, describe a downward curve from between the eyes to indicate the curved bill of the eagle. This same sign is given for *Roman nose*, but hold the back of the hand forward.

Fr. *l'aigle;* Ger. *der Adler.*

Early. See *Soon.*

Early evening. Sign *Sunset* and *Little of*. (C) The Cheyennes understood this, but preferred to swing the *Sun* sign down to near, but not quite, level.

Fr. *au commencement du soir;* Ger. *früh am Abend.*

Early morning. Sign *Little* and *Daybreak*, or *Sunrise*.

Fr. *de bon matin;* Ger. *frühmorgens.*

Ear-rings. Make a ring of each index and thumb and apply to each ear-lobe, backs of hands out, other fingers raised.

Fr. *les boucles d'oreilles;* Ger. *das Ohrgehänge.*

Earth, the World (All land). Sign *All* with both flat hands, palms down, then pat down with both hands twice. Compare *Land*.

Fr. *le monde;* Ger. *die Erde, die Welt.*

Earth, Soil, or **Dirt.** Point down, then with thumb and finger tips, lift and rub some imaginary soil as in *Powder*.
Fr. *la terre;* Ger. *die Erde, der Schmutz.*

Easy, Softly, or **Gently.** Hold flat hand at face height, fingers half spread and a little curved, palm forward, leaning toward the person and gently and slightly shake the hand from side to side. (Sioux and Blackfoot.) With slight modification, much used on the railway in shunting. Compare *Rub it out, Question,* and *Do not.*
Fr. *doucement;* Ger. *sachte.*

Eat or **Food.** Throw the nearly compressed right hand lightly in a curve past the mouth several times. Compare *Water* and *Drink.*
Fr. *manger;* Ger. *essen.*

Eaten enough (Full to throat). Sign *Eat,* then lay L hand on breast, palm in, and raise it to opposite chin. Compare *Hang.*
Fr. *assez mangé;* Ger. *satt gegessen.*

Effect. See *Result.*

Effort. See *Try.*

Egg. Sign *Bird* and *Born;* then indicate the size of the egg with finger and thumb of one or both hands.
Fr. *l'oeuf;* Ger. *das Ei.*

Either, Or. Hold out left V hand, back up; tap each finger in turn with right G. Compare *Both.*
Fr. *l'un ou l'autre, ou . . . ou;* Ger. *entweder . . . oder.*

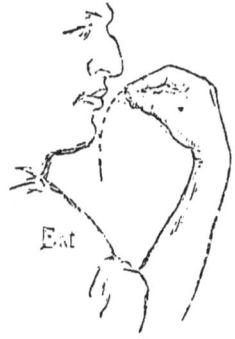

Elk or **Wapiti.** Hold the hands above the head at arm's length on each side, thumb and first two fingers of each spread, others closed; jerk them forward two or three times for three or four inches. Compare *Deer, Moose,* and *Caribou.*

Fr. *le cerf du Canada;* Ger. *das Elentier.*

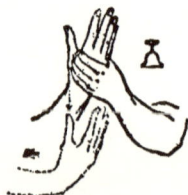

Empty, Absent, Gone, or **Out of.** Place the right 5 hand, points up, in the left C hand, which is back, forward, and down; drop the right hand down out of the left, closing left to O. Compare *All gone.*

Fr. *vide;* Ger. *leer.*

Encamp. See *Camp.*

Encircle. See *Surround.*

Enclosure. Hold out both 5 hands level, palm to palm, finger tips touching; swing them apart in a horizontal circle; draw them back; end with fingers wide apart and heels touching. A much-used sign. See *Corral.*

Fr. *l'enclos;* Ger. *die Einzäunung.*

End. See *Done.*

Endure, Suffer, or **Stand it** (Suffering, but strong and erect). Hold flat curved right hand close in front of breast, breathe heavily, swinging the hand near and from; then raise the right A hand in a curve out and up, about head high. (Sheeaka.) Understood, but not used by Cheyennes.

Fr. *supporter;* Ger. *aushalten, leiden.*

Enemy. Sign *Shake hands* and *Not.* Sometimes use *Hate.*

Fr. *l'ennemi;* Ger. *der Feind.*

Engaged or **Betrothed** (Ring-bound). Sign *Prisoner*, then with right index indicate a ring on ring finger of left hand. (D)

Engaged. Sign *Bye and bye, Marry.* See *Courting.*
Fr. *fiancé;* Ger. *verlobt.*

Engagement (i. e., Business). Swing the flat hands, palms up, up and down for six or eight inches, as in *Road*, but not progressing. Or, sign *Road* and *Meet.*
Fr. *l'engagement, l'obligation;* Ger. *die Verabredung.*

Enlist. Sign *Work* and *Soldier.*
Fr. *enrôler;* Ger. *sich anwerben lassen.*

Enough or **Full** in general sense (Levelling off a full measure). Hold out left O hand, back to left, and across the top from right to left pass the flat palm of the open right hand. Sometimes add *Strong*, to mean *Plenty.* See *Eaten enough.*
Fr. *assez;* Ger. *genug.*

Enter or **Come into.** Hold out hollow left, back up, and pass compressed right hand under and beyond.
Fr. *entrer;* Ger. *eintreten.*

Equal, Even, Same, Too, Also (Even race). Hold G hands in front of breast, side by side, backs up, pointing to front, about two inches apart; push them forward together and a little up in a sweep. A much-used sign. Compare *Race, Parallel, Marry,* and *Mate.*
Fr. *égal, le même;* Ger. *gleich, egal, genau so.*

Erase or **Annul.** Sign *Wrong* and *Wipe out.* See *Rub it out.*

Fr. *effacer;* Ger. *auslöschen, ausstreichen.*

Escape. See *Free.*

Even or **Same.** See *Equal.*

Evening. Sign *Night* and *Little of.* (C) See *Early evening.*

Fr. *le soir;* Ger. *der Abend.*

Ever. See *Always.*

Evil or **Sin.** Sign *Work* and *Bad.*

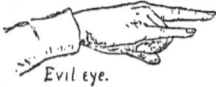

Evil Eye. Close all fingers of right hand, except index and little finger; to point these at any one means " You have the Evil Eye." In Italy this is an insult. (Pop.) In France it means " Shame on you," or " I put you to shame." (Pop.)

Evil eye.

Fr. *la main à corne;* Ger. *das Hexenauge.*

Except or **Unless.** See *But.*

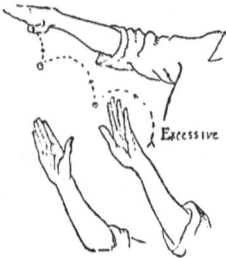

Excessive, Too much, Unjust, Too (Extremely, piled up). With right palm down, make a succession of curves, marking stages each higher than the last, beginning very low; then finish by swinging both hands, palm down, away up and forward. (Sheeaka.) Or sign *Heap.* Sometimes use *Enough.*

Excessive

Fr. *excessif, trop;* Ger. *übermässig, zu viel.*

Exchange. See *Trade.*

Excite, Agitate (Heart flutters). Sign *Heart*, then hold the 5 hand near the heart, back to right, pointing upward; raise it a foot shaking the fingers. The Blackfeet use this for *Glad*, and in most cases among the Cheyennes it implies pleasant excitement.

Fr. *exciter;* Ger. *aufregen.*

Excuse. See *Wipe out.*

Exist. See *Be.*

Expect. See *Hope.*

Explain. See *Describe.*

Exterminate, Annihilate, Crush, Destroy, etc. (Crushed and wiped out). Drop flat right on flat left, palm to palm, grind them together, then brush the right over the left tips, to front and beyond. Compare *Wipe out.*

Fr. *exterminer;* Ger. *vernichten.*

F

Face. Sweep the flat right hand, palm in, across the face and down. This is sometimes used for *Person.*

Fr. *la figure;* Ger. *das Gesicht.*

Fade. See *Melt.*

Faint. Signs for *Die* and *Recover.*

Fr. *s'évanouir, faible, épuisé;* Ger. *ohnmächtig werden, schwach.*

Fall or **Tumble.** The right flat hand in front of breast, back up, swept briskly out, *forward* up and down, to rest palm up. Compare *Another* and *Lie Down.*

Fr. *tomber;* Ger. *hinfallen.*

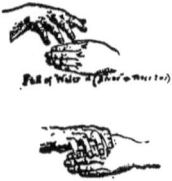

Fall. See *Autumn.*

Fall (Of water). Sign *River* or *Creek*, then hold out flat left, back out, and push flat right over it, bending right fingers over far edge, making them tremble.
 Fr. *la cataracte;* Ger. *der Wasserfall.*

Fail, that is, to lack success. See *Cannot.*

Fail (In business). Sign *Work, Backward.* (Blackfoot.) The *Backward* is indicated by holding the flat left well forward, drawing the flat right back in jumps.
 Fr. *faire faillite;* Ger. *bankerott werden.*

False. See *Lie.*

Fame. See *Glory.*

Famous (Standing on a hill). Sign *Hill*, then over that hold right G, palm forward, index just above left thumb. Or, sign *Chief* and *Brave.*
 Fr. *fameux, célèbre;* Ger. *berühmt.*

Far object, Distant or **Far forward, Over there.** Move the G hand forward and upward in a long slow arch, finishing at arm's length with down curve.

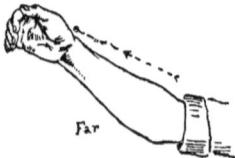

Far (In general). Flat right hand curved, pointing to left, back forward, pushed out and up at arm's length. Compare *Close.*
 Fr. *loin;* Ger. *entfernt.*

Farm. Sign *Land* and *Planting.*
 Fr. *la ferme;* Ger. *der Pachthof.*

Farmer. Sign *Corn* and *Chief*.

Fr. *le fermier;* Ger. *der Ackerbauer*.

Fast, Quick, Rapid, or **Swift** (Pass by). Hold out the flat left hand, back to left. Bring the flat right hand, back to right, several inches in rear of and slightly to right of left, pointing to front and downward; carry right hand swiftly past left and close to it, and as it passes, by wrist action, raise the hand so that fingers will point upward and in front, making a curve; at the same time, draw back the left a little.

Fr. *rapide, vite;* Ger. *schnell*.

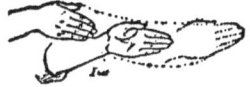

Fat (Shape of a fat animal's hips). Hold the fists out side by side, thumb to thumb, then swing them apart in two curves, up, out, down, and a little forward. Compare *Done* and *Break*.

Fr. *gras;* Ger. *fett*.

Fat or **Grease.** See *Oil*.

Father (Nurse, male). With compressed right hand, pluck at the right breast two or three times, as though drawing out milk. Sometimes add *Male*. Compare *Mother*.

Fr. *le père;* Ger. *der Vater*.

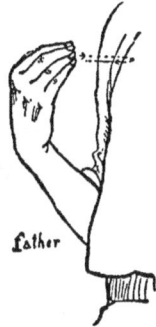

Father-in-law. Sign *Brother-in-law, Old,* and *Man*.

Fault-finding (Striking, knocking). With flat right hand, arm at full length, make a succession of short chops down. This is fault-finding with another. For "fault-finding with me" chop toward the breast. (Sheeaka.) See *Abuse, Chop,* and *By itself*. The Cheyennes use *You, All time, Scold*.

Fr. *blâmer, censurer;* Ger. *das Tadeln*.

Fear, Cowardice, Coward. The head stooped down and the right arm thrown up, palm out, as though to ward off danger. (Sheeaka.) The Cheyennes understand, but prefer *Woman, Heart.* See *Afraid.*

     Fr. *la peur;* Ger. *die Furcht.*

Feather (Small). Pluck an imaginary feather from left arm with index finger and thumb of right hand and blow it away from the mouth with one puff, at same time opening the finger and thumb to let it go.

Feather, i. e., **Quill Feather.** Sign *Wing,* then make as though pulling out and holding up *One* feather.

     Fr. *la plume;* Ger. *die Feder.*

Feel (That is, heart feels). Place the tip of the middle finger, others extended and lifted, against the heart; then draw it up a little way. (D)

     Fr. *sentir;* Ger. *empfinden.*

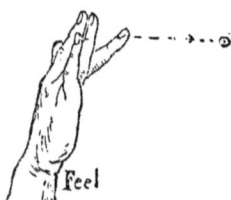

Feel or **Touch** (to touch). The hand as above, but pushed forward and moved a little from side to side. (Sheeaka.) See *Hot.*

Feel or **Touch.** Hold out left flat hand, back up; press tip of right flat hand on it at various places. Compare *At.*

     Fr. *toucher;* Ger. *tasten, berühren.*

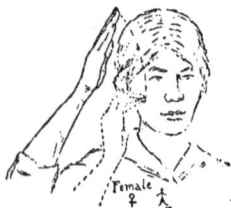

Female or **Woman.** Draw the flat right hand, palm in close to the side of the head, finger tips about on line with the top of head; lower the hand, at the same time curving fingers as though combing with them the hair over ears and cheeks; finish with a snap at line of shoulders. Two hands are used in the north. Compare *Comb.* For *White woman* indicate an immense hat. (Sheeaka.)

Fr. *la femme;* Ger. *das Weib.*

Fetch. See *Bring.*

Few. See *Small.*

Fight or War. Hold loosely clenched A hands well out in front of body, thumbs toward body, about height of shoulders and about three inches apart; bring right hand in toward body few inches, at same time move left out about same distance; then carry right out and bring left in, repeating these two or three times, making them by wrist and elbow action. This is a fight of many; for a fight of two, use the G fingers same way. In old days, according to Father Isadore, the signal for *Battle* was a handful of dust thrown in the air. The gesture of doing this came to mean *Fight.*

Fr. *le combat, la guerre;* Ger. *der Streit, der Krieg.*

Find. Sign *Look* around here and there, then shoot out the V hand and pick up an imaginary something with finger and thumb. Compare *Choose* and *Hunt.*

Fr. *trouver;* Ger. *finden.*

Fingers crossed, To claim Sanctuary. Also called *Bar up, King's X, King's Cross, Pax, Truce, Fins, Fines,* etc. Hold up right hand with first and second fingers crossed. This means "I claim privilege, what I do now is outside the game." (Universal in our schools and probably very ancient.)

Fr. *être exempt;* Ger. *die Immunität, verschont sein.*

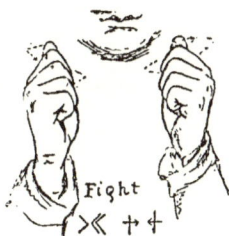

Finish. Hold out flat left, palm up; rub flat right on it, palm down, making two sunwise circles. Also use *Done*.

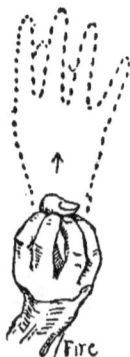

Fire (Blaze, flaring up with smoke). Hold the right hand down and forward at arm's length, back in front of the body; fingers hooked so the tip of thumb is over the nails of first three fingers and holds them down; raise the hand six inches and spring the fingers upward, free, separate, and straight. Do this twice. Compare *Aurora*.

Fr. *le feu;* Ger. *das Feuer.*

Fire, Spark of. Hold up right thumb and index as though holding something and blow it steadily; add *Fire* if needed for clearness. Compare *Feather* (small).

Fr. *l'étincelle;* Ger. *der Funke.*

Fire, Set it afire. Make the motion of striking a match on the side of the thigh and thrusting it forward.

Fr. *allumer;* Ger. *anzünden.*

Fire off, Shoot, or **Gun-Fire** (Blaze shooting forward). Right hand in front of right shoulder; throw palm forward six inches and at same time straighten and spread all fingers with a jerk. Some add a hand clap or many for *Volley firing.*

Fr. *décharger, faire feu sur, tirer;* Ger. *schiessen, abfeuern.*

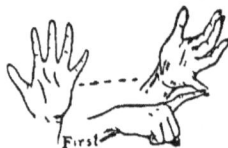

First (Of all, number one). Hold up left 5 hand, palm to right; push it forward, then tap the little finger with the right G. (Sheeaka. A Sioux sign, but understood by Cheyennes.) Compare *Last* and *Guide*.

First.   Sign *Ahead.*
   Fr. *le premier;* Ger. *der Erste.*

Fish.   Make sign for *Water;* then hold flat right hand, back to right, in front of right shoulder, elbow high; and move the hand sinuously forward.   Often omit *Water.*   Compare *Snake.*
   Fr. *le poisson;* Ger. *der Fisch.*

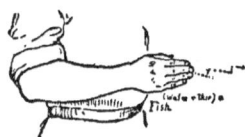

Fisher or **Pekan.**   Sign *Marten* and *Big* (suggested, not established).
   Fr. *le pékan;* Ger. *der kanadische Marder.*

Fix.   Lay low edge of flat right hand on upper edge of flat left near thumb base.   Push right forward and down, turning left back up.   (C)   Or, sign *Work* and *All right.*   Compare *Mend, Council,* and *Law.*
   Fr. *ajuster, arranger;* Ger. *herrichten, in Ordnung machen.*

Fix, In a Fix.   See *Quandary.*

Flag.   Hold flat right well out, back to right.   Lay left G on wrist of right.   Wave right sidewise.
   Fr. *le drapeau;* Ger. *die Flagge.*

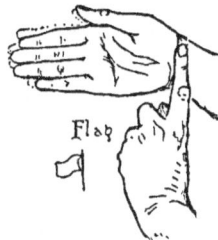

Flat.   See *Prairie.*

Flesh.   See *Meat.*

Float.   Flat left hand, back up; place flat right on it, palm down, and move both to right as on waves.   (C) Understood by Cheyennes.
   Fr. *flotter;* Ger. *oben auf schwimmen, auf dem Wasser treiben.*

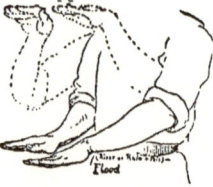

Flood. Indicate source of *Water*, then hold up both flat hands, backs up, side by side, waist high; raise them neck high and sign *Charge*. Omit *Charge* unless needed.

Fr. *l'inondation;* Ger. *die Flut.*

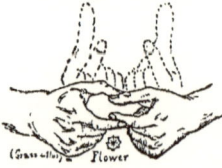

Flour. Sign *Bread* and *Powder*.
Fr. *la farine;* Ger. *das Mehl.*

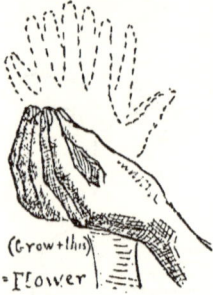

Flower, Bloom, or **Blossom.** Sign *Grass*, but higher; then clasp right index and thumb over left ditto, others closed; then turn the hands so the little fingers touch and the thumbs point up. (C)

Flower. Sign *Grow;* hold both compressed hands together in front, pointing up, backs out; spring them out into 5 hands, forming a circle pointing up.

Fly (The insect). Sign *Bird, Small;* then point here and there on the arm anywhere. Sometimes omit *Small.*
Fr. *la mouche;* Ger. *die Fliege.*

Fly (To). With flat hands held near shoulders simulate wings, beating exactly as in *Bird*, but move the hands forward a foot or more horizontally. Compare *Bird*.
Fr. *voler;* Ger. *fliegen.*

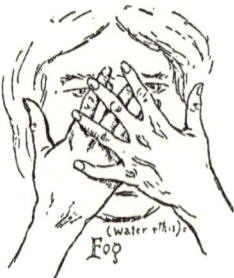

Fog (Water, peep through). Sign *Water* and hold the 5 hands, fingers crossed, in front of the eyes. (C) The Cheyennes understand this, but prefer the next:

Fog (Mud in the sky). Sign *Turtle*, then raise both 5 hands, palms forward, from the horizon up high; then spread them out. This expresses "turtles in the sky";

probably because the sky is clouded as is the water
when the turtle moves in it.

Fr. *le brouillard;* Ger. *der Nebel.*

Follow or **Chase.** Left G hand pointing nearly up,
moved ahead and variously pursued six inches behind
by right G hand. Sheeaka used his thumbs for this.

Fr. *suivre;* Ger. *folgen, nachlaufen.*

Fond, Fondness, Love, Affection, Regard, etc. (Pressed
to the heart). Cross wrists of A hands, backs out, over
the heart, right nearest body, few inches from it; draw
both against the body and bend the head over them.
With one hand it is *Like;* with two hands, *Love.* (Blackfoot.) Compare *Blanket.*

Fr. *affectueux;* Ger. *zärtlich, liebevoll.*

Food. See *Eat.*

Fool, Do you take me for a. With the right G index,
draw down the lower eyelid a little; as though to say,
" Can you see any green there?" (Pop.)

Fr. *le sot, me croyez vous bête?* Ger. *der Narr, denken
Sie ich bin dumm?*

Foolish. See *Crazy.*

Foolish or **Unwise.** Sign *Crazy* and *Little of.*

Fr. *imbécile;* Ger. *närrisch.*

Football signs. See page 233.

Footprints (Visible walk). Sign for *Walk* and for *See*
with the fingers pointed down. This is *Human tracks;*
for *Horse tracks,* sign *Walk* with the index and thumb
of each hand in a three-quarter circle, other fingers
closed, and then add *See* as here.

Fr. *les empreintes des pieds;* Ger. *die Fusztapfen.*

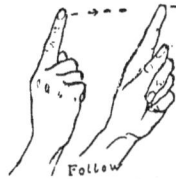

Footrace. Sign *Walk* quickly, and *Race.*
Fr. *la course à pied;* Ger. *der Wettlauf.*

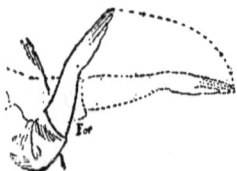

For (Giving to). Throw the flat right hand forward and palm down, slowly toward the object. Compare *Stop*, *Give*, and *Wait.*

For. Sometimes use *Belongs.* Hold out the two G hands nearly back up, a foot apart; swing them together till the G tips are about two inches apart. (Sheeaka.)

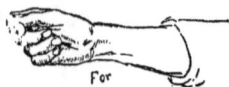

For. Lightly close the right as though it held some object, push it forward and upward, back to right. (Blackfoot.)
Fr. *pour;* Ger. *für.*

Forbid. See *Defend.*

Forest, Timber, or **Woods.** Hold both forearms upright, with all the fingers much spread, meaning *Trees*, the right hand nearest the body, its back against the palm of left; then separate them, drawing right hand toward the body, moving the left away and upward in a curve. See *Tree.*
Fr. *la forêt;* Ger. *der Wald.*

Forever. See *Always.*

Forgive. See *Excuse.*

Forget or **Forgot** (Swept from my brain). Touch the forehead with the right N finger. Shake the head and motion as though to brush away an imaginary fly from near the nose. (Sheeaka and Pop.) See *Remember not.*

Forget or **Forgot.** Clap right hand down on left (for surprise); lay right G, palm forward, on forehead, and add *Hid.*

    Fr. *oublier;* Ger. *vergessen.*

Forward (In space). See *Ahead.*

Forward (In time). See *Future.*

Found it. Sign *I Saw,* then reach forward and with index and thumb pick up an imaginary object. Compare *Choose.*

Found it. At a distance, hold both hands high above the head, fingers closed, thumbs pointing toward each other. (Pop.)

    Fr. *je l'ai trouvé;* Ger. *ich habe es gefunden.*

Found out, i. e., **You are found out.** Point forefinger at the person. (Sheeaka.) Or sign *You, I, Understand.*

    Fr. *démasqué;* Ger. *ertappt.*

Four-foot. See *Animal.*

Fox. Indicate the size of animal and bushy tail.

    Fr. *le renard;* Ger. *der Fuchs.*

Free, Escape, Safe, Save, Relief, Permit, Turn loose (Unbinding). S hands crossed at wrists. With an effort, break the imaginary bonds and throw the hands apart, turning palm sides up. Sometimes add *Go.* See *Pardon.*

Free, Wild, or **Free of Incumbrance** (Cut loose). Hold flat right hand in front of breast, fingers forward, back down; move by wrist action sharply to left a few inches; then jerk back to place two or three times as though cutting something loose. Compare *Chop* and *Wild Animal.*

Fr. *libre;* Ger. *frei.*

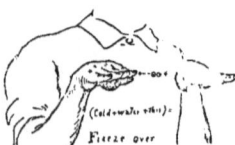

Freeze over, Form ice. Sign for *Cold, Water,* then raise and move till the flat hands are touching in front, side by side, backs up and at arm's length. (C) See *Ice.*

Fr. *geler;* Ger. *gefrieren.*

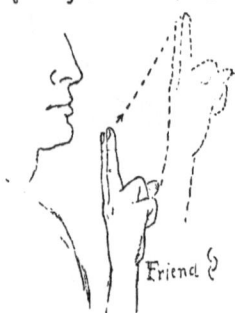

Friend, Friendship, or **Chum** (Brothers growing up together). Hold right N hand in front of neck, palm forward, pointing up; raise it head high, slightly advancing it. *Alliance* is sometimes used, or even *Peace.*

Fr. *l'ami;* Ger. *der Freund.*

Frog (Water hopper). *Water;* then with compressed right hand make long hops forward.

Fr. *la grenouille;* Ger. *der Frosch.*

From. Touch digit of right G hand to right shoulder, then throw it in a long sweep up and forward. Sometimes Indians use flat hand for this.

Fr. *de;* Ger. *von.*

Frost. Sign, *Cold, White,* and *Strong.*

Fr. *la gelée;* Ger. *der Frost.*

Fruit. Sign *Tree*, then make a ring of right index and thumb, others closed, and place it here and there in the branches, and add *Eat*. Compare *Berry*, *Leaf*, and *Money*.

Fr. *le fruit;* Ger. *die Frucht.*

(Tree+This+Eat')
= Fruit

Full. See *Enough*.

Future (Time ahead). Make the signs for *Time* and *Far ahead*. See also *Will*.

Fr. *futur, l'avenir;* Ger. *zukünftig, die Zukunft.*

G

Gallop. Sign *Ride*, then hold out flat hands, palm to palm, right in advance; work them up and down together, the tips describing vertical curves. Compare *Fast* and *Work*.

Fr. *galoper;* Ger. *galoppieren.*

Gamble. Hold the hands out level, six inches apart; swing to left and right simultaneously, in easy curves down and up, keeping them near each other as though swinging a tom tom. Compare *Drive* and *Herd*.

Fr. *jouer;* Ger. *spielen.*

Gap, Gorge, or **Mountain Pass.** Sign *Mountains*, then hold out left L hand, thumb pointing to left and upward, pass flat right between, touching at bottom.

Fr. *le défilé;* Ger. *die Kluft, die Schlucht.*

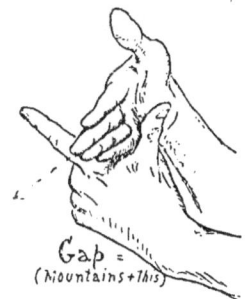

Garden. Strike down with right G as in *Here*, but in several directions, then add *Plant* and *Eat*.

Fr. *le jardin;* Ger. *der Garten.*

Gap = (Mountains+This)

Gather. See *Together*.

Generous. Sign *Heart* and *Big;* or, *Heart, Pities.*
Fr. *généreux;* Ger. *groszmütig, freigiebig.*

Gentle. See *Kind.*

Gently. See *Easy.*

Get or **Obtain** (That is, he gets, or obtains). Reach
out left hand, back up; then with right hand, grasp
something on top of it; then close and draw back the
right. If it is the first person who *gets*, finish by drawing the hand toward oneself. Sometimes omit left
hand.
Fr. *obtenir;* Ger. *erlangen, erhalten.*

Get well. See *Recover.*

Ghost, Soul, or Spirit. Bring right G hand in front of
centre of body, pointing down; then draw it upward,
as though drawing the forefinger out of the mouth,
upward and to the front and at the same time exhale a
breath. (Scott.) The Cheyennes sign *Big eyes* (as in
Owl), and shaking the hands at the same time. See
Spirit.
Fr. *l'esprit;* Ger. *der Geist.*

Gift. Hold left hand, hollow up; with right hand pick
an imaginary object out of the left; carry it forward, at
the same time turning right hand flat, palm up, and fingers pointing down and forward. Or, sign *Give* and
Free (2nd).
Fr. *le cadeau;* Ger. *das Geschenk.*

Girl (Woman sprout). Sign *Female, Young.*
Fr. *la fille;* Ger. *das Mädchen.*

Give. Hold out flat right, back to right, shoulder high; swing it out and down.

Fr. *donner;* Ger. *geben.*

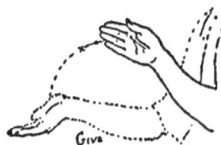

Give you. Swing the hand from the person giving toward *you.* This, with the sign below, shows the beginning of a conjugation.

Give me. Bring the flat right hand well out in front of body, about height of neck, back of hand nearly to left, lower edge nearest to body, pointing upward; draw the hand in toward the body and a little down; at the same time, bend the hand and the wrist so the fingers touch the chest. Compare *Tell me* and *Half-Breed.*

Fr. *donnez moi;* Ger. *geben Sie mir.*

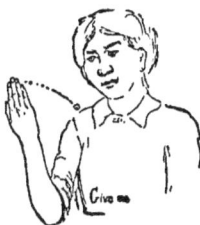

Give it up. See *Abandon.*

Give up, Lose hope, or **Discouraged.** See *Sorrow.*

Glad, Pleasant, Happy, or **Merry** (Sunshine in the heart). Sign *Heart* and *Day.*

Fr. *heureux;* Ger. *froh, glücklich.*

Glitter or **Shining** (The mirror signal). Hold out the L hand with index pointing forward, back up. Rotate with a flash, or jerk so the thumb is upright and back to its original pose. Do this once or twice. See *Courting* and *Sweetheart.*

Fr. *étinceler;* Ger. *glitzern.*

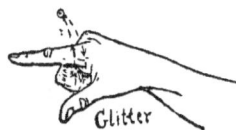

Gloomy, Cross, or **Sullen** (Clouds close). Sign *Clouds,* then draw them down near head. (C) Or, sign *Thinking* and *Bad.* Compare *Cross* and *Angry.*

Fr. *sombre;* Ger. *finster, trübe.*

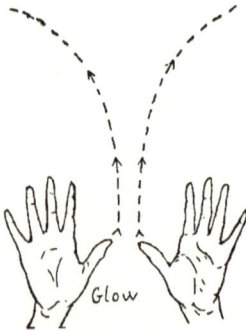

Glory or **Fame.**   Sign *All, Good, Know.*   See *Famous.*
Fr. *la gloire;* Ger. *der Ruhm.*

Glow, Splendor, Wonderful (Spread in the sky). Hold up both 5 hands, palms forward, pointing up, at arm's length, nearly level; raise up very high and at the same time spread widely. A much-used and very plastic sign. May sometimes mean *Weather.*
Fr. *la splendeur;* Ger. *das Glühen, die Pracht.*

Go, Went, or **Travel.** Hold flat right hand, back to right, breast high, pointing to front and down; swing it up and out till the fingers point forward and upward. Often combined with *Arrive there.*
Fr. *aller;* Ger. *gehen.*

Going. Hold up right G, palm forward; move it forward in short pushes.
Fr. *allant;* Ger. *gehend.*

Go away, Go ahead, Go farther (Imperative). Hold flat right hand in front of body, palm forward, fingers upright; move the hand to front in a slight curve to right; repeat once or twice. See *Begin.*
Fr. *allez!* Ger. *gehen Sie!*

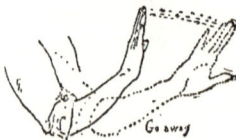

Goat. Sign *Horns,* with the straight G fingers on each side of head, and *Beard.* Sometimes omit *Horns,* signing only *Beard.*
Fr. *la chèvre;* Ger. *die Ziege.*

God (The Great Mystery). Sign *Medicine* and *Great.*
Fr. *Dieu;* Ger. *Gott.*

Gold. Sign *Money* and *Yellow*, or *Hard* and *Yellow*.

For *Gold coin* sign, *Chief, Money*.
Fr. *l'or;* Ger. *das Gold*.

Gone. See *Absent*.

Good, All right, Level, Fair, Just (Level with the heart). Hold the flat extended right hand, back up, level, touching the left breast; swing the hand briskly out to front and slightly up in a curve.
Fr. *bon;* Ger. *gut*.

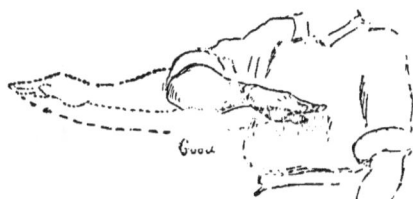

Good-bye. Hold right hand flat, palm down, pointing forward horizontally at height of head and shake the hand up and down by wrist action. A whiteman's sign recently adopted by Indians.
Fr. *adieu, au revoir;* Ger. *lebe wohl!*

Good-morning. Sign *Day* and *Good*.
Fr. *bonjour;* Ger. *guten Morgen*.

Goose. Sign *Bird*, moving the wing hands slowly; hold both flat hands low, side by side, a little apart, backs up; push them down sharply a few inches, for flat feet. Sometimes also make the *honk* sound.
Fr. *l'oie;* Ger. *die Gans*.

Gorge. See *Gap*.

Gossip. See *Telltale*.

Grain, of any kind. Hold both hands hollow together, as in *Bowl;* shake, then point to the hollow of the left with right G. (Sheeaka.) The exact kind must be specified. In Cheyenne, *Wheat* is *Bread* and *Sow; Oats* is *Horse, Eat, Sow.*

Fr. *le grain;* Ger. *das Getreide.*

Grandchild. With the flat right, pat one's own back where the baby is carried. Among the Cheyennes, only the grandmother uses this.

Grand Coup. See *Count Coup.*

Grandfather. Sign *Old* and *Father.*

Grandfather (Father once removed). Sign *Father,* then hold curved left hand in front of body, palm in; and on outer side make the sign *Father* again. For *Great grandfather,* repeat the sign for *Father* once more. For *Ancestors,* many times. (Crow signs given me by La Forge.)

Fr. *le grandpère;* Ger. *der Groszvater.*

Grandmother. As above, but use *Mother* sign. (LaF.)

Grandmother. Sign *Old, Mother.*

Fr. *la grand'mère;* Ger. *die Groszmutter.*

Grasp. See *Keep.*

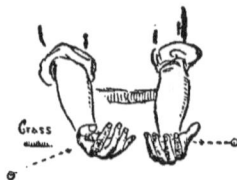

Grass. Hold both hands low, palms up; turn all fingers upward straight and swing hands slightly apart. For *Grass growing,* raise the hands a little. Compare *Children.*

Fr. *l'herbe, le gazon;* Ger. *das Gras, der Rasen.*

Gratitude. Use *Thank you* sign. Or else raise the flat right hand, palm forward and face high; draw it downward in a sweep several times as though stroking the other person's breast. For emphasis use both hands.

Fr. *la reconnaissance;* Ger. *die Dankbarkeit.*

Grave. Hold out both flat hands, thumbs up, six inches apart, pointing level forward; draw them back level to you, sign *Die;* then hold out left flat hand as before and slap on it two or three times with the flat right, for *cover up.*

Fr. *le tombeau;* Ger. *das Grab.*

Great. Hold out the slightly curved 5 hands in front of breast, few inches apart, palms toward each other, pointing to front; separate hands the right to the right and up a little and near the body; the left to the left and down a little and farther away. Compare *Big* and *Wide.* Sometimes use *Much* or *High.*

Fr. *grand;* Ger. *grosz.*

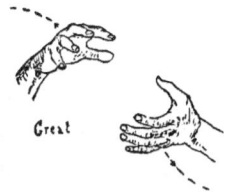

Greater than. Sign *Ahead, Great.* So also *Less than* would be *Behind, Small.*

Fr. *plus grand que;* Ger. *gröszer als.*

Grief. See *Sorrow.*

Grieve. Sign *Heart, Down.* See *Give up* and *Mourn.*

Fr. *se chagriner, pleurer;* Ger. *trauern.*

Ground. See *Land.*

Grouse or **Prairie Chicken.** Sign *Bird* and show size; then with right hand low, palm up, fingers closed except first curved up like neck, imitate forward walking. (Sioux.) Sign *Bird* then indicate fast wing beats and whirring. (Blackfoot.) Sign *Bird* and *Tail cut off*. (Cheyenne.)

Fr. *la gelinotte;* Ger. *das Waldhuhn.*

Grow, Become, or **Turn into.** Hold right G hand low, back down, index finger pointing upward, in front of body; raise the hand by gentle jerks.

Fr. *pousser, croître, devenir;* Ger. *wachsen, werden.*

Guide (Verb). (Show trail and Lead.) Point with right index forward and downward; then add *Lead*. (Sheeaka.)

Fr. *conduire;* Ger. *führen, leiten.*

Guide (Noun). Hold up left 5 hand, little finger forward, and ahead of the right G, all moved forward in easy swings.

Fr. *le guide;* Ger. *der Führer.*

Gun. Make the motion of holding and aiming a gun; then add *Fire-off*. For *Rifle*, add the working of the lever.

Fr. *le fusil, la carabine;* Ger. *das Gewehr.*

Gun, i. e., *Shot-gun,* sign *Gun,* then clasp the hands twice and hold up two fingers. See *Revolver*.

Fr. *le fusil de chasse;* Ger. *die Flinte.*

Gun-fire. See *Fire*.

Gun-powder. Sign *Gun* and *Powder*.

Fr. *la poudre à canon;* Ger. *das Schiesspulver.*

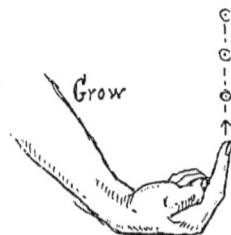

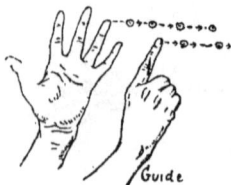

H

Habit (Thought bound). With G forefinger draw a small circle on forehead, then sign *Prisoner*. (D)

Habit (Road smoothed by repeated strokes). Sweep the flat hands, palms down, back and forth; then strike three times down with the right G. (Sheeaka.) Or sign *Way* and *Keep*. (Seger.)

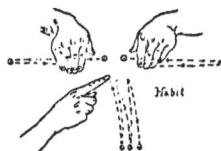

Habit (Long time the same). Hold out left G, draw right G back from left knuckles to shoulder; add *Same*. Fr. *l'habitude;* Ger. *die Gewohnheit*.

Hail. Sign *Rain, Cold,* and with curved right index on thumb indicate size of stones. Fr. *la grêle;* Ger. *der Hagel*.

Hair (Of animal). Hold out left forearm horizontally in front of body and sweep the curved right 5 hand, palm up, along it from elbow to wrist. For *Human hair,* touch one's own hair. Compare *Wing*. Fr. *le poil;* Ger. *der Pelz*.

Half. Hold left flat hand in front of breast, back out. Lay the lower edge of right flat hand on upper edge of left index, in middle, and jerk it toward the tips of left. Sometimes the right hand alone is used edge downward, drawn back and down as though its under side were cutting something. Compare *Part*. Fr. *le demi, la moitié;* Ger. *die Hälfte*.

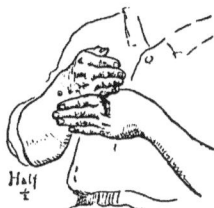

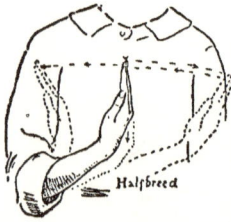

Half-breed. With flat right hand pointing up, little finger next middle of the breast, palm to right, halve the body down breast, swing it far to left, return to centre, then swing far to right and give the tribal sign for each half. Or, give the first sign only; that is, the hand cutting in the middle.

Fr. *le métis;* Ger. *der Mischling.*

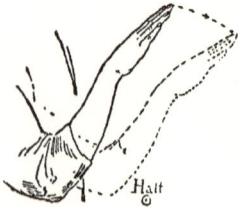

Halt or **Stop.** Hold the right flat hand, palm outward and downward, in front of the body, pointing upward and to front, hand about height of shoulders; move the hand sharply to front and downward, stopping it suddenly. Sometimes merely raise the hand flat forward.

This means also *Keep quiet, Wait a moment,* etc., when made gently. "This sign is world wide. In a journey around the world, I have used it in every country visited and found it instantly recognized. I saw a train stopped by it in the Himalayas, also jinrikishas stopped in Java, Singapore, Saigon, Canton, Hong Kong, Nagasaki, and Manila." (Scott.)

Fr. *Halte!* Ger. *Halt!*

Halve. Same as *Half;* but jerk one part to right and one to left. (C)

Fr. *couper ou diviser en deux;* Ger. *halbieren.*

For *One-Quarter*, lay the "knife hand" at last joint of left index; for *Three-Quarters*, near base; see also *Quarter.*

Fr. *le quart;* Ger. *das Viertel.*

Handsome. See *Beautiful.*

Hang (To be executed). Swing the right L hand over the head down to the neck, palm in; close the thumb and

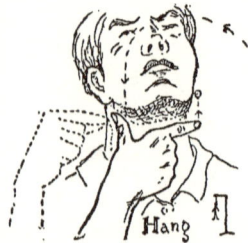

index, then draw it up to height of head, index pointing
down.   This is done in two graceful sweeps.
>   Fr. *pendre;* Ger. *hängen.*

Hang.   Hang right G index like a hook on straight left
G index.
>   Fr. *accrocher;* Ger. *aufhängen.*

Hanker.   See *Want.*

Happen.   See *Luck.*

Happy.   See *Glad.*

Happy Hunting Ground.   Sign *Die, Beyond,* and *Dwell.*
>   Fr. *les Champs Elysées des Indiens;* Ger. *die seligen*
>   *Jagdgefilde.*

Hard (Like rock).   Hold out the left hand flat, edge
down, and strike the palm with the knuckles of the right
two or three times.
>   Fr. *dur;* Ger. *hart.*

Hat (Head cover).   Bring the L right hand, back outward, in front, close to, and a little above the head;
lower the hand until thumb and index are about opposite the eyes; spread thumb and index, passing down
close to forehead.
>   Fr. *le chapeau;* Ger. *der Hut.*

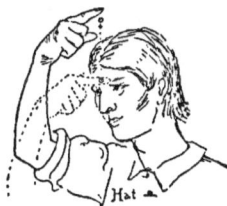

Hatchet.   See *Axe.*

Hate. Hold up both hands opposite left side of face in pose for *Fire-off*, back of each to its side; spring both out as in *Fire-off*, to left side, turning the left very little, so that it shoots forward; the right shoots to the left. Compare *Abandon* and *Scorn;* also *Defiance.* Sheeaka used only *Defiance* sign.

Fr. *détester;* Ger. *hassen.*

Have (To possess). See *Possession.*

Have to, Bound to, Must, Obliged to, Compelled to (Bound down). Sign *Prisoner* and *Work.* Or, *That, Work, Strong.*

Fr. *être obligé;* Ger. *müssen.*

Hawk. First make *Bird* sign, then imitate the seizing of the prey with both feet hawk-fashion, by means of both hands placed in front of body opposite neck, palms outward, make grasping motion forward. (Scott.) Or sign *Bird* and with curved G indicate bill. See *Eagle.*

Fr. *le faucon;* Ger. *der Habicht.*

He. Make the sign *Male;* or point with the thumb, other fingers closed.

Fr. *il;* Ger. *er.*

Headache. Touch head; then hold curved flat hand near and flirt the fingers from behind the thumb two or three times to show the throbbing.

Fr. *le mal de tête;* Ger. *das Kopfweh.*

Healthy. See *Well.*

Heap or **Very Much.** With curved hands show shape, beginning at the lowest points. Compare *Many*, *Mound*, and *Much*.
> Fr. *l'amas, le tas;* Ger. *der Haufe(n).*

Hear. Move the right G hand (pointed forward) from behind the right ear, past the ear and forward. Compare *Listen* and *Indian Nez Percé*.
> Fr. *entendre;* Ger. *hören.*

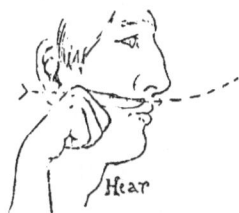

Heart. Bring the compressed right hand against the left breast, over heart and pointing downward.
> Fr. *le coeur;* Ger. *das Herz.*

Heat. See *Hot.*

Heaven. Simply point up with right G, back to right and head high. Compare *Heavens* and *Happy Hunting Ground;* also, *Tall.*
> Fr. *le paradis;* Ger. *der Himmel, das Paradies.*

Heavens, Skies, or **Sky.** Hold both flat hands palms down, tips touching, over and in front of the head; sweep them down sidewise in outline of the dome. Compare *Clouds, Carriage, Hot Weather.*
> Fr. *le ciel;* Ger. *der Himmel.*

Heavy (Cannot hold up). Hold flat hands, a few inches apart, at same level, backs down, in front of body and pointing to front. Raise them slightly and let them drop several inches, finishing low. Compare *Light.*
> Fr. *lourd;* Ger. *schwer.*

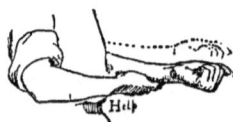

Help. Hold left forearm horizontally in front of body, hand A, and place flat right hand under left forearm and lift it slightly. (Sheeaka; borrowed from the Deaf.) Or, sign *Work* and *With*.

Fr. *aider;* Ger. *helfen.*

Her. See *Possession.*

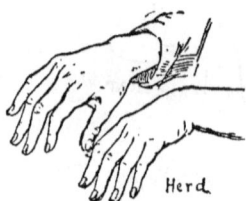

Herd of Animals. Hold out left 5 fingers a little curved, level, far advanced, shoulder high, backs up and out; moved forward and a little down together. For *Herd grazing* hold right 5 over left 5 wrist; draw right back toward body in a slight arc up and down.

Fr. *le troupeau;* Ger. *die Herde.*

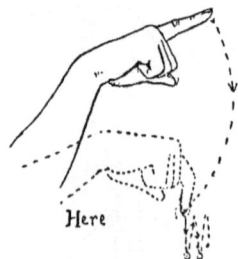

Herd (Verb). See *Drive.*

Here (This spot). Swing the right G, back up, from pointing up, to forward and down; then stab toward the ground two or three times. Compare *Down, Earth, Place.*

Fr. *ici;* Ger. *hier.*

He who. See *Doer.*

Hide, To Cache, Conceal, or **Lose.** Swing the flat or else compressed right hand, palm down, under the flat left hand held in front, palm down; the left hand rests on the right at end of sign. (Sheeaka.) Sometimes add *Hush.* Compare *Enter* and *Night.*

Fr. *cacher;* Ger. *verstecken.*

Hide (Skin). Hold extended left hand, back up, in front of body, and with the right thumb and forefinger gather up, with a pinch, the loose skin on the back of left hand. Sometimes sign *Robe*.

Fr. *la peau;* Ger. *das Fell.*

High or **Height.** Hold the flat right hand, back nearly up, pointing to front, in front of right shoulder; raise the hand according to the height intended. If it refers to humans, hold the right hand (compressed or G) vertically pointing upward. (C) To show height of small objects or animals, hold the flat left, palm up, under right. See *Tall.*

Fr. *haut;* Ger. *hoch.*

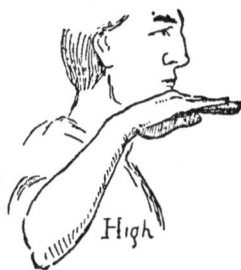

Higher. See *Superior.*

Hill, Bluff, or **Butte.** Push right A fist, back out, straight up, face high. For plural use both hands moved alternately up and down at different places. Compare *Ridge, Lump,* and *Mountain.*

Fr. *la colline;* Ger. *der Hügel.*

His. See *Possession.*

History or **Story** (Pictures of the past). Hold up flat left, palm forward, and sketch on palm with right G; then sign *Past.* (C) Or, Sign *Long, Past, Tell me.*

Fr. *l'histoire;* Ger. *die Geschichte.*

Hit (To make a hit). See *Count Coup.*

Hoax (To wolf or beguile). Sign *I, Make, Him, Wolf.* (Seger.)

Fr. *mystifier;* Ger. *jemandem etwas aufbinden.*

Hog or **Pig.** Indicate size, then with a circle of two thumbs and two index fingers in front of mouth show muzzle; last, with flat right hand, or flat fist back up, make a snout and root. Usually give only the last sign.

Fr. *le cochon;* Ger. *das Schwein.*

Hold (to hold a prisoner). Arms in a level circle, flat right hand inside flat left and overlapping, both palms toward you; swing to right and left. Compare *Defend, Keep,* and *Corral.*

Fr. *tenir prisonnier;* Ger. *gefangen halten.*

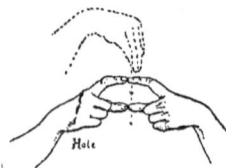

Hole. Form a circle with thumbs and fingers of L hands. If need be, for clearness, hold left hand in position and pass the compressed right through the imaginary hole. Compare *Cook* and *Boil.*

Fr. *le trou;* Ger. *das Loch.*

Holler. See *Yell.*

Home. Sign *My, Teepee.*

Fr. *la demeure, le foyer, le chez-soi;* Ger. *das Heim.*

Home-sickness. Sign *Heart, Want,* and *Teepee.*

Fr. *le mal du pays;* Ger. *das Heimweh.*

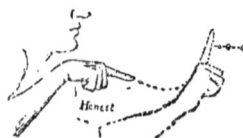

Honest (Straight walk). Point right G straight forward from near throat; push it down and up in a slight curve till it is upright, then push it forward in two or three little jerks. See also *True.*

Fr. *honnête, intègre;* Ger. *ehrlich.*

Honor (Upon my honor). With right index draw a small cross on the heart. (Pop.)

Fr. *parole d' honneur!* Ger. *auf Ehre! bei meiner Ehre!*

Hope.   Sign *Heart, Want.*
   Fr. *l'espoir;* Ger. *die Hoffnung.*

Horse.   Hold the flat left hand, back to front, before face, fingers level; move it to right; and then, for a moment, place the first and second fingers of right astride it, as in *Ride.*   Some omit the last gesture.   The movements of the hand indicate the height, action, and speed of the horse.
   Fr. *le cheval;* Ger. *das Pferd.*

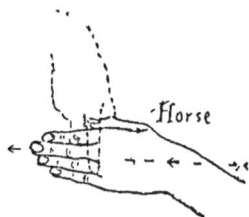

Horseman.   Sign *Man* and *Ride.*   Or, place the V right astride of the flat left and push both to right.
   Fr. *le cavalier;* Ger. *der Reiter.*

Hot or **Heat** (As water or iron).   Hold the hand as in *Feel;* touch the middle right finger tip to tongue; reach it forward and down, as though touching a hot iron, quickly jerking it back.   (A northern sign understood by Cheyennes.)   The use of the middle finger is general, no doubt because it is longest.
   Fr. *chaud;* Ger. *heisz.*

Hot weather (Rays of sun beating down).   Hold the 5 hands a few inches apart, backs up, above and in front of head, pointing toward each other.   Lower the hands to level of face.
   Fr. *les grandes chaleurs;* Ger. *das heisze Wetter.*

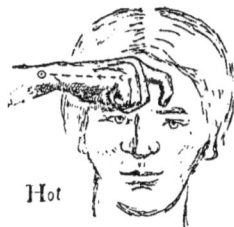

Hot or **Sweating** (Personally).   Draw right index crooked across the brow, left to right, as though to run off the sweat, others and thumb closed.

Hotel.   See *Restaurant.*

Hour. See *Time.*

House

House. Indicate the double slope of the roof by flat hands, pointing nearly up and joined together at the tips. Some use only the next sign for *House.*
　　　Fr. *la maison;* Ger. *das Haus.*

Log-house

House of logs (Corners of a log house). Bring the hands in front of body and interlock the fingers near tips, fingers at nearly right angles and horizontal. Some add *Roof* by joining tips of flat hands as in *House.* Compare *Basket.*
　　　Fr. *la cabane en bois, la hutte;* Ger. *das Blockhaus.*

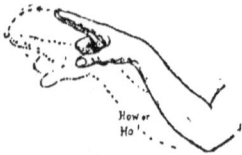
How or
Ho!

How! or **Ho!** The Indian salutation is sometimes used with hand salute; that is, all fingers closed except index and middle, as in *Friend.*
　　　Fr. *Ho!* Ger. *Grüsz Gott!*

How? See *Question.*

How many? See *Question.*

How much? See *Question.*

100

Hundred (Whole circle of tens). Hold up both 5 hands, palms forward, opposite right shoulder; thumbs nearly touching; swing to left and down. Precede this with *one* for *one hundred,* *two* for *two hundred,* etc.
　　　Fr. *cent;* Ger. *hundert.*

Hungry

Hungry or **Hunger** (Cuts one in two). Draw the lower edge of flat right hand, back down, across the stomach; emphasize by drawing back and forth.
　　　Fr. *avoir faim, la faim;* Ger. *hungrig sein, der Hunger.*

Hunt or **Searching for** (In the sense of seeking for).
The fingers of the right V hand brought near the eye,
but pointing forward; then swing horizontally from side
to side, the eye looking wherever they point. Compare
Choose, Find, and *Look*. Or, shade the right eye with
the right hand and swing the head. (Pop.)
   Fr. *chercher;* Ger. *suchen*.

Hunting (With gun or bow). Hold out both G hands,
one behind the other; swing in up-curves forward and
sidewise, but always one behind the other.
   Fr. *chasser;* Ger. *jagen*.

Hurry, to *Come* or to *Go quickly*. Make the sign for
Come (or *Go*) three or four times, very quickly and
emphatically. (Sheeaka.)

Hurry (Ride fast). Jump the flat hands up and down
before you, quickly, palms up. Compare *Light*, which
is similar. but slower.
   Fr. *se dépêcher;* Ger. *eilen*.

Husband. Make sign *Male* and *Marry*.
   Fr. *le mari;* Ger. *der Mann; der Gatte*.

Hush. See *Silence* and *Halt*.

Hypocrite. Sign *Wolf* and *Like*. Or *Face* and *Two*.
According to Ruggles, the Paiutes sometimes use this
second combination for *Liar;* the Cheyennes understand
it but do not use it.
   Fr. *le hypocrite;* Ger. *der Heuchler*.

I

I, Me, Myself, Mine. For *I* touch the centre of the breast with the right thumb extended, other fingers closed. This and the next are used indiscriminately by the Cheyennes.

Me is touching the breast with point of compressed fingers.

My. Lay the A hand on the forehead, palm to left, thumb pointing up; swing it forward and down **level**; that is, sign *Possession*, assuming the first person.

Fr. *je, moi, mien;* Ger. *Ich, mich, mein.*

Ice. Sign *Water* and *Hard.* Sometimes add *Cold.*
Fr. *la glace;* Ger. *das Eis.*

Icicle. Sign *Water* and *Cold;* then hold up right G, pointing downward and dropped a little.
Fr. *le glaçon;* Ger. *der Eiszapfen.*

Idea, Thought (Thought expressed). Lay the right G on the forehead, pointing up, palm to left; swing it down to horizontal at mouth level, then push it straight forward and up in a curve. Compare *So.*
Fr. *l'idée; la pensée;* Ger. *die Idee, der Gedanke.*

Idle. Sign *Work* and *Not.*
Fr. *paresseux;* Ger. *müszig.*

If, Doubt, Undecided, Perhaps, or **Maybe so** (Heart looking two ways). Lay the right V hand on the heart, pointed down and to left front; rotate the hand on the wrist so the back is alternately up and out. When

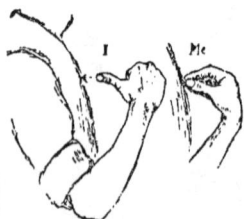

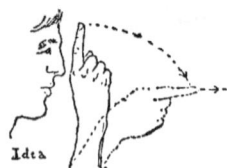

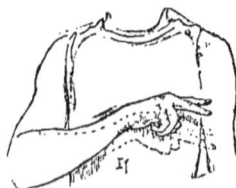

many emotions (i. e., *perplexity*) are to be expressed, use all fingers extended. See *Consider*.

Fr. *si, peut-être;* Ger. *wenn, ob, vielleicht.*

Ignorance (I don't know). Shrug shoulders and raise one flat hand. (Pop.) Or, sign *Know, Not.* Compare *Forget.*

Fr. *l'ignorance;* Ger. *die Unwissenheit.*

Imperative Mood. Sign the verb in question, then strike the flat right, palm down, onto the flat left, palm up. Or add *Push.* (C)

Impossible. Sign *Can* and *Not.* See also *Cannot.* The Cheyennes use *True, Not.*

Fr. *impossible;* Ger. *unmöglich.*

Imprison. See *Arrest.*

In, Inside, or **Within** (To put into). Make a semi-circle of the left arm held out level; then drop the compressed right hand downward between the left and the body. *Outside* begins the same, but the right drops outside the left.

In

Inside, i. e., **in a Hole.** Make a horizontal ring of the left index and thumb, then drop the right index down into it. For a house, use *Enter.*

Fr. *en, dedans, dans;* Ger. *in, drin, im Innern.*

Incite. Sign *Push, Talk,* and *Go;* that is, try to talk into going.

Fr. *inciter;* Ger. *anreizen.*

Inside

Increase. Hold out the flat hands, palm to **palm, well** apart at same height; separate them more and more in slight jerks; or, if it is more explicit, do it with the flat hands one above the other. See *Add to*. Compare *Decrease*.

Fr. *augmenter;* Ger. *vermehren, vergröszern.*

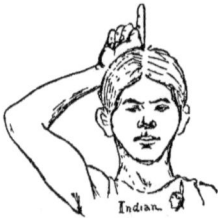
Indian.

Indian. With the tips of right flat fingers, rub the side of the flat left held out back up, in short strokes; meaning reddish, because all men's hands out west are red at this place. Compare *Smooth*.

Indian.

Indian. Indicate the eagle feather at back of head. (Sheeaka.) Or sign *Man* and *Red*. (Scott.)

Fr. *l'Indien;* Ger. *der Indianer.*

Indian Tribe or **Nation.** Give the *Tribal* sign and add *All* in each case.

Indian Tribal signs:

Apache.

Apache (Probably using the notched-stick fiddle). Draw the right G finger *up and down* along the left G several times, from near the point to the base, a foot long each stroke. Compare *Poor*.

Arapahoe. With all fingers of right hand compressed so the points are together, tap the left breast, that is, sign *Mother*. As Sherman Coolidge tells me, the Arapahoes claim theirs to have been the mother of all tribes. In the south, the sign is rub the side of the nose with the right G, referring to their one-time salutation of nose-rubbing.

Indian Tribal Signs—*Continued:*

Banak. Sign for *Lodge* and *Bad.* (C)

Blackfeet. Sign for *Moccasin* and *Black.*

Caddo. Draw the right N over the left N from the tips back to the knuckles (because they wore pants). (Father Isadore.)

Cheyennes. (Perhaps meaning "striped tail," because they used turkey feathers; or, more likely, " finger-choppers," because they chopped their fingers when in mourning). Hold out left G finger and cut it with the edge of the right G finger drawn across it once or twice, each time further up the hand. Compare *Often* and *And all the time.*

Cheyenne

Chippewa. See *Ojibwa.*

Comanche. Sign for *Snake,* pushing the hand forward. Compare *Shoshoni.* (Seger.)

Cree. Sign *Rabbit, People;* but usually omit *People.*

Crow. Sign *Bird* slowly. Sometimes only one hand. Or hold S hand, palm forward, at brow for " Pompadour Indians."

Dakota. See *Sioux.*

Flathead. See *Koutenais.*

Gros Ventre. Sign *Big Belly.*

Hopi. Sign *Dance* and *Snake.*

Indian Tribal signs—*Continued:*

Kiowa. With the tips of the flat right, palm up, back to left, describe an upright ellipse near the right ear; because they used to cut their hair on that side to show the ear ornaments or ear painted red.

Koutenai. Sign for *White-tailed Deer.* (C)

Mandan (Tattooed chin and cheek). With right hand compressed so all tips touch, tap the chin and jaw. (C)

Navaho (Makers of striped blankets). Sign for *Work, Blanket,* and *Striped.*

Nez Percé (Pierced nose). Pass index of right G hand level under nose from right to left. Compare *Hear.*

Ojibwa or **Chippewa** (Living in the Woods). Sign *Tree* and *People;* or sign *Paddle, People.* (Blackfoot.)

Osage (Shaved heads). Rub the flat right hand, palm out, over the side of the head and down, as though shaving the head; the little finger being the sharp edge.

Paiute. Sign *Rabbit, Robe.*

Pawnee (Wolf). Hold up the right V hand, palm forward, near right ear; then swing finger-tips forward.

Piegan. Rotate half closed hand, palm in, near right cheek.

Indian Tribal signs—*Continued:*

Pueblo. Sign *Two Quivers;* that is, *Arrow, Two;* then drop compressed left once or twice into C right hand.

Sac (Shaved heads). Same as *Osage* sign.

Shoshoni or **Snake Indians.** Sign for *Snake* and sometimes add *Bad, Lodge.*

Sioux (Cut throats). Draw the right G finger across the throat.

Uncapapa (From their position in camp). Sign for *Sioux* and *Encamp*, then make an incomplete circle with index fingers and thumbs; then, holding left in pose, strike last joint of index with tip of right G and similarly right index with tip of left G. (C)

Ute. Sign *Black* and *Red.*

Wichita (Tattooed rings). With right G finger tap the forehead in a circle.

Yankton. Sign for *Sioux* and *Nez Percé.* (C)

Indian Agent. See *Agent.*

Indifference (*None of my business*). Both hands held down by the thighs; at the same time a shrug of the shoulders. (Pop.)
    Fr. *l'indifférence;* Ger. *die Gleichgültigkeit.*

Infantry. Sign *Soldiers* and *Walk.*
    Fr. *l'infanterie;* Ger. *die Fusztruppen, die Infanterie.*

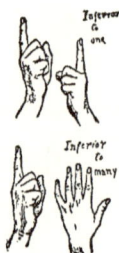

Inferior (To one). Hold up both G fingers, the one representing the inferior much lower.

Inferior (To many). For several inferiors use the 5 hand to represent them, while the G of the other hand up high represents the superior.

Fr. *inférieur;* Ger. *untergeordnet.*

Inhabit. See *Dwell.*

Injure, Doing evil to. If with reference to another person, make sign for *Work* and *Bad.* If with reference to one's self, make signs *Do, to me, Bad.*

Fr. *faire du mal;* Ger. *beschädigen.*

Innocent. See *Clean-handed.*

In order that. See *So that.*

Inside. See *In.*

Interrogate. See *Question* or *Query.*

Intervene. See *Come between.*

Invalid. See *Sick one.*

Investigating. See *Searching;* also *Consider.*

Iron. See *Metal.*

Island (Round thing surrounded by water). Sign *Land,* then with L hands make a horizontal circle; hold left hand in pose, sign *Water* with right hand; then com-

press it and draw it point down around the circle just
made. Compare *Lake*.

Fr. *l'île;* Ger. *die Insel.*

Itching. Scratch the left palm with nail of the right G
index; or else the thigh.

Fr. *la démangeaison;* Ger. *das Jucken.*

J

Jealous (Elbowing aside). Hold the fists near the
breast; alternately swing each elbow out and back a
little. (C)

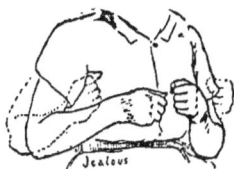

Jealous (Hide and stab). Hold out flat left, back up,
and with right G stab under it once or twice.

Fr. *jaloux;* Ger. *eifersüchtig.*

Jesus (The Cross above). The right G finger upright
and crossed on top with the left G; this cross then
placed above the eyes, the face looking upward; then
the cross pushed toward the sky to the full extent of the
arms. The real meaning being, " He who was crucified
and is now in heaven." (Scott.) Or sign *Big, Medicine, Child.*

Fr. *Jésus;* Ger. *Jesus.*

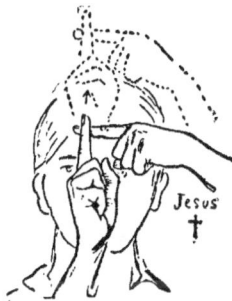

Joke (Play talk). Sign *Play;* that is, hold the right
5 hand near the mouth, back down, fingers a little
curved; swing the hand forward and upward; then add
Talk.

Fr. *la plaisanterie;* Ger. *der Scherz.*

Joyous. Sign *Heart, Glad,* and *Sing.* (C) Sign *Heart, Happy,* or *Playing*.
Fr. *joyeux;* Ger. *fröhlich*.

Judge. See *Consider*.

Jump (Human). Stand right V on left palm; assume these to be legs and make them jump up and down. (Sheeaka.)

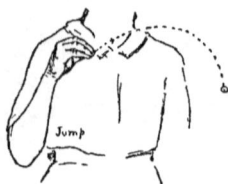

Jump or **Spring** (Anything). Hold compressed right hand, pointing to left, near right shoulder; swing it up forward and down in a long curve. Also used for *Animal,* in which case use several short jumps.
Fr. *sauter;* Ger. *springen*.

Junior. See *Younger;* also *Inferior*.

Just or **Fair.** From a position near each side, bring the extended O hands, palms inward, together so the tips of right thumb and index touch tips of left thumb and index, like two balance pans side by side. (D) Or, sign *True* and *Same,* or *Good*.
Fr. *juste;* Ger. *gerecht*.

Just so. Make the sign *Yes* once or twice; or else, use *True*.
Fr. *justement, précisément cela;* Ger. *genau so, ganz richtig*.

K

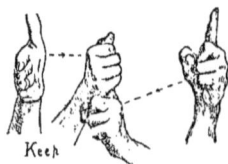

Keep, Grasp, or **Remember.** Hold out flat right hand, back to right, fingers level; hold up left G hand, back to left; swing them together; grasp left index in closed right hand and move the hands slightly to right and left. Compare *Hold* and *Remember.*

Fr. *tenir, retenir;* Ger. *halten, behalten.*

Keep close. Sign *Good* and *Near.* (C)

Keep quiet. Sign *Stop* and *Sit down,* or simply *Stop.* See *Hush.*

Fr. *taisez vous, tenez vous tranquille!* Ger. *ruhig sein! schweigen!*

Kettle. Indicate the shape of the mouth with both L hands; then, holding left unchanged, pass the right G into it; then, with right, lift as if by a handle. Some omit the "handle." Compare *Basket* and *Cook.*

Fr. *le chaudron, la chaudière;* Ger. *der Kessel.*

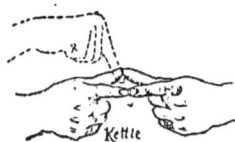

Kidney. Hold up the two compressed hands, then swing them back against the kidneys.

Fr. *le rein, (d'animal) le rognon;* Ger. *die Niere.*

Kill, Overcome, Win, or **Be victor** (Striking with a club). Hold the right A hand, back nearly up, in front of shoulder, back of hand making a slight angle with wrist; strike to the front, downward and little to left, stopping hand suddenly and giving it slight rebound. For *Kill me* or *Beat me,* make the sign toward one's self,

Fr. *tuer, vaincre;* Ger. *tot schlagen, siegen.*

Kin, Kinsman, or **Kinship.** Sign *Brother* and *Distant* or *Near,* as the case may be.

Fr. *le parent;* Ger. *der Verwandte.*

Kind or **Gentle.**   Sign *Heart* and *Good.*
    Fr. *aimable;* Ger. *freundlich, sanft.*

King's X.   See *Fins.*

Knife (Penknife or Jack-knife).   (Whittling a stick.)
With right A hand make motion of whittling the index
finger of the left G hand.   (Blackfoot and Pop.)   The
Cheyennes sign *Cut* and *Bend.*
    Fr. *le canif, le couteau;* Ger. *das Messer, das Taschen-
messer.*

Knife or **Dagger.**   Thumb up straight, rest of fingers
closed, hand at side.   (Pop.)   Compare *He, Turn
down,* and *Opossum.*

Knife.   Hold left hand near mouth, then with lower
edge of flat right make as though cutting off a piece of
meat held between the left hand and the teeth.   Understood but not used by Cheyennes.   They indicate
length with right G on flat left back and add *Cut.*
    Fr. *le couteau, le poignard;* Ger. *das Messer, der Dolch.*

Know or **Be acquainted with.**   Sign *Know,* as below.
    Fr. *connaître;* Ger. *kennen.*

Know or **Understand** (See, it is in my heart).   Lay the
right L hand, back up, on heart; swing it out, up in a
slight curve, and down a little, palm up.
    Fr. *comprendre, savoir;* Ger. *wissen, verstehen.*

Know, I don't.   Shrug the shoulders and shake the head
and raise the right hand open, palm up, to level of
shoulder, inclining the head to the side.   (Pop.)   Compare *Don't care.*

Know, I know what I'm doing (Perhaps " I smell a rat " is the verbal form of the sign). Lay the right index on right side of nose. (Pop.)

Fr. *je ne suis pas aveugle;* Ger. *ich weiss was ich mache.*

Knowledge or **Intelligence.** Tap the forehead and add *Big.* Compare *Conceit.*

Fr. *le savoir, l'intelligence;* Ger. *die Kenntnis, das Wissen.*

L

Labor. See *Work.*

Lake. Sign *Water* and with both L hands make an incomplete horizontal circle, then bring wrists together and swing finger tips apart. The last gesture is to suggest *Wide.* Compare *Island.*

Fr. *le lac;* Ger. *der See.*

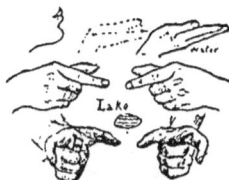

Lame (Bobbing of horse's head). Right A hand out in front, *back up,* moved forward a little and at the same time jerked down by wrist action and to left; repeat. Compare *Old* and *Kill.*

Fr. *boiteux;* Ger. *lahm.*

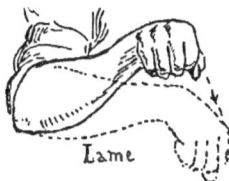

Land, Country, Ground, or **Earth** (Flat and extended). Pat toward ground with one or both flat hands; then swing them apart, flat, palms down, on a broad upward sweep left and right.

Fr. *la campagne, la terre;* Ger. *das Land, die Erde.*

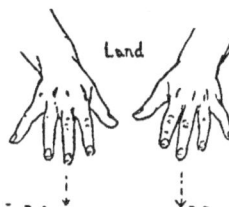

Lantern. Sign *Enclosure,* but make it perpendicular; then in the same space sign *Fire* twice.

Fr. *la lanterne;* Ger. *die Laterne.*

Large. See *Big* and *High.*

Lasso. Sign *Rope,* then hold right L hand over right shoulder, back nearly to right, index pointing up; throw it forward, upward, and down, close index and thumb and jerk the hand back. Often omit *Rope.*

Fr. *le lasso;* Ger. *die Wurfschlinge.*

Last. Hold up the left 5 hand, thumb nearest you; push it straight away, then tap the thumb with the G of the other hand. (Sheeaka.)

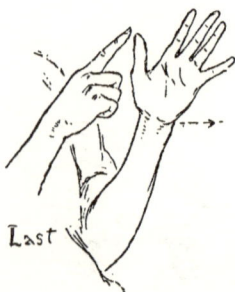

Last (One, After). Hold up 5 left hand and, away behind it, the G right. (Blackfoot.) Compare *First* and *Guide.*

Fr. *le dernier;* Ger. *der Letzte.*

Last

Last year. Sign *Winter, Beyond.*

Fr. *l'année passée;* Ger. *voriges Jahr.*

Late. See *After.*

Laugh. Hold both curved 5 hands, palms up, near the sides, a foot apart; then shake them up and down. Compare *Play.*

Fr. *rire;* Ger. *lachen.*

Law (Written road). Sign *Write,* then *Across* two or three times. Compare *Council* (No. 2.)

Fr. *la loi;* Ger. *das Gesetz.*

Lawyer. *Whiteman, Law,* and *Know.*
    Fr. *l'avocat;* Ger. *der Advokat.*

Lazy or **Tired.** Shake the head, throw it back, then drop both nearly open hands limply, one held out at each side motionless. Compare *Weak* and *Tired.*
    Fr. *paresseux, fatigué;* Ger. *faul, träge, müde.*

Lead. With right hand fingers grasp the flat left hand and drag it forward. (Sheeaka; borrowed from the Deaf.) Sometimes used also for *Teacher.*

Lead. Hold right A hand high in front of right shoulder, back to right; move it forward by gentle jerks, as though leading a pony. See *Guide.*
    Fr. *conduire;* Ger. *führen.*

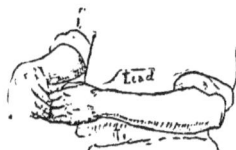

Leaf. Sign *Tree,* then shake right hand shoulder high, with thumb and index pointed nearly up, forming an incomplete circle, others closed. Compare *Money* and *Fruit.*
    Fr. *la feuille;* Ger. *das Blatt.*

Learn. Sign *Book,* then follow the lines with the right G finger and last draw it to *Me.* Or sign *Book, Look, Know,* making the last sign once or twice toward the *Book.* See *Lesson.*
    Fr. *apprendre;* Ger. *lernen.*

Leggings. Draw the L hands, backs out, one on each leg from well down to near hips.
    Fr. *les grandes guêtres;* Ger. *die ledernen Gama-schen.*

Lend, Loan, or **Borrow.** Sign *Give you* (or me) and *By and By, Give me* (or you). Or, *Give, Little while.*
   Fr. *prêter, emprunter;* Ger. *leihen, borgen.*

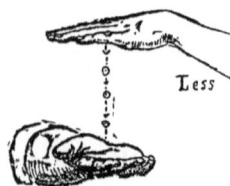

Less (Compressed). Hold the open flat hands a foot or two apart, palm to palm, one above the other. Hold the lower hand stationary and then draw the upper in jerks down toward the lower. See *Decrease.*
   Fr. *moins;* Ger. *weniger.*

Let it alone. See *Abandon.*

Letter (Sticking on the stamp). Indicate size of letter, then close right hand, thumb extended; wet thumb end on lips and press on open left palm.
   Fr. *la lettre;* Ger. *der Brief.*

Level, All right. See *Good,* also *Prairie.*

Liar. Make sign for *Lie;* then indicate the person. To add the intensive *Very much* makes it equivalent to the strong and unprintable English expression that is used in extreme cases.
   Fr. *le menteur;* Ger. *der Lügner.*

Liberal. See *Generous.*

Liberate. Sign *Prisoner,* throw the hands up and apart, then add *Go.* (C) See *Pardon.*
   · Fr. *délivrer;* Ger. *befreien.*

Lie or **False** (Two tongues or forked tongue). Hold the right V hand, back out, a little in front and to the right of mouth, and pointing to left; move the hand to left, past mouth, and downward.

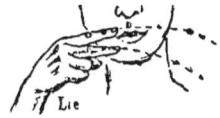

Fr. *le mensonge;* Ger. *die Lüge.*

Life. See *Alive.*

Light (Not dark). See *Day.*

Light (Not heavy). Hold out both flat hands, palms up; raise briskly together in one or two jerks. Compare *Heavy*, which is the same in pose, but in which the hands drop briskly. See *Hurry*, which is similar but much faster and raised each time in one movement.

Fr. *léger;* Ger. *leicht.*

Lightning or **Thunderbolt.** With right G index held high, make a quick zigzag downward.

Fr. *l'éclair;* Ger. *der Blitz.*

Like (To be partial to). Sign *Want.*

Like or **Alike.** See *Equal.*

Listen, I will not. Cover both ears with the hands and shake head. (Pop. and Blackfoot.)

Fr. *je n'écouterai pas;* Ger. *ich will nicht zuhören.*

Listen. Hold right L hand back to right near and around right ear; rotate the hand by wrist action (Cheyenne). Or hold hollowed right hand behind the right ear. (Popular sign understood by Cheyennes.) Compare *Hear.*

Fr. *écouter;* Ger. *horchen.*

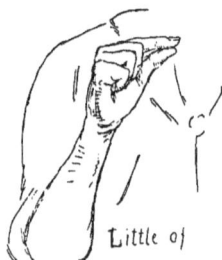

Little of

Little of, Small, Piece of, Part. Hold right hand in front of body, shoulder high, back to right, end of thumb pressing against under side of index so that only about half an inch of index is seen beyond the thumb, other fingers closed. For emphasis, point at right with left G.

Little or **Small of Stature.** For small animal, person, etc., indicate the stature by holding out flat right, palm down, above the ground or above the flat left, palm up. See *Boy*.

Little

Little or **Small degree or matter, Weak.** Hold the right fist above the left as though both were grasping a thin stick, backs out. Twist the right hand and draw it in a little to the breast, turning it so the palm is a little upward instead of a little downward. Compare *Few*. Note *Strong* is its analogue.

Fr. *petit, peu;* Ger. *klein, wenig.*

Live. See *Alive.*

Live in. See *Dwell.*

Liver. Compress the right hand, bend it much at the wrist, hold it so the back is forward and down, fingers level and pointing back; lay it on the right side under the ribs, draw it to the middle of the body following under side of ribs.

Fr. *le foie;* Ger. *die Leber.*

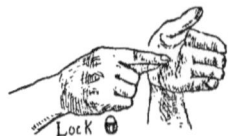

Lock

Lock. Against flat left palm turn thumb and index of right as a key.

Fr. *fermer à clef, la serrure;* Ger. *schlieszen, das Schlosz.*

Long. Fully extend the left arm forward and downward, hand flat, palm down; lay right G finger on the left wrist; then draw it up to the shoulder. Often use *Big.*

Fr. *long;* Ger. *lang.*

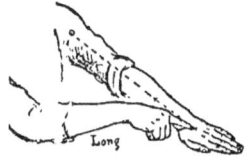

Longing. Sign *Heart* and *Want;* or *Heart, Want,* and *See.*

Fr. *le désir ardent;* Ger. *das Verlangen.*

Long time (Drawn out). Slowly draw the hands very far apart as though pulling out a piece of gum or elastic. See *Time.*

Fr. *longtemps;* Ger. *lange.*

Look. Make V hand and point with fingers in line of sight. Compare *Hunting* and *See.*

Fr. *regarder;* Ger. *ansehen, hinsehen.*

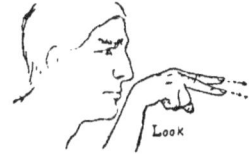

Look at that. Point with forefinger at object and add *See.* Compare *There.*

Fr. *regardez cela, voyez;* Ger. *sehen Sie das an.*

Look out. See *Warning.*

Loose or **Set Free.** See *Liberate.*

Lose, Lost, or **Astray** (Hid, find, and not; apparently referring to the game of hide in the hand). Hold out both fists together, palms up, for *Hid;* then look about and point with right G hand behind here and there and to one side; add *Not.* (Sheeaka.)

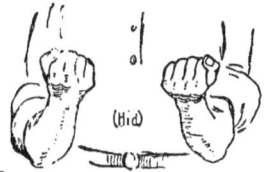

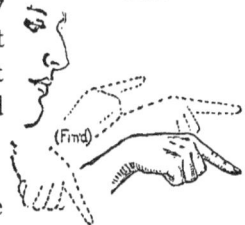

Lose. The Cheyennes use *Hide,* which see. Compare *Night.*

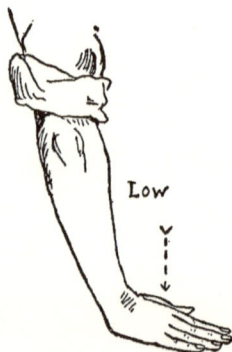

Low

Luck

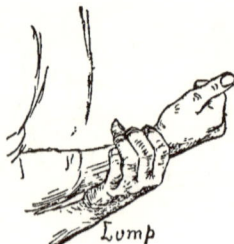

Lump

Lost, I am lost. Sign *Look, Way, See, Not*. (Blackfoot.)

Fr. *perdre, perdu;* Ger. *verlieren, verloren*.

Love.   See *Fond*.

Low.   Hold flat right hand low, back up.
Fr. *bas;* Ger. *niedrig*.

Luck, Happen, Chance, or **Accident** (What turns up).
Extend both G hands in front, palm side up; turn them
in toward each other till the backs are up; forefingers
still extended.   Then add *Good* or *Bad*.   (D)   This
suggests the gambling sticks in the Indian game.   See *Of*.

Luck (Whatever befalls me).   Sign *Medicine*, or shake
the head and the flat hand in front of the neck, then
swing right G in a curve till it strikes the breast.
(Sheeaka.   A doubtful Sioux sign.)

Fr. *la chance, l'accident;* Ger. *der Zufall*.

Lump (Apparently "hill" that can be held in the hand).
Hold up the right A hand, waist high, palm to you,
thumb pointing up, wrist bent so arm is nearly level.
Compare *Hill*.

Fr. *la petite masse;* Ger. *der Klumpen, die kleine
Masse*.

Lunch or **Luncheon.**   Sign *Noon* and *Eat*.
Fr. *le déjeuner;* Ger. *das Mittagessen*.

Lungs.   Hold the 5 hands on the breast, one at each
side, and indicate slow heaving.   Compare *Sick*.
Fr. *les poumons;* Ger. *die Lungen*.

Lynx. With the C hand at each side of the face indicate ruffs; with rings of index fingers and thumbs, show the eyes; then on the G right with the G left show the bob tail. (Sheeaka.) This is a description rather than a name.

Fr. *le lynx;* Ger. *der Luchs.*

Lynx, Bay, or **Bob-cat.** Sign *Cat* and *Short tail.* (Scott.) The Cheyennes, who do not know the true Lynx, sign *Animal* and *Short tail.*

Fr. *le lynx rouge;* Ger. *der Rotluchs, die amerikanische Wildkatze.*

(Whiskers + Big Eyes + Short Tail) = Lynx

M

Mad. See *Angry* and *Crazy.*

Make or **Manufacture.** Hammer the top of one fist with the other two or three times, giving both hands a twisting motion. (Sheeaka. Adopted from the Deaf.) Compare *Work,* which is mostly used by *Indians* for *Make.*

Fr. *fabriquer;* Ger. *anfertigen.*

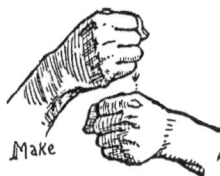

Make

Make up one's mind. See *Decide.*

Man or **Male** (The one alone; the erect one). Right G held up at height of chin, palm forward; many Cheyennes make it back forward. For *Boy* sign *Man* then drop the hand down to a level that indicates height, and turn it palm to you.

Fr. *l'homme;* Ger. *der Mann.*

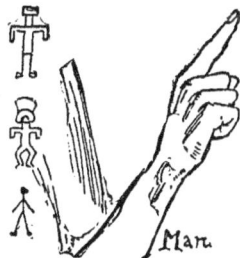

Man

Mandan. See *Indian Tribes.*

Manitoba (Red River Country). Give signs for *Country, River, Red* (suggested).

Manner. See *Way.*

Man who. See *Doer.*

Many (Many tens). Hold up both hands, face high, half closed, palms forward; throw them forward in 5 shape. Repeat several times. See also *Heap* and *Much.*
　　　Fr. *plusieurs;* Ger. *viele.*

Many times, Often, or **All the time.** Hold out left arm level, hand flat palm in; tap it a few times with right G hand from near wrist, moving each time an inch or so toward elbow. Compare *Cheyenne.*
　　　Fr. *souvent;* Ger. *oft.*

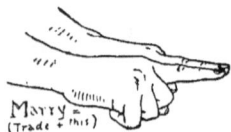

Married or **Marry** (Side by side, united as one). Sign *Trade,* that is, *Bargain;* then lay right G beside left G touching, both pointing forward level, not moved. (C) The Cheyennes omit *Trade.* Compare *Equal, Parallel,* and *Mates.*
　　　Fr. *marié, épouser;* Ger. *verheiratet, heiraten.*

Marten or **Sable.** Sign *Weasel;* that is, curve right G and push it forward, back up, in bounds; indicate size, yellow throat; then, running up a tree. This is a suggested description, as I found no established sign.
　　　Fr. *la marte, la zibeline;* Ger. *der Marder, der Zobel.*

Match. Strike an imaginary match on right thigh, or left arm.

Fr. *l'allumette;* Ger. *das Streichholz.*

Mate or **Partner** (One teepee and side by side). The G fingers in tent form, then up side by side, touching. (Sheeaka.)

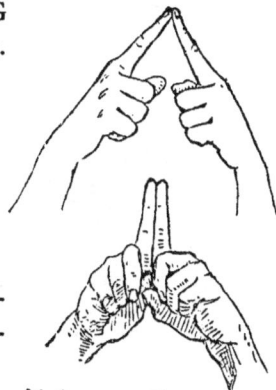

Mate or **Chum.** Sign *Friend, Same.*

Fr. *le camarade, le compagnon;* Ger. *der Kamerad.*

May or **Maybe.** See *Perhaps.*

Me. Touch one's own chest with the tips of the compressed fingers of the right hand. (Sheeaka.) Compare *I.*

Fr. *moi;* Ger. *mich.*

Mates or Partners

Meals. For *Breakfast*, sign *Eat* and *Sunrise;* for *Lunch*, sign *Eat* and *Noon;* for *Dinner*, sign *Eat* and *Sundown.*

Fr. *les repas;* Ger. *die Mahlzeiten.*

Mean or **Intend.** Sign *Want* and *Say.*

Fr. *avoir en vue, vouloir dire;* Ger. *beabsichtigen, meinen.*

Mean or **Stingy.** Sign *Heart* and *Few.*

Fr. *avare;* Ger. *geizig.*

Meanwhile. See *While.*

Meat (1). Hold out the flat left, back up; then with the flat right, palm up, slice pieces off the left palm. This is generally used, but often with left palm up.

Meat

Meat or **Flesh** (2). With right index finger and thumb, grasp the flesh between left index finger and thumb. (Sioux and Blackfoot.) Note, if this be done by putting the right at the under side of the left, it is the same as the next sign.

Meat (3). Lay the flat left hand, little finger down, between the thumb and fingers of the flat right, as far in as possible; then pat the back of the left by opening and closing the right a little and add *Buffalo*. In conversation, *Buffalo* without the first sign is often used for *Meat*, just as we use *Beef*. The first part of this is much like *Thick* and *Thin*, but the whole of the left fingers are involved and the right hand is not slid along.

The right in this, it will be noted, shows the pose of the hand when holding a thick piece of meat to be cut up for drying.

Clark says there is no sign for *Meat;* yet, obviously, his sign for *Bacon* is compounded of *Meat, Thin,* and *Greasy;* and the sign he gives for *Cutting up*, means *Cutting up meat.*

Meat (4). With right index and thumb, pinch the flesh at the palmar base of the left thumb. (Father Isadore says this is fixed and universal among the Comanches.)

Fr. *la viande;* Ger. *das Fleisch.*

Medal. Make a circle of right thumb and index (other fingers closed); lay it little finger in, on the centre of the breast. (C) Compare *Policeman.*

Fr. *la médaille;* Ger. *die Medaille.*

Medicine, Mystery, Holy, Sacred, or **Wonderful** (In the sense of Sacred Mystery). Hold V right hand close to forehead, palm forward, pointing up, separated; move the hand upward, twisting it so that the tips of the extended fingers will describe a spiral curve. This is hardly translatable.

    Fr. *le mystère sacré;* Ger. *das heilige Geheimnis.*

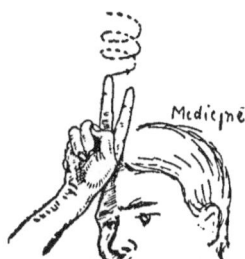

Medicine (A curative drug or potion). Hold out left C back to left and pour into it from a bottle in right C hand. If a powder, pour on flat left palm. If a pill, pour on palm and afterward pick up with index and thumb. (Pop.) Sign *Medicine* and *Eat.* (Cheyenne, recent.)

    Fr. *la médecine, le remède;* Ger. *die Arznei.*

Medicine-Man or **Shaman.** Make signs for *Man* and *Medicine.*

    Fr. *le magicien, le médecin;* Ger. *der Medizinmann, der Schamane.*

Meet. Hold forefingers of both G hands a foot apart, pointing up, left farthest off; move together till touching at the tips. Compare *Trade, Mistake,* and *Avoid.*

    Fr. *rencontrer;* Ger. *treffen, begegnen.*

Melancholy. Incline the head slightly forward and rest forehead on left hand, left forearm close to body. Understood by Cheyennes, but they prefer *Heart on the Ground.*

    Fr. *triste;* Ger. *schwermütig.*

Melt, Fade, Die out, Dissolve. Hold up both "5" hands six inches apart, fingers pointing up, palms toward

you; let the hands drop and slide aside, gradually assuming compressed position, backs up. (Sheeaka.)

Melt. Sign *Wipe out*, but slide the right palm over the left toward the tips in small jerks, then over and beyond.

> Fr. *fondre;* Ger. *schmelzen, vergehen.*

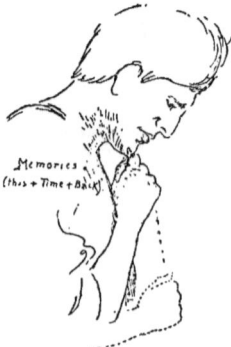

Memories
(this + Time + Back)

Memories. Head hung forward; right A hand dropped a foot under chin; then sign *Time, Back.* (Blackfoot.)

> Fr. *les souvenirs;* Ger. *die Erinnerungen.*

Memory or **Remembering.** Sign *Heart* and *Know.*

> Fr. *la mémoire, se rappeler;* Ger. *das Gedächtnis, sich erinnern.*

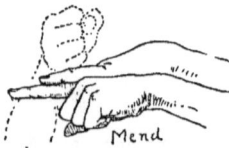

Mend

Mend. Lay the right G along to overlap the left G, then hammer on the left with right fist. (Sheeaka.) Note, this is mending iron or wood; to mend clothes, lay one index on other as above, then with right sew over edge of left. (Blackfoot.) The Cheyennes usually sign *Make* and *Good.* Compare *Fix.*

> Fr. *raccommoder;* Ger. *ausbessern, reparieren.*

Mercy. In the Roman Arena, the appeal for mercy was made by stretching the hand with first and second fingers raised and touching; others closed. (Pop.)

> Fr. *la clémence, la miséricorde;* Ger. *das Erbarmen, die Gnade.*

Mercy on Another. See *Pity.*

Mercy on Me. See *Pity.*

Merry. See *Glad.*

Message, i. e., **Spoken.** See *Speech.*

Metal. Sign *Hard* and describe or point to a piece of the metal in question. Or sign *Strong, Hard.*
Fr. *le métal;* Ger. *das Metall.*

Meteor. Sign *Star* and with hand up high sign *Fire* and let it drop in a wavy line across the sky.
. Fr. *le météore;* Ger. *das Meteor, die Feuerkugel.*

Midday or **Noon.** *Sun* and *Straight up.*
Fr. *le midi;* Ger. *der Mittag.*

Middle (The point dividing in half). Hold out the left G hand, finger level. Drop the right G hand down onto it at the middle joint. Compare *Half* and *Centre.*

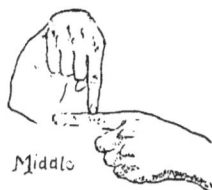

Middle. Strike down with lower edge of flat right between the fingers of left V held pointing up.
Fr. *le milieu;* Ger. *die Mitte.*

Middle

Middle one. Hold up three fingers of left, tap the two outer with right G, then bend the middle one down.
Fr. *celui au milieu;* Ger. *der Mittlere.*

Midnight. Sign *Night* and *Middle.*
Fr. *le minuit;* Ger. *die Mitternacht.*

Mile (Stake, measure, and stake). Hold out closed left at arm's length in front of shoulder, back up, index and thumb joined at top; drop it six inches, point down; then place index and thumb of similar right against it and swing right out level to right for two or three feet and drop it as before.
Fr. *le mille;* Ger. *die Meile.*

Milk. With both S hands make motion of milking.
Fr. *le lait;* Ger. *die Milch.*

Milky Way (Spirit's Trail). *Die* and *Way*, and sweep
the right hand high across the sky to show where.
Fr. *la voie lactée;* Ger. *die Milchstrasze.*

Mingle. See *Mix.*

Mink. Sign *Water, Creek,* and *Animal.* (Blackfoot.)
Sometimes indicate size.
Fr. *le foutereau, le mink;* Ger. *der Mink, der Nerz.*

Minute (Division of time). See *Time.* Hold left O
hand horizontal for *Watch;* tap around it with right G
finger for *hours;* then for minute add *One, Small,* and
Time. Second would be the same with added signs *Few*
or *Very.* (Sheeaka.)
Fr. *la minute;* Ger. *die Minute.*

Minute (Very small). Sign *Small.*
Fr. *trés petit;* Ger. *winzig.*

Mirage. Hold right 5 hand high, opposite left shoulder,
back out, pointing to left; move it horizontally to right
with a tremulous motion. (C)
Fr. *le mirage;* Ger. *die Luftspiegelung.*

Mirror. Flat right, points up, opposite face, shaken
a little forward and back as though adjusting the
distance. Sometimes sign *Look* first.
Fr. *le miroir;* Ger. *der Spiegel.*

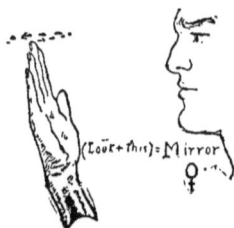

Mislead. Sign *Way*, then thrust right G to right and to left, but not straight.   Or sign *Tell, Straight, Not.*
 Fr. *égarer;* Ger. *verleiten.*

Miss. See *Avoid.*

Mist. See *Fog.*

Mistake (Mark missed).   Hold up left G hand, then pass it by with right G hand.
 Fr. *l'erreur;* Ger. *der Irrtum.*

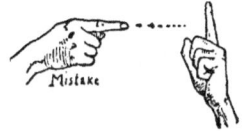

Mix or **Mingle.** Hold up the 5 hands, face high, points up, palm to palm touching; rotate one against the other. If in cookery, imitate the movement of stirring. Compare *Play.*
 Fr. *mélanger;* Ger. *mischen.*

Moccasin.   Pass the open hands over feet from toe to ankle.   Usually but one hand is used, and it need not touch the foot.
 Fr. *le mocassin;* Ger. *der Mokassin.*

Mockery or **Insolent defiance.** Spread the right hand with fingers straight, point of thumb to point of nose, little finger toward the enemy. (Pop.) Not Indian originally, but all understand it now.
 Fr. *la moquerie, la dérision;* Ger. *die Verspottung.*

Modesty.   Cover the eyes with one flat hand, its fingers well apart. (Pop.) See *Ashamed* and *Fog.*
 Fr. *la modestie;* Ger. *die Sittsamkeit, die Bescheidenheit.*

Money (Coin).   With right thumb and index, others closed, make a horizontal circle.   Compare *Sun, Fruit,* and *Leaf.*
 Fr. *l'argent;* Ger. *das Geld.*

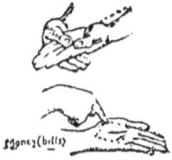
Money (bills)

Money (Paper).   Sign *Writing* and *Money*

Money (Bills).   Draw the flat left hand edgewise between the thumb and fingers of the right; then on left palm indicate shape.   (C)

    Fr. *billets de banque;* Ger. *die Banknoten.*

Snow Moon.
Jan.

Monkey (Man's face, dog's run).   Sign *Face, Man, Dog, Goes.*

    Fr. *le singe;* Ger. *der Affe.*

Hunger Moon.
Feb.

Month (One Moon).   Sign for *One* and *Moon* and *Die.*

    Fr. *le mois;* Ger. *der Monat.*

Each tribe had, of course, its own names for the months.   I have selected the ones most likely to be widely popular, without regard to their origin.

Wakening Moon
Mar.

January (Snow Moon).   Sign *Moon* and *Snow.*

    Fr. *le janvier;* Ger. *der Januar.*

Grass Moon.
Apr.

February (Hunger Moon).   Sign *Moon* and *Hunger.*

    Fr. *le février;* Ger. *der Februar.*

Planting Moon
May

March (Crow Moon).   Sign *Moon* and *Crow.*

    Fr. *le mars;* Ger. *der März.*

April (Grass Moon).   Sign *Moon* and *Short grass.*

    Fr. *l'avril;* Ger. *der April.*

Rose Moon
June

May (Planting Moon).   Sign *Moon* and *Planting.*

    Fr. *le mai;* Ger. *der Mai.*

June (Rose Moon).   Sign *Moon* and *Rose.*

    Fr. *le juin;* Ger. *der Juni.*

July (Thunder Moon).   Sign *Moon* and *Lightning*.
  Fr. *le juillet;* Ger. *der Juli*.

Thunder Moon.
July

August (Red Moon).   Sign for *Moon* and *Red*.
  Fr. *l'août;* Ger. *der August*.

September (Hunting Moon).   Sign *Moon* and then draw a bow as in hunting.
  Fr. *le septembre;* Ger. *der September*.

Red Moon
Aug.

October (Leaf-falling Moon).   Sign *Moon* and *Leaf-falling*.
  Fr. *l'octobre;* Ger. *der Oktober*.

Hunting Moon
Sep.

November (Mad Moon).   Sign *Moon* and *Mad*.
  Fr. *le novembre;* Ger *der November*.

December (Long Night).   Sign *Moon, Night,* and *Long*.
  Fr. *le décembre;* Ger. *der Dezember*.

Falling-leaf Moon
Oct.

Moon (Horns in the sky, or crescent).   Close right hand except thumb and first finger, which forms a half-circle or crescent, held above the right ear, back of hand forward.   Sometimes expressed as *Night* and *Sun*.
  Fr. *la lune;* Ger. *der Mond*.

Mad Moon.
Nov

Moose (Elk with flat horns).   Hold up flat hands for horns; but swing both backward and forward to indicate width; then, with both " L " hands, indicate the hanging muzzle.   (Blackfoot.)
  Fr. *l'orignal;* Ger. *das Elentier, der Elch*.

Long-Night Moon
Dec

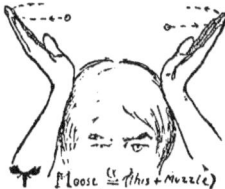

Moon

Moose = (this + Muzzle)

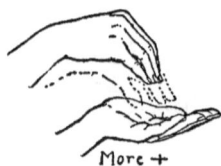

More. Hold out the flat left hand, palm up; then with right make as though throwing sand on it more and more, three times. (Sheeaka.) Compare *Most.* See *Repeat, Add to*, and *Ahead.*

Fr. *plus;* Ger. *mehr.*

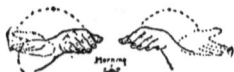

Morning or **Day** (Opening up). Both hands palms down, flat, near together. Sweep them up, out, and apart; turning the palms up. The same as *Day.*

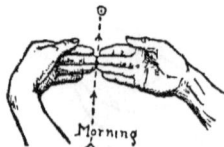

Morning or **Dawn.** Hold out both arms level, full length, side by side, hands flat, backs forward, tips touching; raise them slowly to half height.

Fr. *le matin;* Ger. *der Morgen.*

Mosquito. With right index and thumb make as though pricking right cheek with a thorn; then slap the place with right palm.

Fr. *le moustique;* Ger. *der Moskito, die Stechmücke.*

Most. Sign *More*, then raise the right flat hand high above it. (Sheeaka.) Or sign *Ahead, All.*

Fr. *le plus;* Ger. *meist, am Meisten.*

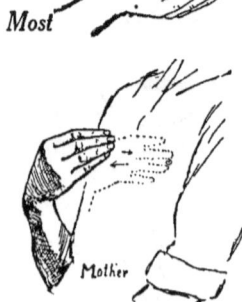

Mother (Nurse or parent, female). With the finger tips of the right hand, make as though drawing milk from the left breast; add the sign for *Female* if necessary. (Scott.) Note the left breast for *Mother*, nearer the heart; the right breast is for *Father.*

Fr. *la mère;* Ger. *die Mutter.*

Mother-in-law. Sign *Brother-in-law, Old, Woman.*

Fr. *la belle-mère;* Ger. *die Schwiegermutter.*

Motor car. Make signs for *Wheels, Horse, Not.* Or sign *Fire* twice then make as though holding and turning steering wheel.

 Fr. *l'automobile;* Ger. *aas Automobil.*

Mound or **Low Hill.** Flat hands together, backs up; separated and swept down to show shape. Compare *Heap*, which is just the reverse; also see *Box.*

 Fr. *la petite éminence;* Ger *der Erdhügel.*

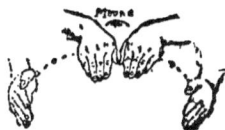

Mount (A horse). Hold right V to right side pointing up; swing it up to right, over and down, points down, onto flat left, which is held thumb up. Or, omit left. (Blackfoot.)

 Fr. *monter;* Ger. *steigen.*

Mountain. Hold up A hand as in *Hill*, but higher, and add *Hard.* Use both hands alternately up and down in various places for plural. Compare *Hill* and *Lump.*

 Fr. *la montagne;* Ger. *der Berg.*

Mountain Lion, Cat. Sign *Cat, Long tail,* and *Jump.* (C) Or with both L hands indicate large round tracks; then, with right G, pointed down, raised and down, each time, indicate the zigzag trail. (Paiute sign, given me by C. B. Ruggles.)

 Fr. *le couguar.* Ger. *der Kuguar.*

Mountain Pass. See *Gap.*

Mourn. With the flat hands used like knives, backs up, little fingers as though sharp edges, make as though to cut off the hair at each side of the head, and add *Cry.*

 Fr. *s'affliger;* Ger. *trauern.*

Mouse = (Animal
+Size + Night + this)

Mouse (Night nibbler). Sign *Animal*, with very small jumps, indicate size and *Night;* then, with right forefinger and thumb, nibble at left G forefinger.

Fr. *la souris;* Ger. *die Maus.*

Move

Move, To move camp (Teepee poles, travois). Both G hands in front, backs out; lay right forefinger on left at middle joint, crossing at an angle of 45 degrees, and push both hands forward in slight jerks, each jerk a day's journey.

Fr. *changer de place, déménager;* Ger. *fortziehen, weg-rücken.*

Mowing machine. Sign *Grass* and *Knife;* the last at right lower than waist. Add *Wagon* if needed to indicate horse mower.

Fr. *la machine à faucher;* Ger. *die Mähmaschine.*

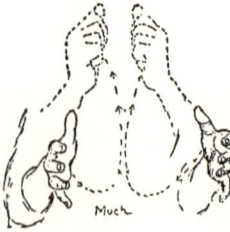
Much

Much or Many. Hold curved 5 hands, palm to palm, a foot apart; swing down together and up face high, closing them; swing a little apart at the finish.

Much

Much (Heap.) Hold the flat hands so the palms are toward each other, the left lower, and draw them apart, the left downward, the right upward. The extent to which they are drawn apart indicates the quantity. Compare *Big, Great, Heap, Increase,* and *Decrease.*

Fr. *beaucoup;* Ger. *viel.*

Much, Too. See *Excessive.*

Mud. See *Soft.*

Mule. Hold extended hands alongside of ears, palms to front, fingers pointing upward; by wrist action, flop the hands to front and rear, representing motion of mule's ears.

Fr. *le mulet;* Ger. *das Maultier.*

Murder. Sign *Kill* and *Free.* Meaning an unjustified killing.

Fr. *le meurtre;* Ger. *der Mord.*

Must. See *Have to;* also *Begin* or *Push.* See *Imperative.*

Muskrat or **Musquash.** Sign *Beaver* and *Small.*

Muskrat (Tail, swimming and lump). Hold out right G, back up, nearly level, pointing forward and to left; shake it, draw it to right; then hold up compressed right hand, back up, pointing forward, and grasp right wrist on lower side with left hand. (Blackfoot.)

Fr. *le rat musqué du Canada, l'ondatra;* Ger. *die Bisamratte.*

My, Mine, or **My own.** Sign *Possession;* that is, hold out the A hand, thumb straight up; then swing it in till it touches the breast; or sometimes lay the spread flat hand on the breast. (Sheeaka.) See *I.*

My, Mine, or **My own.** Touch breast with point of compressed right, then sign *Possession.*

Fr. *mon;* Ger. *mein.*

Mystery. See *Medicine.*

N

Name (Of a man). Sign *Called*. " What is your name?"
would be *Question, You, Called.*

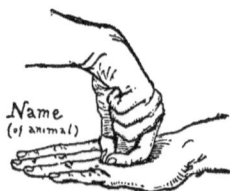

Name (of animal)

Name (Of animal). With right forefinger and thumb,
others closed, make an incomplete circle and lay it
palm down against the palm of the flat left hand, held
forward, back to left. Compare *Brand* and *Called*.
Scott gives it as illustrated.

   Fr. *nommer, le nom;* Ger. (*be*) *nennen, der Name.*

Name, To sign one's (Thumb print). Press the thumb
tip of the A hand against the palm of the flat left. Compare *Letter*.

   Fr. *signer son nom;* Ger. *seinen Namen unterschreiben.*

Named. See *Called*.

Narrow

Narrow. Hold flat hands out, palm to palm, about six
inches apart, fingers level and pointing forward; move
them toward each other until but one inch apart. Compare *Fast, Between, Few,* and *Road.*

   Fr. *étroit;* Ger. *eng.*

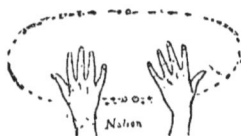

Nation

Nation (People all). Hold up both 5 hands, swing
them toward each other and away in a great circle.
(Sheeaka.) Not well established.

   Fr. *la nation, le peuple;* Ger. *die Nation, das Volk.*

NATIONALITIES:

American. Sign *Thirteen, Fires*. This was once used
on the Ohio, referring to the Council Fires of the
thirteen original colonies. Then add *Country* by

patting the ground with both flat hands and swinging them apart and up.

According to Clark, sometimes called *Long Knives*. Draw a long line east and west; then with flat hand, point up, indicate all south of it. (Blackfoot.)

Fr. *l'Américain;* Ger. *der Amerikaner.*

British (Red coat). Touch the coat; then with fingers brush the cheeks for *red.*

· Fr. *les Anglais, les sujets anglais;* Ger. *die Briten, das britische Volk.*

Canadian (Shaking off the snow). Shake the coat lapel with right hand. (D) The Blackfeet draw a long line east and west then with flat hand point to indicate all north of that line.

Fr. *le Canadien;* Ger. *der Kanadier.*

Chinaman. Indicate long tail by signing *Rope* at back of head.

Fr. *le Chinois;* Ger. *der Chinese.*

Dutchman (Long pipe). Place thumb of Y hand at the mouth, draw it down and outward to indicate the long pipe. (D)

Fr. *le Hollandais;* Ger. *der Holländer.*

Englishman. Sign *White Man, Far.* (Blackfoot.)

Fr. *l'Anglais;* Ger. *der Engländer.*

Frenchman. Hold out the F hand well toward the left, palm up; draw it across in front of self from left to right, turning it palm down. (D) To sign *Hairy Man* would translate the nickname "Poilu."

Fr. *le Français;* Ger. *der Franzose.*

German (The double eagle). Cross the wrists of both 5 hands, thumb palm against thumb palm, and work the fingers. (D)

> Fr. *l' Allemand;* Ger. *der Deutsche.*

Great Britain (Red-coat land). *Land, Coat,* and *Red.*

> Fr. *la Grande-Bretagne;* Ger. *das Groszbritannien.*

Holland. Same as *Dutchman.*

Indian. See *Indian* on p. 106.

Irishman. Hold out left S hand, back up; swing right V around it and end with V resting on back of left. (D) *Green Island Man* would be more acceptable.

> Fr. *l' Irlandais;* Ger. *der Irländer.*

Japanese. Sign *Country* and *Rising Sun.* Or sign *Man, Short, Eyes, Oblique.* The last by pushing up the outer corners of the eyes with G fingers. (These are suggested.)

> Fr. *le Japonais;* Ger. *der Japaner.*

Jew (Long beard). Placing the fingers of the bent 5 hand on the chin, draw them down and off, letting the hand assume the flat position as it leaves the chin. (D)

(As a slang term.) Spread both hands open from opposite each shoulder, palms forward, and rotate them slightly on the wrist back and forth. (Pop.)

> Fr. *le Juif;* Ger. *der Jude.*

Italian.   With the little finger of I hand trace a cross in the centre of the forehead.   (D)

Fr. *l'Italien;* Ger. *der Italiener.*

Mexican (Bearded White Man).   Sign for *White Man* and *Beard.*   In this case, *Beard* is made by rotating and jerking the 5 hand before the chin, points up.

Fr. *le Mexicain;* Ger. *der Mexikaner.*

Negro.   Sign *White Man, Black face.*   (C) Sheeaka also fumbled the open right over the knuckles of the half closed left, to indicate kinky hair.

Fr. *le nègre;* Ger. *der Neger.*

Ontario (Land of Lakes).   Make signs for *Country* and *Lakes.*   (Suggested.)

Fr. *l'Ontario;* Ger. *das Ontario.*

Russian.   Arms akimbo, i. e., C hand on each side of the waist.   (D)   The Cheyennes call them *Ride Easy* from the Cossack circus performers; but it is not an established sign.   *Bear Man* is suggested.

Fr. *le Russe;* Ger. *der Russe.*

Scotchman (Plaid clothes).   Cross the fingers of the right 5 hand with those of the left 5 hand on the chest, then let each drop to continue the lines.   (D)

Fr. *l'Écossais;* Ger. *der Schotte.*

Spaniard.   Sign *Old, Mexican.*

Fr. *l'Espagnol;* Ger. *der Spanier.*

White Man (Hat man).   With G right hand draw first finger across the brow.   (C)   For illustration see *White Man* among W's.

Fr. *l'homme blanc;* Ger. *der Weisze.*

Other countries are indicated in the Deaf Code by making the initial letter in the single-handed alphabet and swinging them in a circle in front of the forehead; but this mode contravenes the fundamental principle of Signs.   (See Introduction.)

Therefore, it is better to wait till a true sign is discovered.

Near or **Nearly**.   Same as *Close*, which see.

Near by.   See *By.*

Nearest.   See *Next.*

Need or **Need to**.   See *Must.*

Needle.   Make the sign for *Sew.*   (C)

Fr. *l'aiguille;* Ger. *die Nadel.*

Neighbor.   Sign *Close* and *Dwell*, or *Sit, Close.*

Fr. *le voisin;* Ger. *der Nachbar.*

Nephew.   Sign *Brother's* (or *Sister's*) *Son.*   (C)

Fr. *le neveu;* Ger. *der Neffe.*

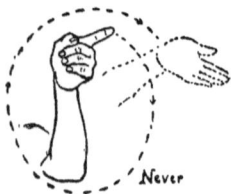

Never

Never (*Ever* and *Not*).   Right elbow fixed at side and with right G hand out straight, describe a complete upright circle, left to right; then throw the hand down to right in *Not*.   (Sheeaka; probably borrowed from Deaf.)

Fr. *jamais;* Ger. *niemals.*

Never mind. See *Rub it out.*

New. Sign *Little time, Traded.* Or, *Little while, Made, Good.*
Fr. *neuf;* Ger. *neu.*

News. With right G struck down to right and left (for *this* and *that*) and *Hear.*
Fr. *les nouvelles;* Ger. *die Nachrichten.*

Newspaper. Sign *Writing* and *Tell* (i. e., *Talk*) to right and left.
Fr. *le journal;* Ger. *die Zeitung.*

Next. See *Neighbor.*

Next or **Second.** Hold out the flat 4 left hand, palm down; with right G draw the left index toward the right; then tap the middle finger of left with right index. Or sign *Close.*
Fr. *prochain;* Ger. *nächst.*

Night (Earth covered up). Bring the flat hands, backs up, well apart, out in front of body, breast high; move them together in outline of a dome, finally resting right wrist on left. Compare *Hide.*
Fr. *la nuit;* Ger. *die Nacht.*

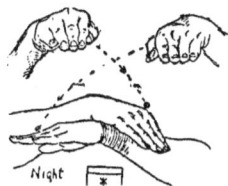

No. Hold flat right hand, back up, in front of body, fingers pointing level and nearly forward. Swing the hand in a graceful curve to right and front, at the same time turning it thumb up, finishing with the back of hand to right and downward; the hand is swept into its

position on a curve.   Usually abbreviated into a short jerk of the flat hand to right, its palm kept facing left. Compare *Bad* and *Different*.

For short range, shake the head; this is simple and universal.   It is so natural that babies and animals do it when offered bitter medicine, for example.   (Popular and Indian generally.)

Fr. *non;* Ger. *nein.*

No, I won't listen; or **Go away, the matter is ended.** Right G hand upraised to level of face, palm out, index upright; wave the finger hand from side to side by wrist action.   Chiefly used by Cheyennes when joking.   It is general in Latin countries.   Compare *White-tailed Deer.*

Fr. *non, allez!* Ger. *Punktum! Schlusz!*

None, Nothing, I have no money.   Turn the flat palms forward, one near each trouser pocket.   (Pop.)

Fr. *il n'y a rien;* Ger. *nichts.*

Noon.   See *Midday.*

Notify.   See *Tell.*

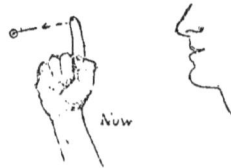

Now (Emphatic "right now").   Hold up right G, back to right and pointing upward about eight inches in front of the face; and, without stopping, carry it a little to front; then stop and give a slight rebound.   Sometimes look up to make it clear that it relates to time of day, that is, the sun's course.   Often it means *this* as in *this day; this moment; this night.*

Fr. *maintenant;* Ger. *jetzt.*

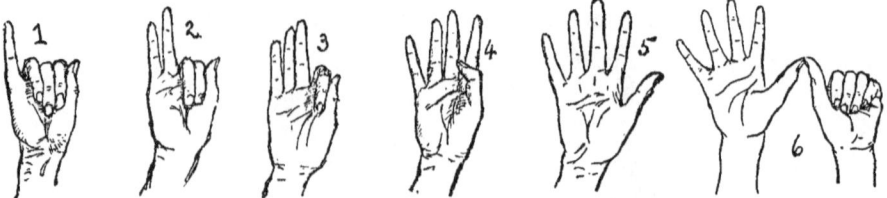

Numbers and **Counting.** Up to *ten* as shown on the fingers at the foot of previous page and this.

For 20—Sign 10, close the hands, then repeat it.

For 25—Sign 20, then drop left, close right, and sign 5.

For 30—Sign 10 three times; or else as below.

For 20, etc., sign 10, then hold out left 5 hand pointing forward and draw right G along each finger from base to tip; each finger so pointed stands for 10.

If over 50, do same with right hand and left index till enough tens are shown.

For 100—Both 5 hands held up, palm forward, thumb tips touching, low, opposite right shoulder; swing in a vertical arch to low opposite left shoulder. This mode of multiplying by ten may be applied to other numbers.

For 1,000—Sign 100 and on flat hands spread and pointing forward, palm down, with index of other hand show number of hundreds as above.

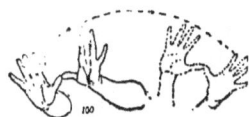

Numbers or **Counting.** Or, with the thumb of the same hand, touch each of the finger tips in succession. (Popular and sometimes used by Cheyennes.)

Fr. *les nombres, les numéros, compter;* Ger. *die Zahlen, zählen.*

Numbers ordinal. Point at or indicate the person or thing; then turn down the first finger for 1st and the second finger for 2d and so on. Also see *First, Next,* and *Last.*

Numeral Sign, Arithmetic, or **Counting.** Hold the left 5 hand, palm up, fingers a little bent; with right G turn one or two left fingers down on left palm.

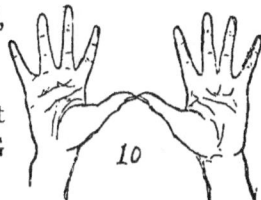

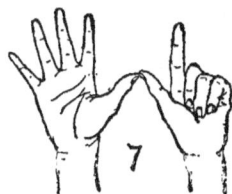

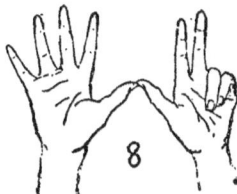

The Deaf mode is the figure-sign, then, without changing position of arm or hand, give the hand a twisting jerk from the wrist, which swings it in a small circle.

Fr. *les nombres ordinaux;* Ger. *die Ordinalzahlen.*

Nun.   Sign *Woman, Black, Hat.*
Fr. *la religieuse;* Ger. *die Nonne.*

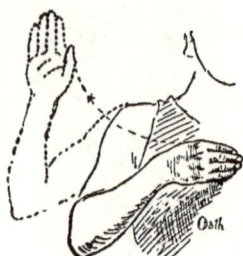

Oath or **Swear.**   Tap the chest with the tips of the flat right hand, then hold it at head height, palm forward. (Sheeaka.)   Sometimes point to Heaven and Earth, then hold up flat right hand.   (C)   Neither is Cheyenne, but both are understood by them.   See *Promise.* With right G make a small cross over the heart.   (Pop.)
Fr. *le serment, jurer;* Ger. *der Eid, schwören.*

Obey.   Make sign for *Listen.*   For emphasis add *Yes. Disobey* is putting the flat hands over the ears.
Fr. *obéir;* Ger. *gehorchen.*

Obliged to.   See *Have to.*   (C)

Ocean.   Sign *Water* and *Very broad.*   Some add *Salt.*
Fr. *l'océan;* Ger. *der Ozean.*

Of (That from that).   Hold right G hand out straight from right side, palm up; rotate the hand so the index tip describes a small half-circle inward and finally the palm is down.   (D)   Compare *Luck.*
Fr. *de;* Ger. *von.*

Offer or **Propose.** Hold the flat hands, palms up, near you, then move forward as though offering something. (Blackfoot.) The Cheyennes sign *Want* and *Give*.

Fr. *offrir, proposer;* Ger. *anbieten, vorschlagen.*

Office. Sign *Writing House.*

Officer. Sign *Chief;* or, if military, sign *Chief, Soldier.* Or indicate with the right index on the left shoulder or arm the insignia of the particular rank.

Fr. *l'officier;* Ger. *der Beamte, der Offizier.*

Offspring. See *Child.*

Often. See *Many times.*

Oil (Blowing oil off surface in pot). With both L hands form a big level circle; then tilt it low on forward side and blow across it. (Blackfoot, but understood by Cheyennes.)

Fr *l'huile;* Ger. *das Öl.*

Oil or **Grease.** Hold out the flat left, thumb up; with right thumb on palm and right index on back (others closed); rub back and forth with short, quick jerks. Compare *Thick, Thin, Bacon.*

Fr. *la graisse;* Ger. *das Fett.*

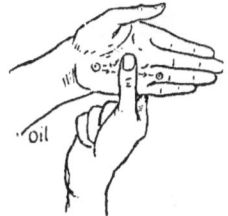

Old (Walking with a stick). Hold right A hand, *back to right*, about twelve inches in front of right shoulder, about height of breast; move the hand a little upward, to front, downward and back into its first position on small curve, repeating motion. Compare *Lame.*

Fr. *vieux;* Ger. *alt.*

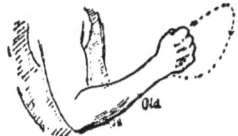

Old Man. Hold up the right index finger as in *Man*, then drop, crook, and swing it in *Old.* See *Decrepit.*

Fr. *le vieillard;* Ger. *der Greis.*

Old, How old are you? Sign *Question, Snows, You;* or *Question, Counting, Colds, You.*

Fr. *quel âge avez-vous?* Ger. *wie alt sind Sie?*

On or **Upon.** Lay the flat right hand, palm down, on back of the flat horizontal left, palm down. Compare *At.*

Fr. *sur;* Ger. *auf.*

Once. Dip the finger ends of the right compressed hand down against the palm of the flat left hand, bringing it away quickly. For *Twice*, do it twice, etc. (Sheeaka.) Compare *This* and *Repeat.*

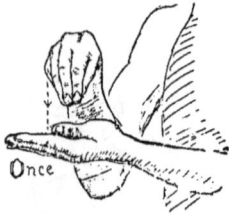

Once (One go). Sign *One* with right G index and push it forward low down. (So, also, *Twice* is *Two* pushed forward, etc.)

Fr. *une fois;* Ger. *einmal.*

One who, or **The man that does.** See *Doer.*

Onion. Sign *Potato* and *Bad, Smell.*

Fr. *l'oignon;* Ger. *die Zwiebel.*

Only. See *Alone.*

Open. The flat hands together, palm to palm, opened out flat as a book. The same as *Book* with *Writing* omitted. Compare *Day, Book, Shell,* and *Shut.*

Fr. *ouvrir, ouvert;* Ger. *öffnen, offen.*

Opossum. Hold out the flat right, fingers doubled on palm, thumb straight up; move it forward level. The thumb represents the tail. This is an Australian sign given by E. C. Stirling. It is offered as a suggestion and as a reminder that the Sign Language is world-wide. The Cheyennes sign *Tree, Climb, Hang by tail.*

Fr. *l'opossum, le (la) sarigue;* Ger. *das Opossum.*

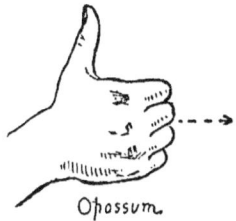

Opposite or **Against.** Hold the G fingers up opposite each other, pointing at each other. Compare *Against.*

Fr. *opposé, en face;* Ger. *gegenüber.*

Or. See *Either.* Sometimes use *Different.*

Orderly or **Put in order.** See *Ready.*

Ordinal Numbers. See *Numbers Ordinal.*

Other. See *Another.*

Other side. See *Beyond.*

Otter (Wrapping the hair plait). With right thumb, index and middle fingers together, others closed, describe a small spiral from near the right ear down. Because the otter skin was the kind used in strips to wrap the plaits of the Indians' hair.

Fr. *la loutre;* Ger. *der (die) Otter.*

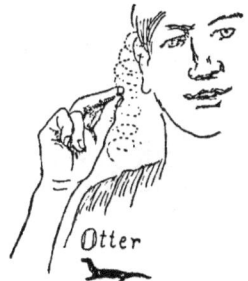

Our. Sign *All, My.*

Fr. *notre;* Ger. *unser.*

Out of. See *Absent.*

Outside or **Out of.** Make a semicircle of the left arm out level; drop the compressed right hand without and beyond the semicircle. Compare *In*, which it resembles, except in the last movement.

Fr. *dehors, hors de;* Ger. *drauszen.*

Over or **Above.** See *Above.*

Overcome. See *Kill.*

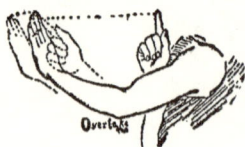

Overtake. Hold out flat left hand at arm's length, palm forward, fingers pointing up; hold the right G hand near the breast, palm out, pointing up; move it forward till it strikes the left hand. Use the left G if only one is pursued. Compare *Arrive there.*

Fr. *atteindre;* Ger. *einholen.*

Owe or **Debt** (Recorded and given). Write on the left palm and swing it from *you* to *me* or otherwise, according to the case. (Sheeaka.)

Owe. Sign *Trade, Time, Money, Give.*

Fr. *devoir;* Ger. *schuldig sein.*

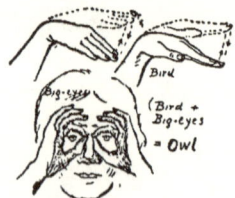

Owl. Sign *Bird* and *Big-eyes;* the latter by putting around each eye a half-circle of thumb and index. (For *Horned Owl* indicate the horns with G hands.) For *Burrowing Owl*, sign *Owl, Hole,* and *Dancing.*

Fr. *la chouette, le hibou;* Ger. *die Eule.*

Own. See *Possession.*

P

Pack. Hold out left flat hand, back to left (this is the horse); bring right flat hand and place palm against left thumb, fingers pointing to front (this is the right pack); raise the right hand and place palm against upper part of left (this is the left pack); repeat these motions quickly.

Fr. *emballer;* Ger. *packen.*

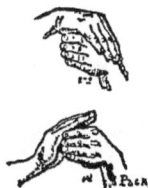

Pain. See *Ache.*

Paint. Use all the fingers of right hand as a brush painting the left palm. Recent Cheyenne. '

Fr. *peindre;* Ger. *anstreichen, malen.*

Paint the cheeks. Sign *Red*, then rub the cheeks and front of the face with palm of flat right hand moved in small circles.

Fr. *se farder;* Ger. *schminken.*

Palsy. Both flat hands, backs up, near breast, shaking.

Fr. *la paralysie agitante;* Ger. *die Schüttellähmung.*

Panther. See *Mountain Lion.*

Paper (Square to write on). With G fingers outline a square, then make as though to write on it with right G.

Fr. *le papier;* Ger. *das Papier.*

Parallel, or **Side by Side.** The index fingers of G hands laid side by side, *not* touching and *not* moving. Some make right index point to left and left to right in this. Compare *Equal, Race,* and *Marry.*

Fr. *parallèle;* Ger. *parallel, gleichlaufend.*

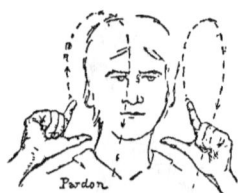

Pardon, Liberate, or Turn Loose (Removing a halter).
Hold both L hands, palms up, near the neck, one on
each side; sweep them up, over, forward and down, as
though removing a halter; at the finish the index fingers
are pointing forward and down. Sometimes add *Go*.
See *Excuse* and *Free*.

Fr. *pardonner;* Ger. *begnadigen.*

Part. If *one-half*, indicate it as in the sign for that
word; if less, hold the right hand nearer end of index,
according to portion desired to be represented. See
Half and *Some*.

Fr. *la partie;* Ger. *der Teil.*

Partner. See *Mate*.

Parturition. See *Born*.

Pass by. See *Avoid*.

Past (Time back). Make the sign for *Time* and jerk
the thumb backward over the right shoulder, all fingers
closed. (Sheeaka.) Or throw the flat hand back over
shoulder. In general, sign *Time, Back*. See *Ago* and *Back*.

Fr. *le passé;* Ger. *die Vergangenheit.*

Pasture. See *Corral*.

Patrol. See *Band*.

Pawnee. See *Indian Tribes*.

Pawnshop (House of three balls). *House* and hold left hand up with thumb, first and second fingers pointing straight down; then make a hoop of right thumb and index and apply it in succession to the three hanging tips. (Pop. and acceptable to Indians.)

  Fr. *le Mont-de-Piété;* Ger. *das Leihhaus, das Pfand-haus.*

Pax. See *Fins.*

Pay (i. e., "Will you give me?" or "Will you pay?"). Hold the right hand forward at level of waist, palm up, fingers half closed, rubbing the tip of first finger and tip of thumb together. (Popular and understood by Sheeaka.) The Cheyennes sign *Money, Give me.*

  Fr. *payer;* Ger. *bezahlen.*

Peace. Clasp the hands in front of body.

  Fr. *la paix;* Ger. *der Friede.*

Peak. Sign *Mountain, Part;* then hold up high all fingers of right hand in a point, back under.

  Fr. *le pic;* Ger. *die Spitze.*

Peas. Sign *Plant,* then with right index and thumb as in *Little of* tap five or six times in a row along the side of the left G.

  Fr. *les pois;* Ger. *die Erbsen.*

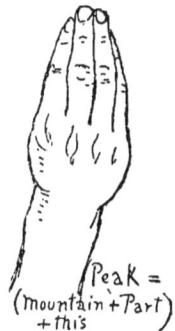

Pekan. See *Fisher.*

Penny. Sign *Red, Money.*

People. Hold up the 5 hands, points up, and add *All.* Compare *Nation* and *Dance.*

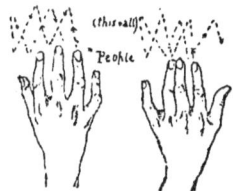

People

People.   Hold up both G hands at various heights, as in *Man* sign.   (Sheeaka.)

Fr. *le peuple;* Ger. *die Leute, das Volk.*

Pepper (Black sprinkler).   Sign *Black*, then use right O hand as tho it held a sprinkler.   A Blackfoot sign understood by Cheyennes.

Fr. *le poivre;* Ger. *der Pfeffer.*

Perhaps.   See *If.*

Permit.   See *Free.*

Perplexed.   See *If* and *Consider.*

Petrol.   See *Spirit.*

Period or **Full stop.**   Use *Done* both No. 1 and No. 2.

Fr. *le point;* Ger. *der Punkt.*

Persevere, Persist, or **Stick to it.**   Hold both fists near breast and firmly push them forward once or twice. That is, sign *Push* repeatedly.

Fr. *persister;* Ger. *beharren.*

Person or **Individual.**   Sign *Man.*

Fr. *la personne;* Ger. *die Person.*

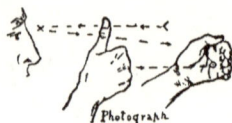

Photograph

Photograph.   Hold out the nearly flat left hand at arm's length, face high, palm to you, fingers level, pointing to right; from near it, draw back right fist, palm to left and up, thumb out straight, as though drawing something to the eye; then near the face change the right hand to flat, slightly curved, back forward, fingers pointing to left, and push it forward against palm of left, as in *Print*.

Fr. *la photographie;* Ger. *die Photographie.*

Picture. Indicate the subject, then hold up both L hands to outline bottom and two sides of a square. With imaginary pencil in right draw on this; left remaining as it was. See *Portrait* and *Photograph.*

Fr. *le tableau;* Ger. *das Bild.*

Pie. Sign *Bread, Round* (i. e., with right G, indicate a horizontal circle of proper size), and *Sweet.* Then sidewise slide the flat right exactly over the flat left, both with palms up. A description, rather than a sign.

Fr. *le pâté, la tarte;* Ger. *die Pastete.*

Piece. See *Little of.*

Pig. See *Hog.*

Pipe. Hold out right G breast high, back down, with index curled up, pointing forward; jerk it forward once or twice.

Fr. *le pipe;* Ger. *die Pfeife.*

Pipe

Pistol. See *Gun.*

Pity or **Mercy** on another (Cry or shed tears for you). Hold G hands, palms downward, index fingers up, in front of and near heart, few inches apart, equally advance and same height; move the hands outward and slightly downward, or toward person. Compare *Cry.*

Fr. *avoir pitié de quelqu' un;* Ger. *jemanden bemitleiden.*

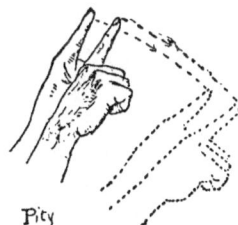
Pity

Pity or **Have mercy on me** (Cry for me). Hold G hands well out in front of body, as described above, but with backs out; bring them toward body, slightly raising them.

> Fr. *plaignez-moi, ayez pitié de moi!* Ger. *haben Sie Mitleid mit mir!*

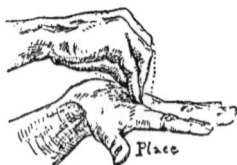

Place or **Put** (Verb). Hold out flat left, back up; swing compressed right over onto it, then open the right a little. Sometimes omit flat left, or use instead compressed left hand held points up. Compare *Bet*.

> Fr. *mettre;* Ger. *stellen, legen, setzen.*

Place (Noun). With right G pointing down, indicate a large circle on the ground. (A Pai-ute sign given by Mallery p. 500, also a popular sign.)

> Fr. *la place;* Ger. *der Ort, die Stelle.*

Plant or **Planting.** With right fingers and thumb, open as though to drop a seed, then closed and moved on to drop another farther, and another, all in the same row. Compare *Animal* and *Jump*. See *Sow*.

> Fr. *planter;* Ger. *pflanzen.*

Play or **Recreation.** Hold up both slightly curved 5 hands, points up and forward, palm to palm, about eight inches apart. Swing them from side to side together, rotating them so the palms are once to front, once to back on each swing. Compare *Dance* and *Children*.

> Fr. *le jeu;* Ger. *das Spiel.*

Playing or **Fooling.** Hold out in front of shoulder the slightly curved 5 hand, palm up; rotate slightly by wrist action. See *Joke* and *Laugh*.

> Fr. *jouer;* Ger. *das Spielen.*

Plenty (Many, piled up). Push forward with both 5 hands, palms first, three times (i. e., sign *Many*); then raise the hands very high, palms forward and down. (Sheeaka.) Or sign *Heap* or *Full*. Compare *Many*.

Fr. *l'abondance;* Ger. *die Fülle.*

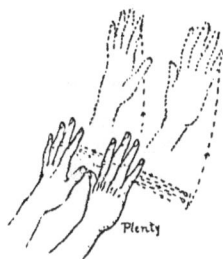

Ploughing. Hold both fists forward as though holding plough, elbows high; and push forward. Also used for cultivation in general.

Fr. *le labourage, labourer;* Ger. *das Pflügen.*

Poison-ivy (Vine, nibbler). Sign *Vine;* that is, hold left forearm upright, as in *Tree*, and with right G finger trace a climbing *Vine* about it; then with thumb and first two fingers of right hand, scratch on edge of flat left, held out back up.

Fr. *le toxicodendron;* Ger. *der Giftefeu, der Giftsumach.*

Polecat. See *Skunk.*

Policeman or **Constable.** Place the curved right index and thumb, little finger out, against left coat lapel. Compare *Medal, Brand,* and *Name.*

Fr. *le sergent de ville;* Ger. *der Schutzmann.*

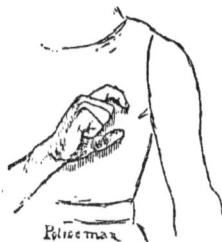

Police-station. Sign *Policeman* and *House.*

Fr. *le poste de police;* Ger. *das Polizeibureau.*

Ponder. See *Consider.*

Poor in property (Scraped bare). With right G finger scrape down the left G finger held up, from tip to base, several times. Compare *Indian Apache,* and *Shame.*

Fr. *pauvre;* Ger. *arm.*

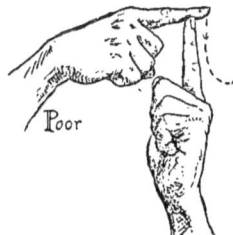

Poor in flesh. See *Thin.*

Porcupine (Prickly hair). Sign *Hair;* then with tips of right 5 hand strike or prick the left palm, held facing the right.

Fr. *le porc-épic;* Ger. *das Stachelschwein.*

Portrait. Hold up the flat left hand, back forward, as though it were a *Mirror,* then sketch on the same with an imaginary pencil, add *Face* and indicate the person. See *Photograph* and *Picture.*

Fr. *le portrait;* Ger. *das Bild*(*nis*).

Positive of adjectives. See *Comparative.*

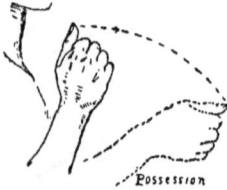

Possesses, Possession, Yours, His own, Belonging to, etc. (Held in the hand.) Hold right A hand, back to right, in front of the neck, or even the forehead, and a few inches from it. Swing it forward and down so the thumb is pointing straight forward.

Fr. *posséder;* Ger. *besitzen.*

Potato. Curved 5 right hand held as low as possible, back down.

Fr. *la pomme de terre;* Ger. *die Kartoffel.*

Pour. Hold out the left O hand, back to left, and pour into it with the right O hand.

Fr. *verser;* Ger. *gieszen.*

Powder. Hold out left hand, palm up; just above it, rub thumb and finger tips of right. Or commonly omit left hand. Compare *Dust.*

Fr. *la poudre;* Ger. *das Pulver, der Puder.*

Power. See *Can.*

Prairie, Smooth land, Flat, or **Level** (Level wide). Flat hands side by side, palms up; then slowly wide spread on same plane. In conversation, usually but one hand is used. Compare *Free* and *Broad.*

Prairie or Flat

> Fr. *la prairie, la plaine;* Ger. *die Prärie, die grosze Ebene.*

Prairie-chicken. See *Grouse.*

Prairie-dog. Sign *Mound, Hole;* then push right G up through hole and add *Talk.*
> Fr. *la marmotte de la prairie;* Ger. *der Präriehund.*

Praise. See *Applause.*

Pray. Lay the flat hands palm to palm, point them to the sky, then draw down toward self; repeat. (Sheeaka.)

Pray. Look up, sign *Talk (No. 1.) straight.*
> Fr. *prier;* Ger. *beten.*

Present (Time). Same as *Now.*

Pretty. See *Beautiful.*

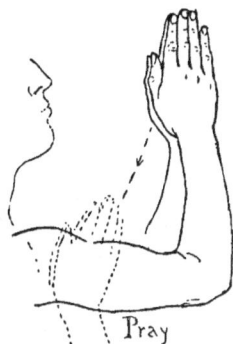

Pray

Pride, Proud, or **Vain.** Draw the flat hand, palm down, over face to breast; throw back head, look up and add *Good.* (Blackfoot.) This is their sign for *Beautiful* with the addition of the head thrown back. Or sign *He, Think, He, Big Chief.* See *Conceit.*
> Fr. *la fierté, fier;* Ger. *der Stolz, stolz.*

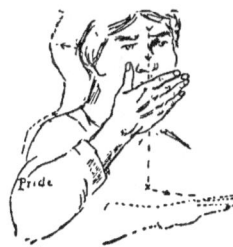

Pride

Priest.   Sign *Robe* and *Black*.
Fr. *le prêtre;* Ger. *der Priester*.

Print.   Push the back of right flat curved hand slowly and firmly against the palm of the left curved ditto, as in *Picture,* only several times.   Compare *Quandary, Approach,* Photograph etc.

Prison (House of bars).   Sign for *House,* then hold 4 hands up, side by side for prison bars.   Add *Man* and *Look through*.

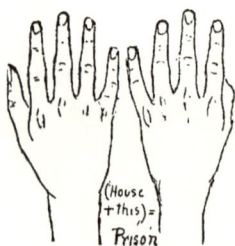

(House +This)= Prison

Prison.   Sign *Prisoner* and *House*.
Fr. *la prison;* Ger. *das Gefängnis*.

Prisoner (Arrested).   Clinch the fists and cross the wrists as though bound, and press down a little.
Fr. *le prisonnier;* Ger. *der Gefangene*.

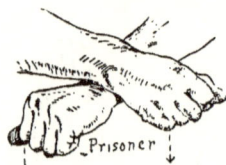

Prisoner

Private.   See *Secret*.

Produce and **Product.**   See *Result*.

Prominent or **Conspicuous** (Stands on a hill).   Sign *Hill* up high, then lay right G against it, pointing up, palm to self, back of right against left hand.   See *Famous*.
Fr. *éminent;* Ger. *hervorragend*.

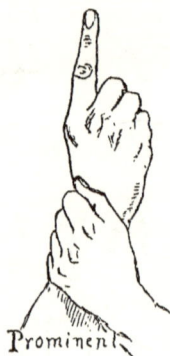

Prominent

Promise (Word bound).   Place the forefinger of right G perpendicularly against mouth; bring down fist and, parallel with it, the other fist, thumbs up; strike both down together twice.   (Sheeaka.)   Also see *Word of Honor,* or *Cross my Heart*.

Promise. Sign *Talk* (i. e., *Word*), *Give*.

Promise, Sworn (I swear). Tap the chest with tips of flat right hand, then raise it, palm forward, and add *Talk*. (Sheeaka.) Compare *Oath*.

   Fr. *la promesse, promettre;* Ger. *das Versprechen, versprechen.*

Proof or **Prove.** See *Show*.

Propose. See *Offer*.

Protect. See *Defend*.
   Fr. *protéger;* Ger. *beschützen*.

Push. The same as *Begin*, which see.
   Fr. *pousser;* Ger. *schieben*.

Put. See *Place*.

Q

Quality. See *Rank*.

Quandary, In a fix, Run against, or **Up against it.** Hold out the curved left hand nearly at arm's length, back forward; push the ditto right from near the breast right out briskly and hard against the left. Sometimes use *Against*. Compare *Approach*, which is similar, but is slow, and right does not touch; also, *Print*, which pushes and is repeated.

   Fr. *l'embarras;* Ger. *die Verlegenheit*.

Quarter (But one of four). Hold up the left 4 hand, back out; then with the right G turn the little finger down on the palm. Sometimes sign *Half*, then again half of the tip portion.

Fr. *le quart;* Ger. *das Viertel.*

Quarrel (Two persons springing at each other). Hold up both G hands and alternately jerk left at right and right at left.

Fr. *la querelle;* Ger. *der Streit.*

Quench. *Fire* and *Wipe out.*

Fr. *éteindre;* Ger. *löschen.*

Question, Query, Interrogation, I am asking you a question, I want to know, usually equivalent to " Is that you? " (Groping or uncertain.) Hold up the right hand toward the person, palm down and forward, fingers and thumb open, spread, but a little curved; by wrist action, swing the hand in small vertical semicircles. The diagram below the illustration indicates the finger tips seen from in front. The motion shown for the little finger is, of course, shared by all. This is a very important and much-used sign; it appears before all questions.

If the person is quite distant, hold the hand higher, more spread, and wave it several times to right and left.

When very near, merely raise the eyebrows. For long distance, raise both arms like Y with hands flat and waved a little. (Crow.) See *Consider.*

Fr. *l'interrogation;* Ger. *die Frage.*

The following are needed in asking questions:

How? Sign *Question* and *Work* and *Way.*

Fr. *comment?;* Ger. *wie?*

Question—*Continued*

How many? or **How much?** Sign *Question;* next
hold the left hand open, curved, palm up, fingers
spread; then with right G digit, quickly tap each
finger on left in succession, closing it back toward the
left palm, beginning with the little finger.

How Many

    Fr. *combien?;* Ger. *wie viele?*

What? (As in " What are you doing?" "What is it? ")
Sign *Question;* follow with the same sign much exag-
gerated; that is, with the arm action, swing the right
5 hand, palm under, fingers slightly bent and separated and pointing forward, in an arc of about a foot
from right over to left and back once or twice. The
Cheyennes in general use this, though they denied
it when questioned. But it seems a good logical sign,
the large arc being equivalent to "object."

(Question + this).
What !

    Fr. *quoi? que?;* Ger. *was?*

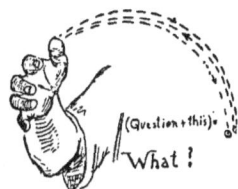

When? If seeking a definite answer as to length
of time, make signs for *Question, How many?* and
then specify time by sign for hours, days, etc. If
asking in general *When?* sign *Question* and *Time.*

When =
(Question + this)

When? If asking for an exact date or point hold
up the left G, make a circle around its tip with right
G, which always points at it. On reaching the starting point, the right G stops, touches the tip of left G.
(Sioux, given by Sheeaka.) This probably represents the shadow going around the tree. See *Time.*

    Fr. *quand?;* Ger. *wann?*

Whence? Strike to left with right G, back up, then
over to right a foot away, then back and again; point

Question—*Continued*

to the person and sign *Come*.   Usually it needs no *Question*.

Fr. *d'où?;* Ger. *woher?*

Where? or **Whither?** (What direction?).   Sign *Question;* then with forefinger sweep the horizon in a succession of bounds, a slight pause at the bottom of each, the head following the finger.   (Sioux and Arapahoe.)   The actual line of the finger is illustrated in the lower plan, the hand being gracefully rotated on the wrist in doing it.   Or sign *Question* and *Somewhere*.

Where?   Sign *Question* and *Look*.

Where? (In an abstract sense).   Extend the open hands, palm up, from the sides out low to the front, and swing them from side to side with a look of inquiry on the face.   (Pop.)

Fr. *où?;* Ger. *wo? wohin?*

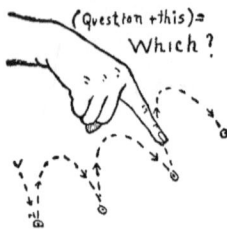

Which? (When the objects are in sight).   Sign *Question* and point with right G in three or four directions, downward or toward the objects in question.

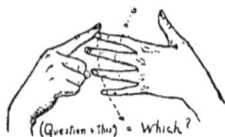

Which? (When the objects are not in sight).   Sign *Question;* then hold left hand in front of you, with palm toward you, fingers to right and held apart; place the end of the right forefinger on that of the left forefinger and then draw it down across the other fingers.

Fr. *quel, lequel?;* Ger. *welcher?*

Question—*Continued*

Whither? Sign *Question* and *Go*, in two or three directions.

  Fr. *où ?;* Ger. *wohin ?*

Who? Sign *Question* and *Man*.

  Fr. *qui ?;* Ger. *wer ?*

Why? Sign *Question*, but do it very slowly. (C)

Why? Sign *Question* and *Want*.

  Fr. *pourquoi ?;* Ger. *warum ?*

Quick. See *Fast* and *Hurry*.

Quiet, be, Be not alarmed, Have patience. The palm of the flat hand held toward the person and gently depressed once or twice. See *Easy*.

  Fr. *soyez tranquille;* Ger. *beruhigen Sie sich.*

Quiet, be. See *Silence*.

Quit. See *Give up;* also *Finish*.

R

Rabbit. Move the M hand straight to the front, back up and undulating on the wrist, to imitate the rabbit hopping forward; then make V right hand and turn it to look back. (Scott.) The Cheyennes omit the second part of this.

  Fr. *le lapin;* Ger. *der Hase.*

Raccoon or **Coon.** Draw the V hand horizontally across the face and nose. If necessary, also indicate *Size* and striped tail.

Fr. *le raton;* Ger. *der Waschbär.*

Race. Move the index fingers forward and up, side by side, as in *Equal;* but keep them moving a long way forward and upward. Compare *Parallel, Marry.*

Fr. *la course, le concours;* Ger. *das Wettrennen, der Wettlauf.*

Rags, In rags. Touch *Coat,* add *Old;* then hold left 5 slightly curved, back up and use ditto right as though to comb out the fingers of left, once or twice.

Fr. *les guenilles, en loques;* Ger. *die Lumpen, zerlumpt.*

Railroad train or **Cars.** Sign *Fire* twice upward for puffs, then add *Fast.* Compare *Motor car.*

Fr. *le train* [*de chemin de fer*]*;* Ger. *der Eisenbahnzug.*

Railroad. Indicate *Train* as above; then push the right G finger quickly along the back of the left V hand and on beyond. (Sheeaka.)

Railroad. Sign *Road;* then with the two G hands, backs up, indicate rails as in *Parallel.*

Railroad. Sign *Hard* (i. e., metal); then hold out two G fingers, backs up, six inches apart, and push both together far forward and a little up.

Fr. *le chemin de fer;* Ger. *die Eisenbahn.*

Railroad Station. Make the signs of *Railway* and *House;* adding, if necessary, *Alight* and *Aboard.*

Fr. *la gare;* Ger. *der Bahnhof.*

Rain (Falling from clouds). Hold A hands, backs up, opposite forehead, near each other; lower them slightly, mostly by wrist action; at the same time open and separate fingers and thumb so they point downward; repeat.

Fr. *la pluie;* Ger. *der Regen.*

Rainbow. Sign *Rain* then indicate the arch with a slow sweep of the flat right hand, back up, high above head.

Fr. *l'arc-en-ciel;* Ger. *der Regenbogen.*

Rank or **Quality** (Of a soldier.) With the right G, indicate stripes on left arm, or else touch each shoulder for epaulets.

Rank or **Quality.** Sign *Chief;* then lay upright right G, palm forward, against back of left ditto, as in *Rising man,* sliding the right up and down to various heights.

Fr. *le rang;* Ger. *der Rang, die Würde.*

Rank, What is his? Sign *Chief, Big; Chief, Little; Question.* Sometimes omit *Chief, Little.*

Fr. *quel rang-a-t-il ?;* Ger. *Welchen Rang bekleidet er ?*

Rapid. See *Fast.*

Rapids. Sign *River, Rock;* and pass the right 5 hand, back up, points first, swiftly forward and down, in an up and down waved course.

Fr. *le rapide;* Ger. *die Stromschnelle.*

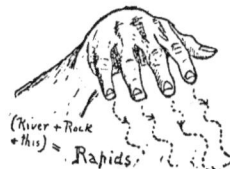

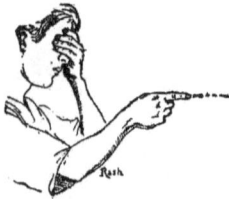

Rash (Going forward blind). Hold left hand on eyes and point right G index forward, moving it to front.
　　Fr. *imprudent;* Ger. *unvorsichtig, verwegen.*

Rattlesnake. Sign *Snake,* then hold right G finger, pointing up, near shoulder, and shake it.
　　Fr. *le serpent à sonnettes;* Ger. *die Klapperschlange.*

Reach. *Arrive there.*

Ready, Orderly, or **Arranged.** Extend the open hands, palm to palm, a few inches apart, pointing outward and parallel to each other, over toward the left side; lift them both together from the wrists, move toward the right a little and let them come down again; repeat the motion until by stages the hands have been moved over to the right side. (D)

Ready. Sign *All, Good;* or use *Arranged,* or combine them into *Arranged, All, Good.* See *Arranged.*
　　Fr. *prêt;* Ger. *bereit, fertig.*

Recall to memory. See *Bring back.*

Receive. Hold out hollow right hand, palm up, half open; draw it back, slightly closing fingers. Compare *Give to me.*
　　Fr. *recevoir;* Ger. *erhalten.*

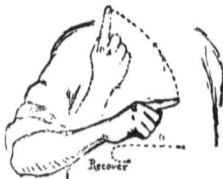

Recover, Get well, Get all right again, Revive, or **Save.** Hold right G hand, back up, in front of breast, pointing to left and front; raise the hand with a graceful sweep, at same time turn it back to front and index pointing

upward.   The actual course of the index tip, if seen
from above, is as in the dotted line under the hand.
   If one is near death by disease, this may be used to
denote recovery; if in great danger, this would mean
escaped.
   Fr. *se porter mieux, se rétablir;* Ger. *sich erholen.*

Recreation.   See *Play.*

Reduce.   See *Decrease.*

Reflect.   See *Idea* and *Consider.*

Refuse.   See *Won't.*

Religion.   Sign *Medicine* and *Way.*
   Fr. *la religion;* Ger. *die Religion.*

Remain.   See *Sit.*

Remember.   Sign *Heart, Know.*   Or, in popular code,
touch the forehead with right G, raise the brows and
nod.

Remember, I; or **Understand.**   Hold right G index upright and grasp it firmly with left hand, face high.
   Fr. *je me souviens;* Ger. *ich erinnere mich.*

Remember not (It slips from my grasp).   As above, but
let the right G index slip down and out.   See *Forget.*
   Fr. *je ne me souviens pas;* Ger. *ich erinnere mich nicht.*

Remembering.   See *Memories.*

Repeat, Again, or **Back.** Place the finger tips of the compressed right hand on the left palm, as the latter is held in front of the body, back down, and strike once or twice. (Sheeaka. Probably borrowed from Deaf.) Compare *Once, Twice, Often,* and *More.*

Repeat. Hold up right G, chin high, back up, pointing to left and forward; lash down with it like a whip twice or more as best fits in. Sometimes sign *Come back.* Compare *All the time.*
Fr. *répéter;* Ger. *wiederholen.*

Reply. See *Answer.*

Request. See *Beg.*

Resemble. See *Alike.*

Respond. See *Answer.*

Responsible. Sign *I* (or whoever it is), *Do, That* Or *My* (or *His*) *Way.* (Seger.) Sign *Carry* and *That* (Suggested.)
Fr. *responsable;* Ger. *verantwortlich.*

Restaurant or **Hotel.** Sign for *House* and *Eat.*
Fr. *le restaurant, l'hôtel;* Ger. *das Restaurant, das Hotel.*

Restrain or **Prevent.** Sign *Hold* and *Keep quiet.* Sometimes use *Do not.*
Fr. *réprimer, empêcher;* Ger. *zurückhalten, verhindern.*

Result. Sign *After, Work, See.*
Fr. *le résultat;* Ger. *das Ergebnis, die Folge.*

Retreat (Of many). Sign *Charge,* then reverse and withdraw the hands.

Retreat (Of one). Sign *Going,* then turn the G hand palm toward you and draw it back with similar action. (Understood; not established.)
Fr. *la retraite;* Ger. *der Rückzug.*

Reverie. Bow the head, resting the mouth on the A fist. Compare *Memories.*
Fr. *la rêverie;* Ger. *die Träumerei.*

Revile. See *Blackguarding.*

Revive. See *Recover.*

Revolver. Sign for drawing from belt behind and present the same, using right G hand, back to right. Add *Fire-off,* if need be. See *Gun.*
Fr. *le pistolet, le revolver;* Ger. *der Revolver.*

Rich. Sign *Possesses, Heap, Money.*
Fr. *riche;* Ger. *reich.*

Ride (To ride an animal). Hold the hands as in *Horse,* and then move the hands to the front on short vertical curves.
Fr. *aller à cheval;* Ger. *reiten.*

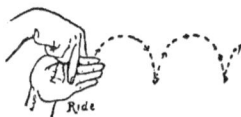

Ridge (Of hills). Hold the A hands touching, thumbs toward face and upright; draw them apart a foot. Compare *Soldiers* and *Hill.*

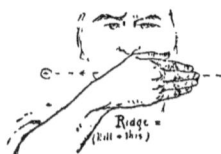

Ridge =
(Rill = this)

Ridge. Sign *Hill* with right, then hold 5 out at arm's length, face high, flat, and bent, so the fingers point to the left; swing it slowly horizontally across to the right. This last seems to mean "lying across the horizon" and appears in several combinations. See *Mirage*.

Fr. *la crête;* Ger. *der Kamm.*

Rifle. See *Gun.*

Right. See *Good.*

Rill. See *Creek.*

Ring (For finger). Hold up left 5 hand; then with right index and thumb make as though slipping a ring on the ring finger.

Fr. *la bague;* Ger. *der Ring.*

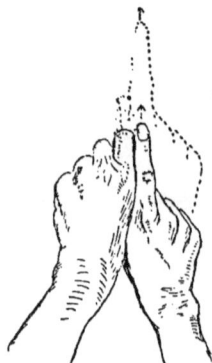

Rising man

Rising man, or **Coming man** (Man rising to stand on a hill). Hold up left as in *Hill;* lay right G behind or beside it, against the thumb, palm forward, pointing up; push right up until the base of the index is sitting on top of the left; that is, becomes *Prominent.* See *Prominent* and *Famous.*

Fr. *l'homme qui arrivera;* Ger. *der Mann der Zukunft.*

River =(this)

River, Big stream, or **Running water.** Sign *Water* then with tremulous movement draw flat right 4 hand, palm down, from opposite left breast to opposite right; fingers always level and pointing to left. Compare *Creek* and *Rill.*

Fr. *la rivière;* Ger. *der Flusz.*

Road (i. e., Highroad; especially between high banks, hills, or fences). Holding the open hands, palm to palm and pointing forward, carry them forward, as if they represented the sides of a road; then add *Going* by pushing the flat right hand forward in line between, palm to left, fingers level. (Sheeaka.) Or sign *Way* and *Wagon.*

Fr. *le chemin, la route;* Ger. *der Weg, die Landstrasse.*

Robe. Sign *Coat;* but instead of ending at waist, sweep the hands as low as possible.

Fr. *la robe;* Ger. *das Kleid, die Robe.*

Rock or **Stone.** Sign *Hard* and sometimes indicate shape. For *Stone* add *Lump.* Compare *Metal.*

Fr. *la roche, la pierre;* Ger. *der Fels, der Stein.*

Root. First sign *Tree* or *Grass*, as may be; then point down, place the 5 hands together at the wrists, backs up and level; pointing left to front and left, right to front and right; then move them out and apart.

Fr. *la racine;* Ger. *die Wurzel.*

Rope (Trailing after the horse and twisted). Sign *After;* then, as right is drawn to rear, make tip of index describe a spiral curve. Commonly omit the left hand.

Fr. *la corde;* Ger. *das Seil, der Strick.*

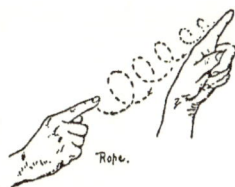

Rose (Flower). Hold the fingers of the left hand straight, little separated, arranged in a circle, back to left and front; in front of body, index finger horizontal and pointing to right and front; with right hand make as though picking berries from the left finger tips. (C)

Fr. *la rose;* Ger. *die Rose.*

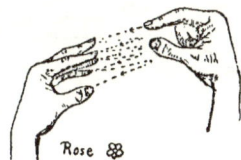

Rotten (Meat). Indicate smell, etc.
Fr. *pourri;* Ger. *faul, verfault.*

Rub it out, Erase, Annul, Never mind, As you were.
Put middle finger of right hand to tongue, then rub
left palm and wipe the palm with under side of right
forearm. (Sheeaka. A white man's sign now understood by Indians.)
Or, if afar, simply shake the flat right hand quickly
and vigorously from side to side as it is held palm forward in front of the face. (Pop.) Compare *Easy* and
Erase.
Fr. *effacer;* Ger. *auswischen, "Schwamm drüber!"*

Rumor (A little flying thing). With flat 5 right hand,
palm down, shoulder high, swing out level from throat
to right, working all the fingers as in playing piano.
(A Paiute sign, given me by Mary Austin.) A combination of *Wind* and *Fly.*
Fr. *la rumeur;* Ger. *das Gerücht.*

Run. Swing the fists at each side as in running.
Fr. *courir;* Ger. *laufen.*

Run against. See *Quandary.*

Run away, Slip away, Clear out, Sneak (Run under
cover). Hold out flat left hand, palm down; push
right G hand under it quickly and sinuously. Sometimes preface it by laying one hand over the eyes. Compare *Jealous.*
Fr. *filer, se sauver;* Ger. *ausreiszen, weglaufen.*

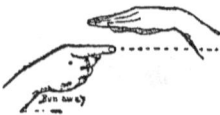

Running Water. See *River*.

S

Sacred. See *Medicine*.

Sad. See *Sorrow*.

Saddle. Hold out both S hands, palms up, side by side (sometimes inches apart), about height of shoulders, forearms vertical, wrists bent so backs of hands are nearly down.
>   Fr. *la selle;* Ger. *der Sattel*.

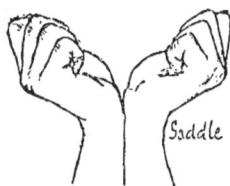

Safe. See *Recover* or *Alive*.

Sage Brush (Bunches). With all finger tips together pointing up, swing the hand to various places in front of right shoulder. (C) Compare *Peak* and *Canoe*.

Sage. Sign *White, Good smell, Grass*.
>   Fr. *la plante aromatique de la prairie;* Ger. *der Präriebusch*.

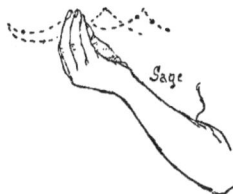

Salt. Sign *Powder*, then the act of sprinkling with finger and thumb. (Blackfoot.) Touch the tongue cautiously with the right G. Compare *Sugar* and *Pepper*.
>   Fr. *le sel;* Ger. *das Salz*.

Same. See *Equal*.

Sanctuary, to claim. See *Bar up*.

Satisfied. See *Contented*.

Save. See *Recover*, also *Free*.

Save or **Except.** See *But*.

Savey or **Sabe.** This word universal in the west is the same sign as *Know*.

Saw. With lower edge of right, thumb up, saw across the upper edge of left wrist held out horizontally.
Fr. *la scie;* Ger. *die Säge.*

Say. See *Call*.

Scalp (To). Point to scalp, make as though pulling it forward and sign *Cutting* under. The last two gestures being done out in front of the body.
Fr. *scalper;* Ger. *die Kopfhaut abziehen.*

Scatter! (A command to scouts). See *Go* and *Scatter*.

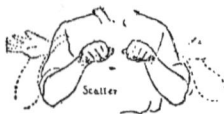

Scatter or **Sow** (As seeds). Hold the closed hands, backs up, near each other and close to breast; move right hand well to front and right, left well to front and left; that is, widely separate the hands, swinging each in a half-circle out, so the palms are a little outward, at the same time extending and separating fingers and thumbs. (C) Compare *Bad* and *Scorn;* in these the hands are not moved apart.

Scatter. Swing closed right to left, there opening to 5 so palm is to left and forward; then same movement with hand opened to right, each time in a graceful sweep. The Cheyennes say the above is *Throw away*.
Fr. *disperser, semer;* Ger. *ausstreuen, säen.*

Schoolhouse. Sign *House* and *Writing;* usually preceded by *Children.*

Fr. *l'école;* Ger. *die Schule.*

Schoolteacher. Sign *Book* and *Chief.*

Fr. *le maître d' école;* Ger. *der Lehrer.*

Scold. See *Abuse;* also *Fault-finding.*

Scorn. Turn the head away and with one hand throw an imaginary handful of sand toward the feet of the person. This is the same as *Bad*, except for the turn of the head.

Fr. *le mépris;* Ger. *die Verachtung.*

Scout. Same as *Wolf*, but hold the hand near the right ear. Sometimes use *Advance Guard*, which see. The Cheyennes sometimes sign it as *Wolf, Soldier.*

Fr. *le coureur (d' armée);* Ger. *der Späher.*

Scout, to. Sign *Wolf* and *Look.*

Fr. *aller à la découverte;* Ger. *spähen.*

Scout; that is, *Boy Scout.* Hold up the right hand with finger and thumb forming a ring, other three fingers straight up. (Pop.)

Fr. *le petit éclaireur;* Ger. *der jugendliche Pfadfinder.*

Scout; of the *highest degree.* Add the sign *Wolf* to the foregoing. (Suggested.)

Scout leader or **Patrol leader.** Sign *Boy Scout;* then lay the 4 left hand on left side of head to indicate plume. (Suggested.)

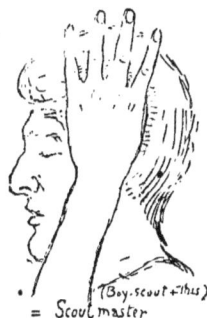

Scout, Tenderfoot. Make signs *Boy Scout* and *Small.* (Suggested.)

Sculptor. Right fist closed, thumb held up straight and free, then used as a trowel on an imaginary wall. (Pop.)
   Fr. *le sculpteur;* Ger. *der Bildhauer.*

Search me. With a hand grasping each lapel, spread open the coat. (Pop.)
   Fr. *examinez-moi;* Ger. *was weisz ich ?* (Pop.)

Seasons. The four seasons are *Little Grass (Spring); High Grass (Summer); Leaf Fall (Autumn);* and *Cold* or *Snow (Winter).* Each is given in alphabetic place.

Secret or **Private** (Talk under cover). Left hand flat, horizontal, near left cheek; with right, sign *Talk* under it. Usually sign *Talk* and *Hide.*
   Fr. *le secret;* Ger. *das Geheimnis.*

Seek. See *Hunt.*

See. The fingers of V hand pointed forward (as in *Look*) then advanced a little in the line of sight; sometimes for extra point, it is changed into G hand and pushed forward. Also compare *Hunt* and *Lie, Look* and *Find.* The difference between *Look* and *See* is not observed by most Indians; but it is well to maintain it.
   Fr. *voir;* Ger. *sehen.*

See me. Point at one's own chin with the right V hand and touch breast.
   Fr. *voyez-moi;* Ger. *sehen Sie mich.*

Seem. See *Appear.*

Seize. Move the open hands forward; grasp and draw back as though seizing some object.
   Fr. *saisir;* Ger. *ergreifen.*

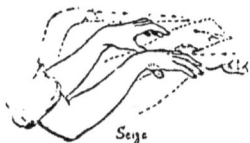

Select. See *Choose.*

Sell. See *Trade.* On the Stock Exchange, the clenched fist thrown forward and down means *Sell.* Probably in imitation of the auctioneer's hammer. See *Kill.*

Sell, Sold or **Bought** i. e., **Marketed.** On middle of side of left G held out, tap two or three times with middle side of right G. This is also used for *Buy*, which see for illustration. It is supposed to have had origin in an old gambling game. See *Trade.*
   Fr. *vendre;* Ger. *verkaufen.*

Send (Command and Go). Hold the right A near the breast; swing it out, up and down a foot; then swing the right G higher and farther. (Sheeaka.)
   Fr. *envoyer;* Ger. *senden, schicken.*

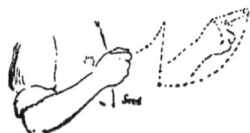

Separate or **Apart.** Lay the G fingers side by side, backs up; spring them apart, widest at tips, moving them forward and out.
   Fr. *séparer;* Ger. *trennen.*

Several. Extend the fingers of the right A hand, one at a time, beginning with the index. (Sheeaka.)
   Fr. *plusieurs;* Ger. *mehrere.*

Sew. Hold flat left hand index edge up, thumb level with index; move right G hand index with extended thumb, across left index once or twice as in 'sewing; each time nearer the body and each time turning the right index nail down, as it is moved forward. Compare *Awl.*

Fr. *coudre;* Ger. *nähen.*

Shade. Sign *Sun, Not.*

Shadow (Of a person). Indicate the person; then sign *Going, There by me, Same.* *There by me* is indicated by pointing to the ground on the left side with right G.

Fr. *l'ombre;* Ger. *der Schatten.*

Shall. See *Will.*

Shaman. See *Medicine-man.*

Shame (On you). (The finger of scorn made sharper.) Point left index at person, all others closed; and with right index similarly held, rub it on back of left index from middle to tip and beyond. (Pop.) See *Ashamed.* In France the idea is conveyed by the *Horns.* See *Evil Eye.*

Fr. *fi! fi donc!* (Pop.); Ger. *Schäme dich!*

Sharp or **Keen.** Hold out flat right hand, palm up; touch little finger edge lightly with ball of left thumb and add *Good.* For *Sharp points* see *Porcupine.*

Fr. *affilé;* Ger. *scharf.*

Shave. Use the flat right hand as a razor, palm to

right, points up, little finger next right cheek as the
edge; move it toward the right ear.
Fr. *(se) raser;* Ger. *(sich) rasieren.*

Shawl. Sign *Blanket* and *Fringe.* For *Fringe,* hold
out the left 5 hand points forward, level; then push the
similar right over it forward several times.
Fr. *le châle;* Ger. *der Schal.*

She. Sign *Female* and point with G finger at the person.
Fr. *elle;* Ger. *sie.*

Sheep, Mountain, or **Bighorn.** With compressed hands
above each eye, pointed backward, trace the sweep of
horns, ending below ears, with points turned forward.
Fr. *le mouton sauvage;* Ger. *das amerikanische
Groszhornschaf.*

Sheep, Common. Sign *Bighorn* and *White Man.*
Fr. *le mouton;* Ger. *das Schaf.*

Shell. Hold the curved hands side by side, close and
open them on the under side, as though hinged on top.
Compare *Boat, Book, Bowl,* and *Open.*
Fr. *la coquille;* Ger. *die Muschelschale.*

Shield (Noun). With both L hands a little apart, index
fingers pointed down, make a large incomplete circle
to left of left breast. See *Protect.*
Fr. *le bouclier;* Ger. *der Schild.*

Shine, Shimmer, or **Glitter.** Hold out the curved right
5 hand, palm down; lower it slightly, shaking it quickly
sidewise. Compare *Snow, Glitter,* and *Easy.*
Fr. *briller, étinceler;* Ger. *scheinen, glänzen.*

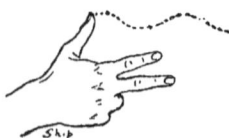

Ship. Raise and spread thumb and two first fingers to be masts, others closed; then push the hand forward slowly in a rising and falling line. (Deaf sign for *Sailing Ship*. For Indian sign see *Boat, Big*.)

Fr. *le navire;* Ger. *das Schiff.*

Shoe. Sign *Moccasin, White Man.*

Fr. *le soulier;* Ger. *der Schuh.*

Shoot (A gun). See *Fire.*

Shoot (An arrow). Sign *Bow*, then snap the index fingers out straight. To add *Hit with an arrow*, hold up the flat left and thrust the right G through it.

Fr. *lancer (une flèche);* Ger. *schieszen.*

Shop. See *Store.*

Short. For things which grow, hold the flat hand back forward, fingers pointing up at desired height. For things which do not grow, use the flat hand, palm down; or else, both flat hands side by side, palm to palm. The same as *Low*.

Fr. *court;* Ger. *kurz.*

Shot-gun. See *Gun.*

Shout. See *Yell.*

Show, Prove, Proof, or **Behold.** Raise flat left hand, palm forward. Lay index of right G on it and turn the two about, pushing them forward as though to show something. (Sheeaka. Borrowed from the Deaf.)

Show, Prove, Proof, or **Behold.** Hold out the flat left, palm up, pointing forward and down. Point to the person in question with right G, then at left palm with right V.
Fr. *montrer;* Ger. *zeigen.*

Sick, Suffering, Sick one, or **Invalid** (Throbbing). Hold flat hands out near breast; move the hands quickly outward and back several times. Compare *Lungs.*
Fr. *malade;* Ger. *krank.*

Side by Side. See *Parallel.*

Sign Language, To talk in Sign Language. Touch the back of left hand with tip of right, the back of right with tip of left and add *Talk.* (C)
Fr. *le langage des signes;* Ger. *die Gebärdensprache.*

Silence, Silent, or **Hush.** Lay the extended index, pointing upward, over the mouth. In the more vigorous form of *Shut up,* lay the flat hand on the mouth (recent).
Fr. *silence! taisez-vous!;* Ger. *schweigen! still!*

Silly. See *Foolish.*

Silver. Sign *Money* and *White.*
Fr. *l'argent;* Ger. *das Silbergeld.*

Sin or **Badness.** Same as *Bad.* See *Evil.*

Since. See *After.*

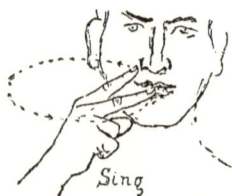

Sing. Hold right V hand, back to right, in front of face; finger tips a little higher than and close to mouth, pointing nearly up. Move the hand briskly so finger tips describe a small horizontal circle. Compare *Lie* and *Abuse*.

Fr. *chanter;* Ger. *singen.*

Sioux. See *Indian.*

Sister. Sign *Woman* and *Brother.*
Fr. *la soeur;* Ger. *die Schwester.*

Sister-in-law. Sign *Brother-in-law* and *Woman.*
Fr. *la belle-soeur;* Ger. *die Schwägerin.*

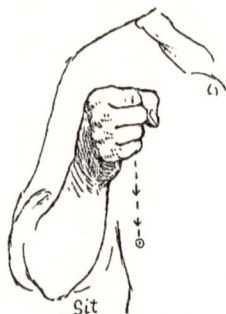

Sit, Sit down, or **Remain.** Hold the right A hand in front of and a little lower than right shoulder, back to right; move the hand emphatically downward a few inches. Compare *Wait* and *Aboard.*

Fr. *s'asseoir;* Ger. *sitzen.*

Skin. See *Hide.*

Skinny. See *Lean.*

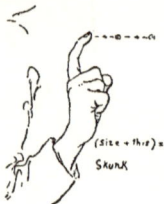

Skunk or **Polecat.** Indicate *Size* and tail up; that is, curving G up, palm forward; move in gentle jerks forward, and then add *Smell, Bad.* Compare *Weasel.*

Fr. *la bête puante, la mouffette;* Ger. *das amerikanische Stinktier.*

Sky. See *Heavens.*

Sled or **Sleigh** (The runners). Both G hands, backs down, 4 inches apart; index fingers curved and pushed forward. The idea is helped by *Snow* on *Ground.*

Fr. *le traineau;* Ger. *der Schlitten.*

Sleep. Hold both flat hands, backs up, in front of breast, same level; swing both over to the left in an up and down curve, in which the right (only) turns palm up; the left continues back up; then lower the head a little to right. Some finish with both palms up.

Journeys are one sleep, two sleeps, etc., on the Plains.

Fr. *le sommeil, dormir;* Ger. *der Schlaf, schlafen.*

Sleepy. Rub the eyes with the fists. (Pop.) Or yawn and lay the head on one side, closing the eyes. (Sheeaka.) Both of these are understood by the Cheyennes, but they use *Want, Sleep.*

Fr. *avoir sommeil;* Ger. *schläfrig.*

Slow. Hold out the flat left hand, palm to right; ditto right hand opposite, palm to left; in slow jerks, move the left hand forward; at the same time, jerk the right, making the latter fall behind. Compare *Fast.*

Fr. *lent;* Ger. *langsam.*

Small, Few, or **Crowded.** Compress both hands so the fingers are straight, but at an angle with the back of the hand; hold them about eight inches apart, backs out, pointed up and forward, right higher; move them together till the right is over the left. Sometimes the Cheyennes made this sign with the closed fists to mean *Few.* Compare *Little.*

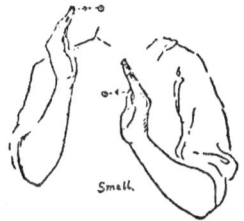

Fr. *peu;* Ger. *wenig.*

Smaller, to make. See *Decrease.*

Smart. See *Cunning.*

Smell.   Hold V hand, back up, fingers pointing to chin; swing fingers up so the nose passes between them.   Compare *Blood* and *Brother*.   Place the palm close before the tip of the nose.   (Pop.)

Fr. *sentir;* Ger. *riechen.*

Smell, A bad smell, or Stink.   Sign *Smell* and hold the nostrils, or sign *Bad*.   (Sheeaka.)

Fr. *la mauvaise odeur, la puanteur;* Ger. *der üble Geruch, der Gestank.*

Smell, A good smell.   Sign *Smell* and *Good*.

Fr. *la bonne odeur;* Ger. *der gute Geruch, der Duft.*

Smoke.   For distant smoke, like a signal-fire smoke, make sign for *Fire* and continue raising hand in a spiral till higher than head.

Fr. *la fumée;* Ger. *der Rauch.*

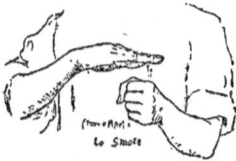

Smoke a pipe (Action of filling it).   Hold up the left A, thumb up, tap on top two or three times with flat right, then add *Pipe*, jerking it forward two or three times.

Fr. *fumer (une pipe);* Ger. *rauchen (eine Pfeife).*

Smoke a cigarette.   Put index and thumb to mouth as though holding a cigarette.   (Blackfoot.)

Smooth or **Level.**   Rub the back of the flat left hand, held palm down, with whole palm of the flat right, back and forth, in long strokes.   Sometimes use *Prairie*.   Compare *Indian* and *At*.

Fr. *lisse;* Ger. *glatt.*

Smooth Ground.   See *Prairie*.

Snake (Its motion). Hold the right H (or sometimes G) hand, back to right, waist high, fingers pointing to front; move it several inches to front in a sinuous line from side to side. Compare *Fish*, *Creek*, and *Rope*.

Fr. *le serpent;* Ger. *die Schlange.*

Sneak. See *Run away.*

Snow. Raise and spread both hands a foot apart, backs up, fingers curved; then softly lower them in slow, short zigzags. For *Rain*, the lines down are straight. *Years* are commonly called *Snows* or *Winters.* Compare *Shimmer.*

Fr. *la neige;* Ger. *der Schnee.*

So, Just so (That's true). Swing the right G index from 45 degree angle down to level; then add *Straight*, swinging index up slightly at finish. Sometimes sign *Yes.* Compare *Idea.*

Fr. *si, précisément cela;* Ger. *so, jawohl.*

So that; In order that (So, that). Strike down a foot with the right G in front of breast, then strike it on the left flat hand held opposite left breast. (Sheeaka.)

Fr. *de sorte que, pour;* Ger. *um, damit.*

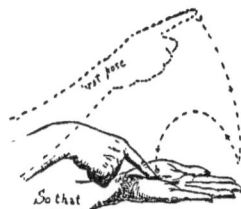

Soap. Rub the hands together as in washing them.

Fr. *le savon;* Ger. *die Seife.*

Soft or Muddy Ground (Animal's legs going down). Form a horizontal half-circle of left index and thumb; drop the right fist into it; reverse the hands and repeat.

Fr. *la terre molle, la boue;* Ger. *die weiche Erde, der Schlamm.*

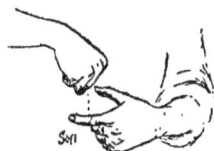

Soft, in general.   Sign *Hard* and *Not.*
    Fr. *mou;* Ger. *weich.*

Soil.   See *Earth.*

Soldiers (In a row, spread out).   Hold the flattened
fists out in front, side by side, backs up so basal joints
of the fingers are nearly level and the middle joints
form a row; then swing them apart.

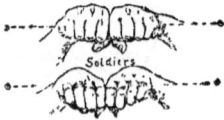

    In many whose fingers are stiff the row is made with
the basal joints plumb, as in the upper cut; but the
correct way is as below.

    "This represents the line of the Indian soldiers that,
pending the order to charge, held back the people in the
buffalo hunt." (Scott.) Compare *Ridge, Done,* and *Fat.*
    Fr. *les soldats;* Ger. *die Soldaten.*

Some (Here and there one).   Point with index finger
downward and at some near spot on the ground, then
change to another farther off, then to another.   (Scott.)
    Fr. *quelques;* Ger. *einige.*

Some, A part of.   Hold out level flat left, back forward
and out; lay flat right thumb up on left index near the
tip; then jerk it toward tip and beyond.   This is much
like *Halve;* but the right is casually brushed along the
edge of the left and at no time precisely placed.
    Fr. *du;* Ger. *etwas.*

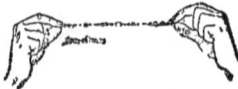

Sometimes (Different times).   Sign *Time,* moving the
hands apart in short jerks.   (Seger.) Compare *By
and by.*
    Fr. *quelquefois;* Ger. *zuweilen.*

Somewhere. Hold right G up near right shoulder; swing it in a curve up and down to opposite left shoulder and back. Also used in the question *Where ?*

Fr. *quelque part;* Ger. *irgendwo(hin).*

Son. Sign *Born* and *Male.*
Fr. *le fils;* Ger. *der Sohn.*

Song or **Poem** (Written singing). Sign for *Sing* and *Write.*
Fr. *la chanson;* Ger. *das Lied.*

Soon or **Early.** Sign *Time,* then stop with the fingers an inch apart. Compare *Sometimes, Time, By and by, Close.*

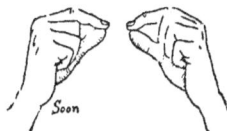

Sorrow, Distress, Discouraged, Down-hearted, Sadness, or **Sad** (Heart on the ground). Lay the right compressed hand on the heart, pointing down; then throw it forward and down, ending the sign with the flat hand very low, palm up, near the ground.
Fr. *le chagrin, la douleur;* Ger. *das Leid.*

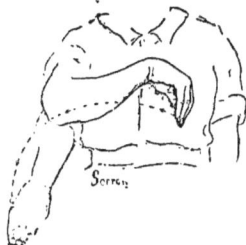

Sorry (It grinds my heart). Rub the fist on heart in circle two or three times. (Blackfoot.)
This is less strong than *Sorrow* and is used as a polite expression of interest, equivalent to " What a pity." (Eastman.) See also *Trouble.*
Fr. *j'en suis fâché;* Ger. *leid tun, es thut mir leid.*

Soul. See *Spirit.*

Sour. See *Bitter.*

Sow. See *Sew.*

Sow Seeds. See *Scatter.*

Spark. See *Fire.*

Speak. See *Talk.*

Spear. Make as though thrusting a spear with both hands.
> Fr. *la lance;* Ger. *der Speer.*

Speech, Message, or **Talk.** That is, a long talk, as at council, by oneself. (Handing out words.) Hold the flat right hand, back down, pointing to left, at lower lip and swing it forward several times. Compare *Discussion* and *Talk.*
> Fr. *la harangue;* Ger. *die Rede.*

Speech to me or **Tell me.** Speech by another addressed to oneself is the same as the preceding, but swing the right hand in toward the chin instead of out. Compare *Drink, Water, Discussion,* and *Talk.*

Spell, that is, **Spell it.** Make writing in the air, then sign *Talk.*
> Fr. *écrivez le;* Ger. *buchstabieren Sie es.*

Spider. Hold the palm of the right hand about one and a half inches from a flat surface; spread the fingers and thumb and work them like legs; the hand represents the body. (Scott.) Compare *Bunch* and *Herd.*
> Fr. *l'araignée;* Ger. *die Spinne.*

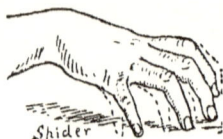

Spirit or **Petrole** (Water of strong power). There is no established sign; but Sheeaka understood this combination: *Water* and *Strong*. A Cheyenne gave it *Lantern, Different, Strong, Pour*.

Fr. *l'essence, le pétrole;* Ger. *das Benzin*.

Splendor. See *Glow*.

Spoon. Use the cupped right hand as a spoon.

Fr. *la cuiller;* Ger. *der Löffel*.

Spotted. Hold out the level left arm and with right curved 5 hand finger tips tap the left arm at various places on the inside, from the wrist up, as though flecking it with the tip of a brush, at both up and down strokes. Compare *Striped*.

Fr. *tacheté;* Ger. *getupfelt*.

Spring (Water coming up and spreading). Make the sign for *Water*, then a large horizontal circle with L hands (as in *Hole*); then push the right compressed hand up through the left L hand and, as it comes up, extend the fingers with a slight snap to represent the bubbling water.

Fr. *la source;* Ger. *die Quelle*.

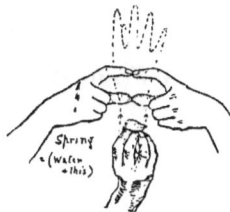

Spring (Little grass time). Sign *Grass* and *Short*. Add *Time* if there is doubt.

Show longer grass for June, etc.

Fr. *le printemps;* Ger. *der Frühling*.

Squeeze. See *Few*.

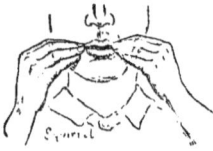

Squirrel. Hold both compressed hands near the mouth and give a quick motion of the lips. (Ruggles.) Or sign *Tree* with left hand, then with compressed right hand as in *Animal* indicate running up and around.

Fr. *l'écureuil;* Ger. *das Eichhörnchen.*

Squirrel, Flying. Sign *Squirrel, Fly;* and then with right hand flat, palm down, simulate flight down and up in a long sweep. This is merely a description, not an established sign.

Fr. *l'écureuil volant;* Ger. *das Flughörnchen.*

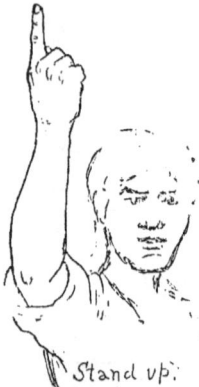

Stand (As a man). Make right V hand stand on left palm, the fingers representing legs. For an animal, use all four fingers of right. See *Alight.*

Fr. *se tenir debout;* Ger. *stehen.*

Stand up (As a tree or pole). Hold G hand, back forward, erect over shoulder. Compare *Tall* and *Up.*

Fr. *être debout;* Ger. *aufrecht stehen.*

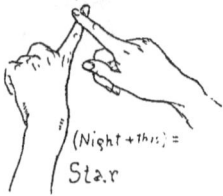

Star. Make the sign for *Night,* then cross the right G with left G near the tips and hold up high. Some flirt the index tip from behind the curved thumb in different directions up high, to mean twinkling. This is nearly like *Talk up high.*

Fr. *l'étoile;* Ger. *der Stern.*

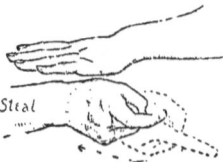

Stay. Sign *Stop, Wait,* and *Sit down.*

Fr. *rester;* Ger. *bleiben.*

Steal (To seize under cover). Hold out flat left hand pointing out, back up; reach right G hand under wrist, then draw it back with a sweep, curving it into a hook at the same time.

Fr. *voler;* Ger. *stehlen.*

Steamboat. Sign *Boat, Big, Fire,* holding the hand above the forehead for the last.

Fr. *le bateau à vapeur;* Ger. *das Dampfboot.*

Stingy. See *Mean.*

Stink. Sign *Bad Smell.*

Stir. Hold left as in C, back out, and make as though stirring its contents with a ladle held in right. Compare *Tea.*

Fr. *remuer;* Ger. *rühren.*

Stone. Sign *Rock* and *Lump.*

Stop. See *Halt.*

Stop or **Full Stop.** See *Period.*

Store or **Shop.** Sign *House* and *Trade.*

Fr. *le magasin, la boutique;* Ger. *der Laden.*

Storm. Sign *Strong* then *Wind,* shaking the fingers when opened and sometimes adding the sound of blowing.

Fr. *l'orage, la tempête;* Ger. *der Sturm.*

Story. See *History.*

Straight. See *Honest;* also *True.*

Stranger. Sign, *My, People, Not.* **Or** *Man, Different.*
Fr. *l'étranger;* Ger. *der Fremde.*

Stream. See *River.*

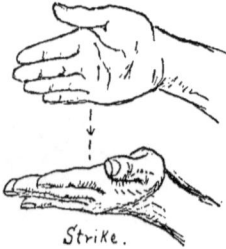

Strike. Hold out flat left, palm up; strike it with the
edge of flat right hand.   Compare *Chop* and *Kill.*
Fr. *frapper;* Ger. *schlagen.*

Strike.

Strike, To make a.   See *Count Coup.*

Striped. Hold out flat left with forearm level and draw
the right flat palm across it at different points on the
upper side.   Compare *Spotted.*
Fr. *rayé;* Ger. *gestreift.*

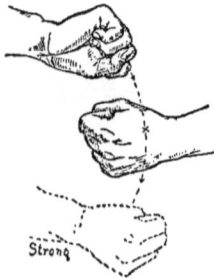

Striped.

Strong. With left fist, back out, grasp an imaginary
stick; then also grasp it four inches higher with right
fist, back in.   Give a strong outward twist to the right,
finishing with the right fist below the left and back
downward.   The left is not moved.   This means
physically strong in most cases, and few Indians distinguish this from *Very much;* which see. Compare *Little.*
Fr. *fort;* Ger. *stark.*

Strong

Subtract or **Take from.** Holding out the flat left, palm
toward you, with all the right fingers and thumb make
as though seizing something on the left palm; draw the
right to you and down.   (Sheeaka. Borrowed from the
Deaf.)   Compare *Place.*
Fr. *soustraire;* Ger. *abziehen.*

Subtract

Succeed. Sign *Push*, *Work*, and *Finish*. Compare *Fail*.

Fr. *réussir;* Ger. *Erfolg haben.*

Suffering. See *Sick.*

Sugar or **Sweet.** Rub the tongue with tips of extended index and second finger of right hand, then add *Good*. Compare *Salt* and *Bitter*.

Fr. *le sucre;* Ger. *der Zucker.*

Sullen or **Sulky.** Sign *Heart, Angry, Hide*. (Blackfoot.) See *Gloomy.*

Summer (Time of high grass). Sign *High, Grass*. Or sometimes sign *Hot* only.

Fr. *l'été;* Ger. *der Sommer.*

Sun. Form a circle with index and thumb of right hand; hold hand toward east and swing it in a great up-curve toward the west. In conversation, the circle is often incomplete.

Fr. *le soleil;* Ger. *die Sonne.*

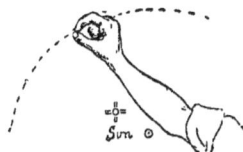

Sunday. Sign *Day* and *Medicine*.
Fr. *le dimanche;* Ger. *der Sonntag.*

Monday is *Day after Medicine Day*.
Fr. *le lundi;* Ger. *der Montag.*

Tuesday is *Two Days after Medicine Day*.
Fr. *le mardi;* Ger. *der Dienstag.*

Wednesday is *Three Days after Medicine Day*.
Fr. *le mercredi;* Ger. *der Mittwoch.*

Thursday is *Four Days after Medicine Day.*
Fr. *le jeudi;* Ger. *der Donnerstag.*

Friday is *Two Days before Medicine Day.*
Fr. *le vendredi;* Ger. *der Freitag.*

Saturday is *Little Medicine Day.*
Fr. *le samedi;* Ger. *der Sonnabend.*

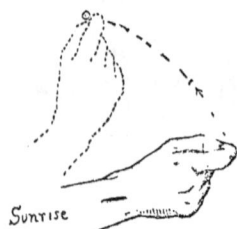

Sunrise. Make a ring of the right index and thumb, others closed, level, at full length toward the east; then raise it, chiefly by wrist action, so the ring is nearly at an angle of 45 degrees.
Fr. *le lever du soleil;* Ger. *der Sonnenaufgang.*

Sunset. The reverse of Sunrise; that is, hold the ring to the west and swing it down from 45 degrees to level or lower.
Fr. *le coucher du soleil;* Ger. *der Sonnenuntergang.*

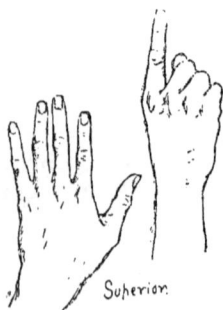

Superior or **Higher** (One above another). Hold both G fingers side by side, upright, one of them higher to represent the person or thing. When it is *One above many* use the left "5" hand instead of left G. See *Rising Man,* also *Chief.*
Fr. *supérieur;* Ger. *höher (stehend), vorgesetzt.*

Superlative. See *Comparative;* also *Very much.*

Supper. Sign *Night* and *Eat.*
Fr. *le souper;* Ger. *das Abendessen.*

Surprise, You surprise me. Hold flat hand on the mouth. This can be made stronger by using both hands. Sometimes also for emphasis precede this with a slap down of the flat right on the flat left, palm to palm. See *Astonishment*.

Fr. *étonner;* Ger. *überraschen*.

Surrender or **Give up.** (No weapons.) Hold both 5 hands, palms forward, at height of head. Sometimes one hand only.

Fr. *rendre, se rendre;* Ger. *sich ergeben*.

Surround or **Encircle.** Hold out both L hands at arm's length, then swing them together to form a level circle. See *Enclosure*.

Fr. *entourer;* Ger. *umgeben*.

Swap. See *Trade*.

Swear. See *Oath*.

Sweat. Draw the hooked right index across the brow as though wiping off sweat. See *Hot*.

Fr. *la sueur;* Ger. *der Schweisz*.

Sweat Lodge or **Turkish Bath.** Sign *Medicine* and *Wickey up*. (C) Or with 5 hands indicate the shape beginning at top, then sign *Open, Enter, Sweat*.

Fr. *le sudatorium, le bain turc;* Ger. *das Schwitz-bad*.

Sweet. See *Sugar*.

Sweetheart or **Lover.** Touch G to lips and add *Heart*. (Modern, but now in general use among Cheyenne boys.)

Sweetheart or **Lover.** Thrust the right L hand forward, level, back up and to right, turning slowly by wrist action so the thumb rises two or three inches up and down on the axis of the index. Compare *Courting* and *Glitter*.

Fr. *le bien-aimé;* Ger. *der Geliebte.*

Swift. See *Fast.*

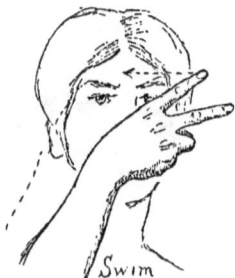

Swim (Probably to suggest a fish tail in action). That is, "Will you come in swimming?" Hold right hand as high as the face, back forward, all fingers closed except index and middle, these are spread like V and pointed to left. Move the hand a little to right. (Pop.)

Fr. *nager;* Ger. *schwimmen.*

Swimming. Sign *Water,* then strike out with hands as in swimming.

Fr. *nageant;* Ger. *schwimmend.*

Swoop. See *Dive.*

T

Table (Flat top, square shape). Swing flat hands, palms down, as in *Broad* turn sharply and draw both toward you; with a V hand on each side, strike down for legs, then sign *On* and *Eat.* A description, not an established sign.

Fr. *la table;* Ger. *der Tisch.*

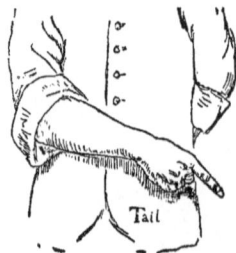

Tail. Right G hand, back up, at left side, pointing back and down.

Fr. *la queue;* Ger. *der Schwanz.*

Take or **Bring** (From some one else). Reach out the
G hand, hook the index and draw it toward you, in and
upward, as though pulling a string up and back. Compare *Steal.*

> Fr. *prendre (de quelqu'un);* Ger. *nehmen (von
> Jemandem).*

Take (From oneself). The same, but point index
toward body, hook it and draw away.

> Fr. *prendre (de soi-même);* Ger. *nehmen (von sich
> selber).*

Take from. See *Subtract.*

Talk or **Say** (A little talk). Hold right hand under
mouth, index and thumb tips together, pointing forward, and move slightly forward, snapping the index
from behind the thumb two or three times. Compare
Called, Telltale, Speech, Bark.

> Fr. *parler;* Ger. *sprechen.*

Talk, to me. Make the same gesture as above, but
point and draw the hand toward the cheek.

Tall or **High.** Move the flat right straight up to arm's
length, back out.

> Fr. *grand, haut;* Ger. *hoch, grosz.*

Tangle or **Tangled.** Revolve the 5 hands, in and out,
one about the other. Compare *Play.*

> Fr. *embrouiller;* Ger. *verwirren.*

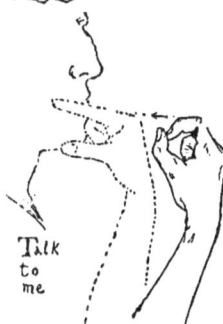

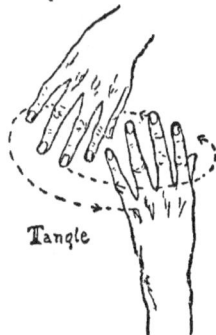

Taste. Join the first finger and thumb, rest their points on the lower lip and work the lips. Compare *Salt, Sugar, Sour,* and *Bitter.*

Fr. *goûter;* Ger. *schmecken.*

Taste bad (To taste and throw away). Sign *Taste* and *Bad.* (Seger.)

Fr. *avoir un goût mauvais;* Ger. *schlecht schmecken.*

Tattler. See *Telltale.*

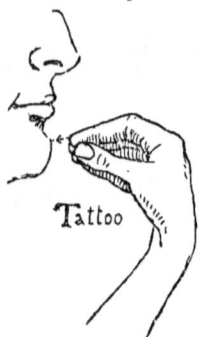

Tattoo. Tap the place with all five finger tips in a point.

Fr. *tatouer;* Ger. *tätowieren.*

Tea (Stirring it). Trace the rim of the left O hand with the thumb and finger tip of the right O hand, other fingers extended. (Sheeaka.) Compare *Stir.* Or sign *Leaf, Drink.*

Fr. *le thé;* Ger. *der Tee.*

Teacher. Sign *Writing* and *Chief.* See also *Guide.*

Fr. *le professeur;* Ger. *der Lehrer.*

Team. Sign *Horse, Two;* with L hand indicate *Halter* and add *Coat* for *Harness.*

Fr. *l'attelage;* Ger. *das Gespann.*

Teepee or **Lodge.** Cross the tips of the G fingers held high. In *Tent* they are not crossed.

Fr. *la loge (la hutte) des Indiens;* Ger. *die Indianer-hütte.*

Telegraph. On forefinger of left G hand, palm up, tap with crooked forefinger of right hand, as though telegraphing; then shoot it along left forefinger and on in line. (Crow sign, La Forge.)

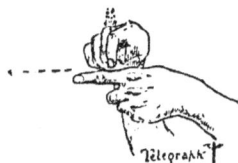
Telegraph

Telegraph. Sign *Wire*, then tap on it two or three times with right G and add *Talk*, shooting it far ahead.
Fr. *le télégraphe;* Ger. *der Telegraph.*

Telephone. Sign *Wire;* raise O hand to the ear like the receiver, then add *Talk.*
Fr. *le téléphone;* Ger. *der Fernsprecher.*

Tell about. See *Explain* and *Speech.*

Tell me. See *Talk* and *Speech.*

Tell-tale, Tattling, or **Tattle** (Magpie or Chatterer). Make a bill with forefinger and thumb; hold it at the mouth, pointing forward; open and shut it, but do not advance it. Note, it does not get anywhere; *Talk* does.
Fr. *le rapporteur;* Ger. *der Ausplauderer.*

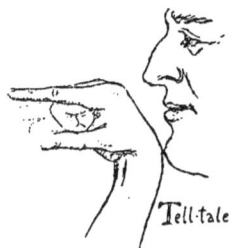
Tell-tale

Tenderfoot. Make signs for *Scout* and *Little.* (Scott.)
Fr. *le novice;* Ger. *der Neuling.*

Tense, of verbs, indicated by *Now*, *Time Back*, and *Future*, that is *Time Ahead.*

Tent. Like *Teepee*, but do not cross the fingers. Sometimes add *White Man.*
Fr. *la tente;* Ger. *das Zelt.*

Tent

Than. See *As.*

Thank you, or **Gratitude.** Raise the open right hand within a foot of the face, back down and to right; then carry it outward and downward toward person, bowing at same time (Pop). For this the Cheyennes use one hand as in *Gratitude*, which see. Sign *Give, Good.* (Blackfoot.)

> Fr. *merci, je vous remercie, la gratitude;* Ger. *ich danke dir* (or *Ihnen*), *die Dankbarkeit.*

That. Point with right G at the person or thing. Compare *This, There,* and *Yonder.*

> Fr. *ce ..là;* Ger. *der, jener.*

That or **Which,** relative pronoun (The one behind that). Left L hand pointing to right. Lay right forefinger on end of left, then turn it up and back to touch the thumb. (D)

> Fr. *qui, que, lequel;* Ger. *welcher.*

That place. Hold out right G, back up, at arm's length, face high, pointing forward; strike it down three or four times, chiefly by finger action. Compare *Then* and *Here.*

> Fr. *là;* Ger. *da, dort.*

Theatre. Sign *House, Look, Big, Many.* (Sheeaka.)

> Fr. *le théâtre;* Ger. *das Theater.*

Their. See *Possession.*

Then (That time). Swing right G, point first, forward and down in an 18-inch curve. Compare *Yonder* and *That place.*

> Fr. *alors;* Ger. *damals.*

There. Simply point with middle finger, others closed, hand held breast high. Compare *Challenge.*

Thick. Hold out flat left, back to left, place right underneath palm up; clasp left with it, rub right fingers and thumb tips back and forth on the middle of the left hand in long, slow rubs. Compare *Meat*, *Thin*, *Oil*, and *Bacon*.

Fr. *épais;* Ger. *dick.*

Thief. Sign for the person and add *Steal.* (C)

Fr. *le voleur;* Ger. *der Dieb.*

Thin (Not thick). Like *Thick*, but rub lower edge and little finger of left with tips of right thumb and index finger united, others closed. Usually the little finger side is the *Edge.* Compare *Bacon*, in which all of the fingers are used; also, *Oil*, *Thick*, and *Meat*.

Fr. *mince;* Ger. *dünn.*

Thin or **Poor in flesh** (Flesh clawed off). Bring both 5 hands, backs forward, in front of breast and touching it. Move each to its side, curving the fingers more.

Fr. *maigre;* Ger. *mager.*

Things. The 5 hands similarly pointing forward, backs up, waist high, one at each side of the body; swing once or twice in small circles nearly vertical, but a little forward in the upper part.

Fr. *les choses;* Ger. *die Dinge.*

Think (Drawn from the heart). Lay right G on the heart, back up, and swing it outward ten inches and a little up.

Fr. *penser;* Ger. *denken.*

Thinking. See *Consider.*

Thirst, Dry, or **Drouth.** Sign *Want* and *Drink.*
Fr. *la soif;* Ger. *der Durst.*

This

This. Hold flat left palm up near body and thrust right G down to it. For *These* repeat it several times.
Fr. *ce* . . . *ci;* Ger. *dieser.*

Thought. See *Idea.*

Thousand. Sign *Hundred* and then *Ten times.* See *Numbers.*
Fr. *mille;* Ger. *tausend.*

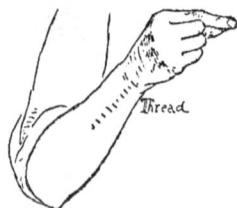
Thread

Thread. Rub thumb and index together, as though twisting a thread, and sign *Sew.* Compare *Powder.*
Fr. *le fil;* Ger. *der Faden.*

Threaten. Shake clenched fist toward the person.
Fr. *menacer;* Ger. *drohen.*

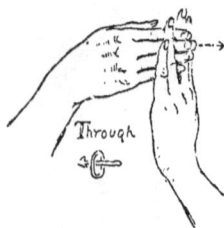
Through

Through. Push the right flat hand edgewise outward between the middle and third fingers of the left, which are held pointing upward. Compare *Between.*
Fr. *par, au travers de;* Ger. *durch.*

Thunder. Clap the hands loudly in front of face and add a rapid zigzag with the right G finger for *Lightning.*
Fr. *le tonnerre;* Ger. *der Donner, das Gewitter.*

Thy or **Thine.** Sign *You. Possess.*
Fr. *ton;* Ger. *dein.*

Ticket. Hold out H left, back up; lay the right G across it at the middle knuckles; add *Writing* and indicate *Railway, Theatre, Pawn*, etc., as needed.

Fr. *le billet;* Ger. *das Billett.*

Till. See *To.*

Time (Duration). Join the index finger and thumb of each hand at tips, other fingers closed; hold back of right hand to right, left to left, thumb tips touching; draw the hands apart, slowly and level. A little apart means *Little time;* a long way is *Long time,* etc. Sign *After, Little time,* for *Bye and bye.* So leaving the hands touching means *Now;* and *Time, Long, Behind* means *Long time ago.* A much-used sign. See *Ago* and *Past.*

Fr. *le temps;* Ger. *die Zeit.*

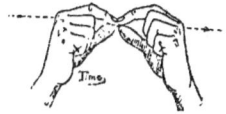

Time afterward, After a little time, Bye and Bye. Hold out the left G level, pointing forward, breast high; lay the right G on the back of the left, draw it back toward the wrist an inch. For *Time ahead,* sign *Time* and *Ahead,* that is, hold up left G and swing right G parallel and far ahead in the same line. Or sometimes for *Time ahead* or *Future* give the *Time* sign first given, but draw the right forefinger and thumb in an up and over curve far ahead, instead of to the right.

Fr. *plus tard;* Ger. *später.*

Time (Shadow around tree). Hold up left G, point right G at it and swing it around, finally touching it at top. (Sioux, Sheeaka.) This is used for exact point or date.

Fr. *l'époque;* Ger. *die Zeit, der Zeitpunkt.*

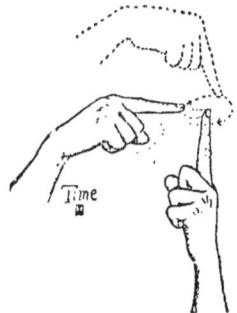

Hour. Indicate in the sky the position of the sun at that hour.

Hour (i. e., sixty minutes). Hold up the left hand with back toward you, index and thumb joining in a complete vertical circle; with right G on this as a pointer, move an inch and add *One*.

Fr. *l'heure;* Ger. *die Stunde.*

Minute or **Moment.** Hold the flat left hand pointed forward, thumb up; lay the right G on it like a pointer and move it the least bit. (Sheeaka.) The Cheyennes sign *Hour* and *Small.* In giving *Time* it is safest to do it in railway style; that is, 45 minutes after 4 would be 4 hours and 45 minutes; not a quarter before 5.

Fr. *la minute;* Ger. *die Minute.*

Second. Make the signs *Minute* and *Very small.* (Sheeaka.)

Fr. *la seconde;* Ger. *die Sekunde.*

Day or **Light** (The opening up, as contrasted with *Night*, the closing over). Hold out the level flat hands in the same horizontal plane, backs up, pointing to front, a few inches apart. Swing them upward apart to right and left, and then downward on a curve, turning the palms up; ending when the hands are about opposite shoulders and a little higher than at the start.

For the days of the week, see under *Sun.*

Sometimes *"one sun"* is *"one day."*

For *To-day* the sign for *Now* is first made.

Fr. *le jour;* Ger. *der Tag.*

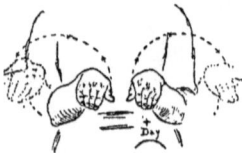

Time of Day, as morning, forenoon, noon, afternoon, etc. Point to the sun's position in the sky at the time. See *Midnight.*

Fr. *l'heure du jour;* Ger. *die Tageszeit.*

Week. Sign *Suns, Seven* (Sheeaka) or *One Medicine Day.* Compare *Sunday.*

Fr. *la semaine;* Ger. *die Woche.*

Month. Crescent or Horns in the sky. See illustration in M.

Fr. *le mois;* Ger. *der Monat.*

Seasons. *Spring, Short grass; Summer, High grass; Autumn, Falling leaf; Winter, Cold* or *Snow.*

Fr. *les saisons;* Ger. *die Jahreszeiten.*

Year. Sign *One Cold* (Cheyenne). Or better perhaps, though not general, sign *Snow,* then swing the right G in a circle to left, down and up on right, then again make *Snow,* meaning from snow around to snow. (Sheeaka.) Sign *One Snow* (Blackfoot).

Fr. *l'an, l'année;* Ger. *das Jahr.*

Tired or **Weary.** Hold out G hands, backs up, six inches apart, drop them and draw them to you a little. Sometimes used for *Quit.* See *Lazy.* Compare *Afraid.*

Fr. *fatigué;* Ger. *müde.*

To, Till, or **Until.** Hold the left G a little forward, palm to you; swing the right G upward till the forefingers meet at tip. (Sheeaka; probably borrowed from the Deaf.) Compare *Meet.*

Fr. *jusqu'à;* Ger. *bis.*

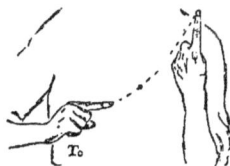

Tobacco (Ground in the palm). Hold flat left hand, back down, in front of body; grind on it the heel of closed right in small circles.

Fr. *le tabac;* Ger. *der Tabak.*

To-day. Sign *Day* and *Now.*

Fr. *aujourd'hui;* Ger. *heute.*

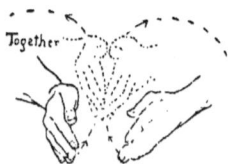

Together or **Gather** (Gathered together). Press the palms of the flat hands together two or three times, swinging them apart and together once or twice, so the tips describe six-inch vertical circles going down on the outside and up on the inside of each. Note this also means *Gather.* See also *With, Meet,* and *Heap.*

Tomahawk. Hold the flat right hand in the hollow of the horizontal left arm (C). Compare *Baby.* Or sign *Axe* and *Smoke.*

Fr. *le tomahawk, la hache de guerre des Indiens;*
Ger. *die Streitaxt der Indianer.*

To-morrow. Sign for *Another* and *Sunrise.* Compare *Yesterday.*

Fr. *demain;* Ger. *morgen.*

Too, Too much. Sign *Enough*, but raise both hands at arm's length above the head. (Scott.) Sometimes use *Heap.* See also *Excessive, Ahead,* and *Over.*

Fr. *trop;* Ger. *zu viel.*

Too or **Also.** Sign *Equal, With,* or **And**.

Fr. *aussi;* Ger. *auch.*

Touch. See *Feel.*

Town. Sign *House;* then, keeping the flat hands at same angle, swing them wide apart, keeping left near body, right far away. Add *White Man* if needed.

Fr. *la ville;* Ger. *die Stadt.*

Track or **Trail; i. e.,** to follow by *Trail.* Sign *Walk* and point to the ground with right G; move it forward in a sinuous course. Sometimes add *Look.*

Fr. *tracer;* Ger. *aufspüren.*

Trade, Exchange, Swap, Bargain, Buy, or **Sell.** Hold G hands pointing up, one at each shoulder; move them together in a down curve till wrists are crossed. See *Avoid.*

Fr. *trafiquer, troquer, faire le commerce;* Ger. *tauschen, handeln, Handel treiben.*

Trail (A road). See *Way.*

Train. See *Railroad.*

Trap or **To trap.** Make a large level circle of forefingers and thumbs for the trap; then snap these up together, index alongside index, thumb alongside thumb to indicate the closing.

Fr. *le piège, prendre au piège;* Ger. *die Falle, mit der Falle fangen.*

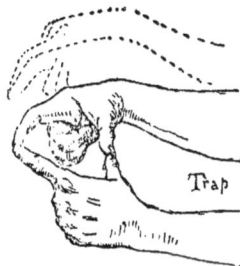

Travel. Hold out the 5 hands, palm to palm, but left a foot advanced and six inches higher, both of them vibrated up and down. This means *Keep on Going.* See *Work, Go,* and *Walk.*

Fr. *voyager;* Ger. *reisen.*

Treaty. Sign *Shake Hands* and *Write;* that is, write with right index on flat left palm.

Fr. *le traité;* Ger. *der Vertrag.*

Tree. Hold right forearm upright in front of shoulder, fingers straight, spread upward. For plural use both hands. For *Forest,* hold left outside and touching right; draw right near body and push left far away. See *Forest.*

Fr. *l'arbre;* Ger. *der Baum.*

Tribe or **Troop.** See *Bunch.*

Triumph. Wave one hand in circle above the head as swinging a flag. At a distance, wave a hat, coat, or blanket.

Fr. *le triomphe;* Ger. *der Triumph.*

Troop or **Tribe.** See *Bunch.*

Trot. Indicate the kind of animal, then with S hands, backs up, indicate movement of feet as in trotting. (C)

Fr. *le trot, trotter;* Ger. *der Trott, traben.*

Trouble or **Perplexity.** See *Consider, Doubt, Sorry,* and *Sorrow.*

Fr. *le trouble, la perplexité;* Ger. *die Sorge, die Bestürzung.*

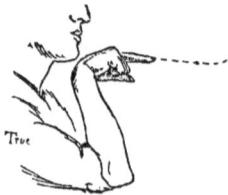

True, Truth, Certain, Sure, Straight (One straight trail). The G forefinger pointing straight forward under the chin, then moved forward with an upward curve. Compare *Honest.*

Fr. *vrai, la vérité;* Ger. *wahr, die Wahrheit.*

Try or **Attempt.**   Sign *Work* and *Begin.*
Fr. *essayer;* Ger. *versuchen.*

Turkey.   Sign *Bird;* then indicate *Beard* with compressed right hand under the chin, pointed down and
shaken.   (C)

Turkey.   Sign *Bird;* then hold right G at forehead, back
up, curved, pointed down, and drop it past the nose
down below chin.
Fr. *le dindon;* Ger. *der Truthahn, der Puter.*

Turkish Bath.   See *Sweat Lodge.*

Turn him down or **Thumbs down.**   This dates from the
Roman arena.   Right arm at full length, fingers closed,
thumb extended and pointing downward; meaning
"Kill him" or "it."   See *Knife.*

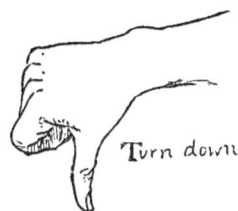
Turn down

Turn into.   See *Grow.*

Turn loose.   See *Free* and *Pardon.*

Turtle or **Tortoise.**   Hold right hand low, back up,
flat, but fingers bent back on palm; push it forward,
giving it by wrist action a serpentine course.   See *Fog.*
Fr. *la tortue;* Ger. *die Schildkröte.*

Turtle

Twice.   See *Once.*

Twinkle.   Sign *Star* and *Talk.*
Fr. *étinceler;* Ger. *funkeln.*

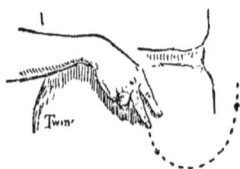

Twins. Lay V fingers, palm in, on abdomen and add *Born*.

    Fr. *les jumeaux;* Ger. *die Zwillinge.*

Typewrite. Sign *Write;* then with both hands strike here and there at keys.

    Fr. *écrire à la machine, dactylographier;* Ger. *mit der Schreibmaschine schreiben.*

U

Ugly. Sign *Face;* i. e., swing the right 5 hand in a circle near the face, and add *Bad.*

    Fr. *laid;* Ger. *häszlich.*

Unable. See *Can't.*

Uncertain. Sign *Perhaps, Know,* and *Not.*

    Fr. *incertain;* Ger. *unbestimmt.*

Uncle. Sign *Father* (or *Mother*) and *Brother.*

    Fr. *l'oncle;* Ger. *der Onkel.*

Undecided. Bow the head forward, resting the right G on the lips. See also *Thinking* and *If.*

    Fr. *en doute;* Ger. *unschlüssig.*

Under. See *Below.*

Understand. See *Know;* also, *Keep.*

Unfair. See *Excessive.*

United. Sign *Alliance* or *With.*

    Fr. *uni;* Ger. *vereinigt.*

United States of America. There is no well-established sign, but the Indian of a hundred years ago referred to the United States as the " Thirteen Fires," i. e., Council Fires. So that *Thirteen* and *Fires* would answer. The Blackfeet indicate the Boundary Line running east and west, then all south of it.

So, also, for the individual States, in the absence of established signs, we may use their nicknames. These, however, are mere suggestions.

Fr. *les États-Unis d'Amérique;* Ger. *die Vereinigten Staaten von Nordamerika.*

Alabama (Cotton State). *Country* and *Cotton.* The latter by pointing to something by cotton.

Arizona (Cactus State). *Country, Trees,* and *Sharp,* as in *Porcupine.*

Arkansas (Bear State). *Country* and *Bear Black,* to distinguish from *Russia.*

California (Golden State). *Country* and *Gold;* for gold pinch the lobe of the ear, or point to any gold or yellow thing in sight; if it is near, take an imaginary pinch of it, to exclude the object that is made of it.

Colorado (Centennial State). *Country* and 100 *Years* or *Snows.*

Connecticut (Nutmeg State). *Country, Fruit,* and *Hard.*

United States—_Continued_

Dakota, North (Flickertail State). _Country_ and holding G hand, palm up, wag the index to express the tail of the Flickertail gopher.

Dakota, South (Coyote State). _Country_ and _Small Wolf._

Delaware (Diamond State). _Country_ and, for _Diamond_, place the right thumb and index on an imaginary stone on ring finger of left; then add _Twinkle._

Florida (Peninsular State). _Country_ and _Water._ The half into the left C hand, held level and facing the right, lay the right N fingers, backs up.

Georgia (Cracker State). _Country, Corn_, and _Grind_, as in _Coffee._ The Crackers were so called because of their cracked corn diet.

Idaho (Land of the Shoshoni). _Country_ and _Snake._

Illinois (Prairie State). _Country_ and _Prairie._

Indiana (Hoosier State). _Country_ and _Who is here ?_

Iowa (Hawkeye State). _Country, Hawk_, and _Eye._

Kansas (Sunflower State). _Country, Flower_, and _Sun._

Kentucky (Blue Grass State). _Country, Grass_, and _Blue._

Louisiana (Pelican State). _Country, Bird, Long bill;_ and with index show outline of the pouch.

United States—*Continued*

Maine (Pine Tree State). *Country* and *Tree.*

Maryland (Terrapin State). *Country* and *Turtle.*

Massachusetts (Bay State). *Country* and *Bay.*

Michigan (Wolverine State). *Country* and *Wolverine* or *Bushy-tailed Bear.* Indicate *Bear*, then *Tail* and *Bushy.*

Minnesota (Gopher State). *Country* and *Small Striped Animal.* With compressed right hand, back up, indicate a small animal; then draw the fingers of left 4 hand along it for stripes.

Mississippi (Bayou State). *Country, Bay,* and *Trees.*

Missouri (Banner State). *Country* and *Flag.* Or else, *"Show me State,"* thus, with flat right hand shade right eye, knit brows, look here and there.

Montana (Land of the Blackfeet.) *Country* and *Blackfeet.*

Nebraska (Shallow River). *Country, River, Broad,* and *Low.* Or *Pawneeland, Country,* and *Wolf,* which is the Pawnee sign.

Nevada (Silver State). Sign *Country, Metal,* and *White;* bring right hand hollow under left and shake as though jingling coins.

New Hampshire (Granite State). *Country* and signs for *Hard* and *Very.*

United States—*Continued*

New Jersey (Blue State). *Country, Color,* and *Blue.*

New Mexico (Sunshine State). Make sign for *Country* and *Sun.*

New York (Empire State). *Country* and *Crowned,* which is indicated by placing both 5 hands on the sides of the head like the feathers in a war-bonnet

North Carolina (Tar Heel State). *Country, Heel,* and *Black.*

Ohio (Buckeye State). *Country, Deer,* and *Eye.*

Oklahoma (Sooners State). *Country* and *Soon,* or else *Country* and *Kiowa.*

Oregon (Beaver State). *Country* and *Beaver.*

Pennsylvania (Keystone State). *Country* and *Keystone,* thus: Hold up right hand, fingers out, pointing up, a space between the ring and middle fingers only; hold all fingers of left hand extended and join at tips to form a wedge; put this wedge in the opening between the fingers of the right hand.

Rhode Island (Little State). *Country* and *Very Small.*

South Carolina (Palmetto State). *Country* and *Leaf;* then indicate the shape of leaf with flat hand and fingers spread to their utmost.

Tennessee (Long Rifles). *Country, Rifle,* and *Long.*

United States—*Continued*

Texas (Lone Star State). *Country,* and *Star, Alone.*

Utah (*Mormon* or *Many Wives State*). *Country, Mates, Many.*

Vermont (Green Mountain State). *Country, Mountain, Color,* and *Grass.*

Virginia (Tobacco State). *Country* and *Tobacco.*

Washington (Evergreen State). *Country, Green,* and *Always.*

West Virginia (Panhandle State). *Country* and *Cook by frying;* then hold out flat spread left hand, palm up, and grasp the wrist with the right.

Wisconsin (Badger State). *Country* and *Badger.*

Wyoming (Land of Cheyennes). *Country* and *Cheyennes* or *Finger Choppers.*

Unjust. Sign *Honest* and *Not.* See *Excessive.*
Fr. *injuste;* Ger. *ungerecht.*

Unless or **Except.** See *But.*

Unlucky. Sign *Medicine* and *Bad.*
Fr. *malheureux;* Ger. *unglücklich.*

Until. See *To.*

Unwise. See *Foolish.*

Up or **Upward.** Point up with flat hand or else the right G, raising the same about head high. The index means specifically "that thing up there"; whereas the flat hand means the abstract idea "up." Compare *Tall* and *Stand*.

Fr. *en haut, haut;* Ger. *auf, hinauf, aufwärts.*

That Up There

Us. See *We.*

V

Vain. Sign *Beautiful;* then draw head and body back with an arrogant look. (Blackfoot.) Sign *Paint, Dress, Good, Love.* (C) See *Pride.*

Fr. *vain;* Ger. *eitel.*

Valise. Hold out both arms, level, low, parallel; hands flat, but bent at right angles to arms; palms to you, tips touching. Add *Clothes* and *Enter* twice or three times.

Fr. *la valise;* Ger. *der Handkoffer.*

Very Much, Heap Much, Strong, Brave, Superlative. Hold left S hand, back out, in front of body; forearm horizontal and pointing to right and front; bring the ditto right hand some six inches above and a little in front of left hand; strike downward with right hand, mostly by elbow action, the second joints of right hand passing close to and about on a line with knuckles of left hand. This is very like *Strong* and seems in some renditions to be the same.

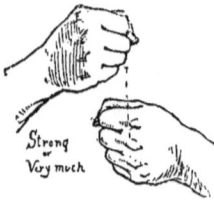

It is also used for *Very, Very Much,* and for a certain strong English adjective that is omitted from the Sunday School readers. Compare *Strong.*

Fr. *beaucoup, très;* Ger. *sehr, viel.*

Vessel. See *Bowl*.

Victor. See *Kill* and *Triumph*.

Vigilant or **Watchful.** Sign *Look,* in different directions, and *All the time.*
 Fr. *vigilant;* Ger. *wachsam.*

Village (Many Lodges). Sign *Lodges* or *Teepees* and *Many.*
 Fr. *le village;* Ger. *das Dorf.*

Vine. Sign *Tree* with left; then with right G trace the vine's course about it.
 Fr. *la vigne;* Ger. *die Ranke.*

Volley. See *Fire.*

Vomit. Hold compressed right hand back up below chin, pointed to left and upward, move it upward forward and down, point first, once or twice.
 Fr. *vomir;* Ger. *(sich) brechen, sich übergeben.*

Vomit

W

Wager. See *Bet.*

Wagon. With index and thumb of each hand make two vertical circles, hands held backs up, a foot apart and shoulder high; by wrist action rotate these circles and move them forward a little.
 Fr. *la voiture;* Ger. *der Wagen.*

Wagon

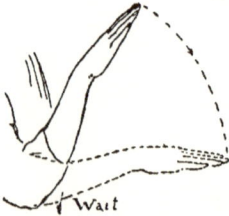
Wait

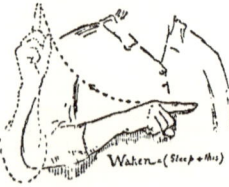
Waken - (Sleep + this)

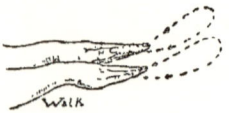
Walk

Walk (animal)

Wall

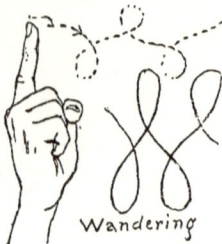
Wandering

Wait (Stop here). Flat hand up, palm forward; then gently bent forward to nearly level, palm down. Compare *Halt*.

    Fr. *attendez!;* Ger. *warten!*

Waken. Sign *Sleep* and *Arise* (That is, lay the right G horizontally on breast and swing it out upright a foot away, back to right). Or sign *Sleep* and *Done*, i. e., *Ended*.

    Fr. *réveiller, s'éveiller;* Ger. *wecken, erwachen.*

Walk or **March.** (For a person.) (Shape and movement of feet.) Hold out the flat hands, backs up, a few inches apart, pointing to front; swing the right forward, upward, and downward to same height as when starting; then the left ditto; draw the right hand to rear. Repeat these motions.

Walk (For an animal). With the S hands, backs up, go through the same as above.

    Fr. *marcher;* Ger. *gehen.*

Wall or **Fence.** Push flat hands straight forward, points up, palms in; then, when well out, turn palms toward you and swing together. Compare *Valise* and *Box*.

    Fr. *le mur;* Ger. *die Mauer, das Gitter.*

Wandering. Hold up right G, palm forward; advance it with excessive sweeping zigzags from side to side, forming loops. These loops are 18 inches across; their plan, seen from above, is in the lower scroll. Compare *Alive* and *White-tail Deer*.

    Fr. *errant;* Ger. *wandernd.*

Want (To), **Crave, Desire, Wish, Anxious for, Will** (Thirsty for). Hold the right hand, back to right, in front of and near chin; form a vertical incomplete circle with G index and thumb. Swing the hand down past the mouth, outward and upward, turning it at the finish so that the little finger is as high as the index.
  Fr. *désirer;* Ger. *wünschen.*

Want

Wapiti. See *Elk.*

War. See *Fight.*

War-cry. See *Battle-cry.*

Warm, To (One's hands). Hold out both flat hands, side by side, breast high, backs up, slightly curved as though over a fire; then rub them together. (Blackfoot.)

Warm
(then rubbed together)

Warm, I am warm. Draw the 5 hands down over breast, then hold out together, palms down, pointing forward. See also *Hot.*
  Fr. *chaud;* Ger. *warm.*

Warning, Beware, Caution, or **Look out.** Raise right index, rest closed; turn hand so as to have right eye, index, and the person in line; at the same time, shake the head a little. (Sheeaka.)
  Fr. *l'avertissement, prenez garde!;* Ger. *die Warnung, Vorsicht!*

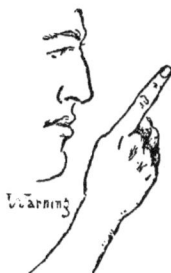

Warning

Warpath, To go to War (The thumb chasing the index). With its index at a right angle with the palm and pointing toward the left, other fingers closed, its thumb ex-

Warpath

tended and upright near base of the index, back of hand
outward; move the right hand forward with a long downward then upward curve in front of the right shoulder.

Fr. *le chemin de guerre;* Ger. *der Kriegspfad.*

Washing Clothes. Rub with both fists as on a rubbing
board. Old gesture was to rub the right fist circularly,
palm down, on the left, palm up.

Fr. *laver;* Ger. *waschen.*

Washington. Sign *White Man, All, Chief, High.* (Sheeaka.)

Watch (A timepiece). Form a horizontal circle with
thumb and index of left hand, others closed; tap around
on this with the tip of right G.

Fr. *la montre;* Ger. *die Taschenuhr.*

Watch. See *Look.*

Water, Running. See *River.*

Water (In general). Bring the slightly cupped right
palm from forward nearly level to near the chin. Compare *Drink* and *Speech.*

Fr. *l'eau;* Ger. *das Wasser.*

Waterfall. See *Fall of Water.*

**Way, Manner, Road, Method, Custom, Plan, Trail,
Law,** etc. Both hands flat, palms up, but thumb sides
higher, side by side, pointing front, breast high, alternately advanced and withdrawn. Much used among

Indians and sometimes equivalent to *-ship* or *-ness*, as in *Kingship* or *Goodness*. Compare *Walk* and *Road*.

>Fr. *le chemin, la manière;* Ger. *der Weg, die Art und Weise.*

We, Us, and **Our** (Me all). Touch one's chest with right thumb, fingers closed, then add *All.* (Sheeaka.) The Cheyennes sign *Me, All,* and *Together.*

>Fr. *nous, notre;* Ger. *wir, unser.*

Weak. Swing the bent arms slowly from side to side as in walking weakly. Or *Strong,* and *No.* See *Tired* and *Lazy.*

>Fr. *faible;* Ger. *schwach.*

Weary. See *Tired.*

Weasel. With right G curved, back up, imitate bounding; then indicate *Tail* and *Half, Black.* (Sheeaka.)

>Fr. *la belette;* Ger. *das Wiesel.*

Week. See *Time* and *Sun.*

Weep. See *Cry.*

Weigh (Metaphorically). See *Consider.*

Welcome. Sign *Come* and *Good.*

>Fr. *bienvenu;* Ger. *willkommen.*

Well, Good Health (Body strong). Flat hands one on each side of the body; draw them away, clench them and move them down with a jerk. (Sheeaka.) The Cheyennes sign *All, Body (as above), Hard.* Compare *Sick* and *Lungs.*

>Fr. *bien portant, la bonne sante;* Ger. *wohl, die Gesundheit.*

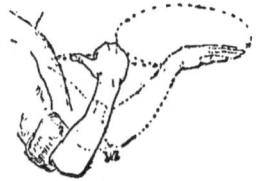

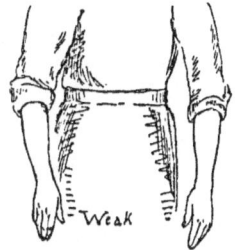

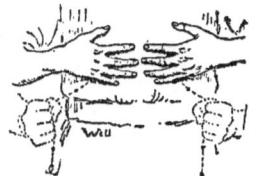

What?   See *Question.*

When?   See *Question.*

Whence?   See *Question.*

Where?   See *Question.*

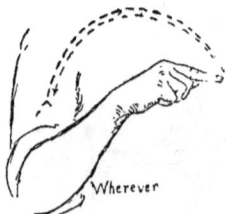
Wherever

Wherever (All places).   Hold right G out, back up, pointing toward horizon.   Swing slowly in a half-circle up and over to left, then back to right; repeat.

Fr. *en quelque lieu que ce soit;* Ger. *wo auch nur.*

Whether.   See *If.*

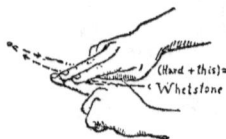
(Hard + this) = Whetstone

Whetstone.   Sign *Hard*, then hold out left N hand and rub right N hand on it, with long, sweeping strokes.

Fr. *la pierre à aiguiser;* Ger. *der Wetzstein.*

Which?   See *Question.*

Which.   See *Who.*

While, After a.   See *Bye and bye.*

Every little While

While, Every Little While.   Hold out left G, pointing to right; with left G tap on it several times, each time moving the right nearer the base of left G.   See, *All the time.*   Compare *Peas* and *Buy.*

Fr. *à chaque moment;* Ger. *jeden Augenblick.*

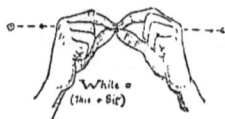
While (This + Sit)

While, Meanwhile, or During.   Sign *Time*, slowly moving hands until about six inches apart.   Some shake the right hand in drawing it back.   Or sign *Time, Sit.* Compare *Time, Sometimes, Soon.*

Fr. *pendant;* Ger. *während.*

Whirlwind. See *Cyclone*.

Whiskey. Sign *Fire* and *Water*, or *Crazy, Water*. Although some Cheyennes call beer fire-water, because of the explosion and froth.

  Fr. *le whiskey, l'eau-de-vie;* Ger. *der Whisky, der Branntwein.*

Whisper, or Speak Privately. Hold up flat right hand, thumb at one side of the mouth, and incline the head. Or sign *Hide* and *Talk*.

  Fr. *chuchoter;* Ger. *flüstern.*

White (Color). See *Colors*.

White or White Man (Hat or Cap wearers). Hold right G hand, back up and to right, in front of, close to, and a little to left of face, pointing to left; draw the hand to right, index finger passing horizontally in front of eyes. Sometimes add *Man*.

  Fr. *l'homme blanc;* Ger. *der Weisze.*

Whither? See *Question*.

Who or Which (This equals that). Hold the two G fingers side by side on left; then, keeping the relative positions, swing them to the right. (W. C. Roe.) Probably modern. This is the same as *As;* the context alone shows which is meant.

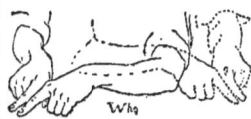

Why? See *Question*.

Wicky-up. Swing the curved G fingers together in dome shape, left tip resting on right tip; then change to curved 4 hands and swing down and apart on a curve. (C)

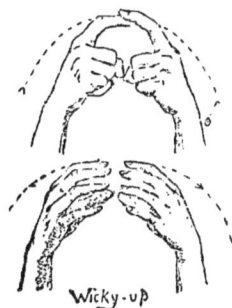

Wide. See *Broad.*

Wife. Make signs for *Female*, then *Marry.* Usually sign *My* (or *His*) *Woman.*
    Fr. *la femme;* Ger. *die Frau, die Gattin.*

Wild. Sign *Bad;* then push both 5 hands forward, thumbs up, six inches apart, switching them simultaneously from side to side. Sometimes use *Crazy* or *Free.*

Wild (Wild animal). Sign *Look* backward, then add *Go* quickly. Sometimes use *Free.*
    Fr. *sauvage;* Ger. *wild.*

Will. See *Want.*

Will or **Shall** (Futurity). Hold the right open flat hand, palm to left, pointing straight out and elevated near ear. Push it straight forward and upward the length of the arm. Sometimes sign *Time Ahead* or *Far Ahead.* Compare *Past* and *Future.*
    Fr. *le futur exprimé par l'inflexion du verbe;* Ger. *werden, wollen.*

Win or **Overcome.** Make sign for *Kill;* and indicate in what way. Thus, a person winning at gambling "Kills" the other in that way.
    Fr. *gagner, vaincre;* Ger. *gewinnen, siegen.*

Wind. Hold up the 5 hands, shoulder high, backs up, a few inches apart, pointed forward and hands moved with a tremulous motion in direction of wind. If

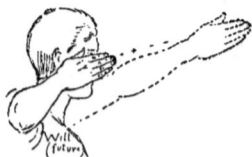

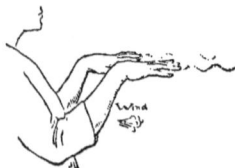

strong wind, preface this with *Fire-off* or *Charge*. Or
Sign *Forward*, using both hands. See *Rumor* and *Storm*.
    Fr. *le vent;* Ger. *der Wind.*

Wing. Hold out left arm level, bent; sweep flat right
5 hand over it from shoulder down. Or, sometimes
flap one hand as in *Bird*. Compare *Hair*.
    Fr. *l'aile;* Ger. *der Flügel.*

Winter (Cold time). Hold closed hands in front of
body, forearms about vertical, hands several inches
apart; give a shivering, tremulous motion to hands;
Sometimes, and particularly with Northern Indians.
the sign for *Snow* is made. Add *Time*, if there is any
doubt.
    Fr. *l'hiver;* Ger. *der Winter.*

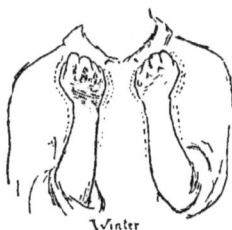

Wipe Out, Excuse, or **Forgive** (To wipe it off). Hold
left hand flat, palm up; smartly brush it with finger
tips of right flat hand, from wrist to fingers and beyond.
Compare *Exterminate* and *Color*. For the stronger
idea, see *Pardon*.
    Fr. *excuser;* Ger. *verzeihen.*

Wire. Hold right G back nearly up, pointing to left,
about face high, near left shoulder; draw it across level
to right shoulder. Compare *Creek* and *Rope*.
    Fr. *le fil de métal;* Ger. *der Draht.*

Wise, Wisdom (Heart and head good). Sign *Heart*,
then touch forehead and sign *Good*. (C) Or, *Heap*,
Understand. Sometimes use *Cunning*.
    Fr. *sage, la sagesse;* Ger. *klug, die Weisheit.*

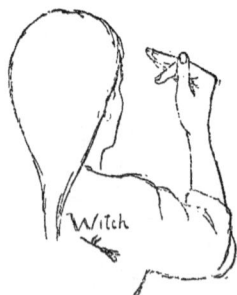

Wish. See *Want.*

Witch. Cross the upright thumb of right hand **on the** middle of the index, which is a little bent, other fingers straight, held so one can sight over the thumb at the person meant. (Ruggles.) Also used for *Distrust* and *Discredited.* Widely established in the mountains.

  Fr. *la sorcière;* Ger. *die Hexe.*

With or **Together.** Hold out the flat left, fingers forward, level, back to left; and lay the side of the right G finger, pointed forward, against the centre of the left palm. Sometimes means *Add.* See *Together* and *Beside.*

  Fr. *avec, ensemble;* Ger. *mit, zusammen.*

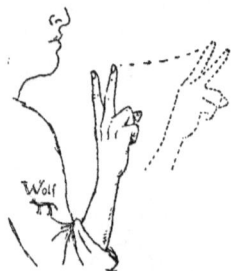

Within or **Inside.** See *In.*

Wolf. Hold the right V hand, palm forward, near right shoulder, pointing straight upward; move it a little forward and up. See *Scout.*

  Fr. *le loup;* Ger. *der Wolf.*

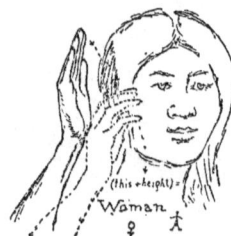

Wolverine. Sign *Bear, Small,* and indicate bushy tail. This is merely a description, not an established sign.

  Fr. *le carcajou, le volverenne;* Ger. *der braune Vielfrasz.*

Woman. Make the sign for *Female;* sometimes also indicate height. Compare *Comb.*

  Fr. *la femme;* Ger. *die Frau.*

Wonderful. See *Glow.*

Wood or **Timber.** Sign *Tree,* then indicate size and shape. Add *Chop* and throw forward (i. e., onto fire).

  Fr. *le bois;* Ger. *das Holz.*

Woodchuck or **Groundhog.** With compressed right, back up, pushed forward, rolling from side to side, indicate the animal, its *Size;* then, with left H hand near upper lip and right H hand near lower, show the action of the front teeth, which differ from those of other rodents its equal in size in being *White.* This is not an established sign, but suggested as a description.

Fr. *la grande marmotte d'Amérique;* Ger. *das virginische Murmeltier.*

Woodcraft Boy. The Y hand; this denotes the Horned Shield, the symbol of the Order. (Not Indian.)

Woodcraft Girl. Make the sign of *Sun* on the heart and then raise it to the zenith. (Not Indian.)

Woodpecker. Sign *Bird,* then hold left arm upright for *Tree* and on this place the partly compressed right; make it hop up and tap the left palm with curved right G.

Fr. *le pic, le pivert, l'épeiche;* Ger. *der Specht.*

Word (One piece of talk). Make C and lay it on the mouth, then swing it forward and a little down. (A very doubtful sign given by Sheeaka.)

Fr. *le mot;* Ger. *das Wort.*

Word of Honor. See *Cross the heart.* (Pop.)

Work, Doing, Make, or **Act.** Hold the flat hands four inches apart, palm to palm, level, left a little ahead; push them forward a little, simultaneously, and, at the same time, swing the points upward and downward briskly by wrist action, so that the finger points follow

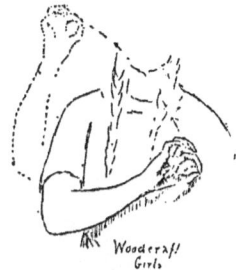

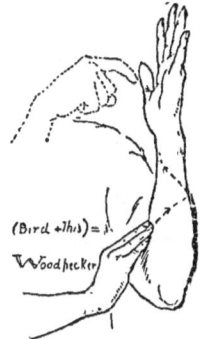

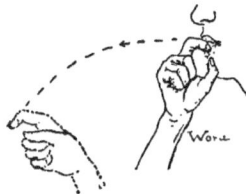

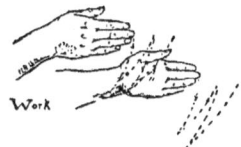

the lines shown in the cut. To complete the sign, the action should be repeated at the left side with the hands reversed with regard to each other; but usually the first only is given. Possibly refers to fleshing a hide, which was about the hardest work in an Indian camp. For *Work hard,* use both A fists instead of flat hands.

Fr. *travailler;* Ger. *arbeiten.*

World. See *Earth.*

Wound (The course of arrow or bullet). Swing the right G hand toward the body, point first, back of hand to left and front, so that the tip just grazes the surface of the body and passes on, as though glancing off. Compare *Ache.*

Fr. *la blessure;* Ger. *verwunden.*

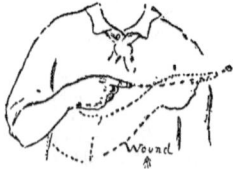

Wrap. Bring the slightly compressed hands, backs outward, in front of body, backs of fingers of right hand resting against inner surface of left, index fingers about horizontal; rotate the hands around each other.

Fr. *envelopper;* Ger. *einwickeln.*

Wrestle. Cross the wrists about two feet in front of the face, hands clenched as in *Prisoner;* then wriggle them from side to side.

Fr. *lutter;* Ger. *ringen, kämpfen.*

Wring. Hold the left A hand palm up and the right A hand back up, index of each touching thumb of the other as though holding a rope; then twist by wrist action till the position of each hand is reversed.

Fr. *tordre;* Ger. *ringen.*

Wrinkle. Wrinkle the skin of forehead and pinch same; also draw lines on face with finger tip. Sometimes omit last.

Fr. *la ride, le pli;* Ger. *die Runzel, die Falte.*

Write or **Writing.** With an imaginary pencil in right fingers, write on left palm; or in the air simply.

This last preceded by *Come* is commonly used in European hotels for *"Give me my bill."*

Fr. *écrire;* Ger. *schreiben.*

Wrong. Sign *Honest* and *Not;* or else *Bad.* Sometimes use *Different* and *Bad.* See *Crooked.*

Fr. *tort;* Ger. *unrecht.*

Y

Year. See *Time.*

Yell, Holla, or **Cry Out.** Place the G hand on the mouth, jerking it much upward and a little forward to show the sound coming out of the mouth and going far. Compare *Called.*

Fr. *holá! hé!* Ger. *holla!; hallo schreien.*

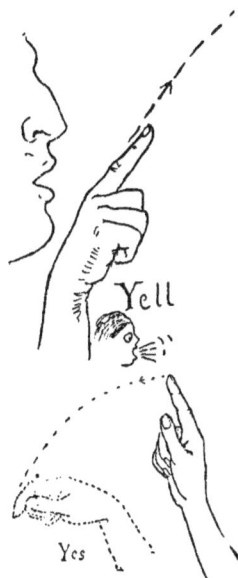

Yes (Bowing of the head and body). Hold right hand upright near shoulder, index and thumb only extended, others closed; move it slightly to the left and a foot downward, at the same time closing the index over the thumb. Or simply nod.

Fr. *oui;* Ger. *ja.*

Yesterday

Yesterday (Beyond the night). Sign *Night;* then, holding left in position, swing the right upward and to right on a curve, finishing at height of left, palm up, i. e., *Beyond.* Or, sign *Before* and *Day.* Or, *One; Sleep, Behind.*

Fr. *hier;* Ger. *gestern.*

Yonder

Yonder, Over yonder. Point as in *There,* or with G, then swing the finger up over and down farther ahead. Compare *Far.*

Fr. *là-bas;* Ger. *drüben, dort.*

You (M)

You or **Thou.** Singular, point at the person; for plural, point, then add *All;* that is, swing the finger in a horizontal circle (You, all).

Fr. *vous;* Ger. *Sie.*

Young (A sprout). Hold the hand as in *Grow;* then lower it emphatically a foot. Sometimes use *Old* and *Not.*

Fr. *jeune;* Ger. *jung.*

Younger. Sign *Born* and *After.*

Fr. *plus jeune, cadet;* Ger. *jünger.*

Your. See *Possession.*

APPENDIX

FOOTBALL SIGNALS
Code of Signals Used to Indicate Various Fouls

Signals.	Fouls.
Grasping of wrist	Holding
Shaking fists	Unnecessary Roughness
Crossed legs	Tripping
Sifting of hands	Illegally in motion
Hands on Hips	Off-side
Arm aloft	Refusal of Penalty
Arms extended sidewise	Incompleted F. Pass
Arms folded	Interlocked interference
Both arms aloft	Score
Military Salute	Loose-ball foul

NOTE—These signals will be given to the press-stand by the referee from behind the offensive team.

FRANK BIRCH, Referee.

BOOKS BY ERNEST THOMPSON SETON

WILD ANIMALS I HAVE KNOWN, 1898
The stories of Lobo, Silverspot, Molly Cottontail, Bingo, Vixen, The Pacing Mustang, Wully and Redruff. Price, $2.00. (Scribners.)

THE TRAIL OF THE SANDHILL STAG, 1899
The story of a long hunt that ended without a tragedy. Price, $1.50. (Scribners.)

BIOGRAPHY OF A GRIZZLY, 1900
The story of old Wahb from cubhood to the scene in Death Gulch. Price, $1.50. (Century Company.)

LOBO, RAG AND VIXEN, 1900
This is a school edition of number one, with some of the stories and many of the pictures left out. Price, 50c. net. (Scribners.)

THE WILD ANIMAL PLAY, 1900
A musical play in which the parts of Lobo, Wahb, Vixen, etc., are taken by boys and girls. Price, 50c. (Doubleday, Page & Co.)

THE LIVES OF THE HUNTED, 1901
The stories of Krag, Randy, Johnny Bear, The Mother Teal, Chink, The Kangaroo Rat, and Tito, the Coyote. Price, $1.75 net. (Scribners.)

PICTURES OF WILD ANIMALS, 1901
Twelve large pictures for framing (no text), viz., Krag, Lobo, Tito Cub, Kangaroo Rat, Grizzly, Buffalo, Bear Family, Johnny Bear, Sandhill Stag, Coon Family, Courtaut the Wolf, Tito and her family. Price, $6.00. (Scribners.)

KRAG AND JOHNNY BEAR, 1902
This is a school edition of Lives of the Hunted with some of the stories and many of the pictures left out. Price, 50c. net. (Scribners.)

TWO LITTLE SAVAGES, 1903
A book of adventure and woodcraft and camping out for boys, telling how to make bows, arrows, moccasins, costumes, teepee, warbonnet, etc., and how to make a fire with rubbing sticks, read Indian signs, etc. Price, $1.75 net. (Doubleday, Page & Co.)

MONARCH, THE BIG BEAR OF TALLAC, 1904
The story of a big California grizzly that is living yet. Price, $1.25 net. (Scribners.)

ANIMAL HEROES, 1905
The stories of a Slum Cat, a Homing Pigeon, The Wolf That Won, A Lynx, A Jackrabbit, A Bull-terrier, The Winnipeg Wolf, and a White Reindeer. Price, $1.75 net. (Scribners.)

BIRCH-BARK ROLL, 1906
The Manual of the Woodcraft Indians, first edition, 1902. (Doubleday, Page & Co.)

WOODMYTH AND FABLE, 1905
A collection of fables, woodland verses, and camp stories. Price, $1.25 net. (Century Company.)

THE NATURAL HISTORY OF THE TEN COMMANDMENTS, 1907
Showing the Ten Commandments to be fundamental laws of all creation. 78 pages. Price, 50c. net. (Scribners.)

THE BIOGRAPHY OF A SILVER FOX, 1909
or Domino Reynard of Goldur Town, with 100 illustrations by the author. 209 pages. Price, $1.50 net.
A companion volume to the Biography of a Grizzly. (Century Company.)

LIFE HISTORIES OF NORTHERN ANIMALS, 1909
In two sumptuous quarto volumes with 68 maps and 560 drawings by the author. Pages 1,267. Price, $18.00 net.
Said by Roosevelt, Allen, Chapman, and Hornaday to be the best work ever written on the Life Histories of American Animals. (Scribners.)

BOY SCOUTS OF AMERICA, 1910
A handbook of Woodcraft, Scouting, and Life Craft including the Birch-Bark Roll. 192 pages. Price, 50c. Out of print. (Doubleday, Page & Co.)

ROLF IN THE WOODS, 1911
The Adventures of a Boy Scout with Indian Quonab and little dog Skookum. Over 200 drawings by the author. Price, $1.75 net. (Doubleday, Page & Co.)

THE ARCTIC PRAIRIES, 1911
A canoe journey of 2,000 miles in search of the Caribou. 415 pages with many maps, photographs, and illustrations by the author. Price, $1.75 net. (Scribners.)

THE BOOK OF WOODCRAFT AND INDIAN LORE, 1912
with over 500 drawings by the author. Price, $1.75 net. (Doubleday, Page & Co.)

THE FORESTER'S MANUAL, 1912
One hundred of the best-known forest trees of eastern North America, with 100 maps and more than 200 drawings. Price, $1.00 in cloth, 50c. in paper. (Doubleday, Page & Co.)

WILD ANIMALS AT HOME, 1913

with over 150 sketches and photographs by the author. 226 pages. Price, $1.75 net. In this Mr. Seton gives for the first time his personal adventures in studying wild animals. (Doubleday, Page & Co.)

MANUAL OF THE WOODCRAFT INDIANS, 1915

The fourteenth Birch-Bark Roll. 100 pages. 25c. paper, 75c. cloth. (Doubleday, Page & Co.)

WILD ANIMAL WAYS, 1916

More animal stories introducing a host of new four-footed friends, with 200 illustrations by the author. Net, $1.50. (Doubleday, Page & Co.)

WOODCRAFT MANUAL FOR BOYS, 1917

A handbook of Woodcraft and outdoor life for members of the Woodcraft League. 440 pp. 700 ills. Price, 50c. (Doubleday Page & Co.)

WOODCRAFT MANUAL FOR GIRLS, 1917

Like the foregoing but adapted for girls. 424 pp., Illus. Price, 50c. (Doubleday, Page & Co.)

THE PREACHER OF CEDAR MOUNTAIN.

A novel. A tale of the open country. Net, $1.35. (Doubleday, Page & Co.)

SIGN TALK

A Universal Signal Code, Without Apparatus, for use in the Army, the Navy, Camping, Hunting, Daily Life and among the Plains Indians. Net, $3.00. (Doubleday, Page & Co.)

BY MRS. ERNEST THOMPSON SETON
(Published by DOUBLEDAY, PAGE & CO.)

A WOMAN TENDERFOOT, 1901

A book of outdoor adventures and camping for women and girls. How to dress for it, where to go, and how to profit the most by camp life. Price, $2.00.

NIMROD'S WIFE, 1907

A companion volume, giving Mrs. Seton's side of the many camp-fires she and her husband lighted together in the Rockies from Canada to Mexico. Price, $1.75 net.